Miss Billy—Married

by

Eleanor H. Porter

Miss Billy—Married
by Eleanor H. Porter

ISBN: 978-93-59955-95-7

Published by

DOUBLE 9 BOOKS

2/13-B, Ansari Road
Daryaganj, New Delhi – 110002
info@double9books.com
www.double9books.com
Tel. 011-40042856

ABOUT THE AUTHOR

American author Eleanor Emily Hodgman Porter was born on December 19, 1868, and died on May 21, 1920. She was best known for her books Pollyanna (1913) and Just David (1916). Frances Fletcher Hodgman and Llewella French (née Woolson) had a daughter named Eleanor Emily Hodgman on December 19, 1868, in Littleton, New Hampshire. She learned how to sing by going to the New England Conservatory for many years. They moved to Massachusetts after getting married to John Lyman Porter in 1892. That's when she started writing and selling short stories and then novels. Her death date was May 21, 1920, in Cambridge, Massachusetts. She was buried at Mount Auburn Cemetery. She wrote several books for adults, such as The Turn of the Tide (1908), The Road to Understanding (1917), Oh Money! Money! (1918), Dawn (1919), Keith's Dark Tower (1919), Mary Marie (1920), and Sister Sue (1921). She also wrote several collections of short stories, such as Across the Years (around 1919), Money, Love, and Kate (1923), and Little Pardner (1926). Porter had a lot of success with his books. In the United States, Pollyanna was the eighth best-selling novel in 1913, the second best-selling novel in 1914, and the fourth best-selling novel in 1915 (with 47 printings between 1915 and 1920). Just David was the third best-selling novel in 1916, The Road to Understanding was the fourth best-selling novel in 1917, and Oh Money! Money! was the fifth best-selling novel in 1918.

CONTENTS

CHAPTER I
SOME OPINIONS AND A WEDDING

"I, Bertram, take thee, Billy," chanted the white-robed clergyman.

"'I, Bertram, take thee, Billy,'" echoed the tall young bridegroom, his eyes gravely tender.

"To my wedded wife."

"'To my wedded wife.'" The bridegroom's voice shook a little.

"To have and to hold from this day forward."

"'To have and to hold from this day forward.'" Now the young voice rang with triumph. It had grown strong and steady.

"For better for worse."

"'For better for worse.'"

"For richer for poorer," droned the clergyman, with the weariness of uncounted repetitions.

"'For richer for poorer,'" avowed the bridegroom, with the decisive emphasis of one to whom the words are new and significant.

"In sickness and in health."

"'In sickness and in health.'"

"To love and to cherish."

"'To love and to cherish.'" The younger voice carried infinite tenderness now.

"Till death us do part."

"'Till death us do part,'" repeated the bridegroom's lips; but everybody knew that what his heart said was: "Now, and through all eternity."

"According to God's holy ordinance."

"'According to God's holy ordinance.'"

"And thereto I plight thee my troth."

"'And thereto I plight thee my troth.'"

There was a faint stir in the room. In one corner a white-haired woman blinked tear-wet eyes and pulled a fleecy white shawl more closely about her shoulders. Then the minister's voice sounded again.

"I, Billy, take thee, Bertram."

"'I, Billy, take thee, Bertram.'"

This time the echoing voice was a feminine one, low and sweet, but clearly distinct, and vibrant with joyous confidence, on through one after another of the ever familiar, but ever impressive phrases of the service that gives into the hands of one man and of one woman the future happiness, each of the other.

The wedding was at noon. That evening Mrs. Kate Hartwell, sister of the bridegroom, wrote the following letter:

BOSTON, July 15th.

"MY DEAR HUSBAND:—Well, it's all over with, and they're married. I couldn't do one thing to prevent it. Much as ever as they would even listen to what I had to say—and when they knew how I had hurried East to say it, too, with only two hours' notice!

"But then, what can you expect? From time immemorial lovers never did have any sense; and when those lovers are such irresponsible flutterbudgets as Billy and Bertram—!

"And such a wedding! I couldn't do anything with *that*, either, though I tried hard. They had it in Billy's living-room at noon, with nothing but the sun for light. There was no maid of honor, no bridesmaids, no wedding cake, no wedding veil, no presents (except from the family, and from that ridiculous Chinese cook of brother William's, Ding Dong, or whatever his name is. He tore in just before the wedding ceremony, and insisted upon seeing Billy to give her a wretched little green stone idol, which he declared would bring her 'heap plenty velly good luckee' if she received it before she 'got married.' I wouldn't have the hideous, grinning thing around, but William says it's real jade, and very valuable, and of course Billy was crazy over it—or pretended to be). There was no trousseau, either, and no reception. There was no anything but the bridegroom; and when I tell you that Billy actually declared that was all she wanted, you will understand how absurdly in love she is—in spite of all those weeks and weeks of broken engagement when I, at least, supposed she had come to her senses, until I got that crazy note from Bertram a week ago saying they were to be married today.

"I can't say that I've got any really satisfactory explanation of the matter. Everything has been in such a hubbub, and those two ridiculous children have been so afraid they wouldn't be together every minute possible, that any really rational conversation with either of them was out of the question. When Billy broke the engagement last spring none of us knew why she had done it, as you know; and I fancy we shall be almost as much in the dark as to why she has—er—mended it now, as you might say. As near as I can make out, however, she thought he didn't want her, and he thought she didn't want him. I believe matters were still further complicated by a girl Bertram was painting, and a young fellow that used to sing with Billy—a Mr. Arkwright.

"Anyhow, things came to a head last spring, Billy broke the engagement and fled to parts unknown with Aunt Hannah, leaving Bertram here in Boston to alternate between stony despair and reckless gayety, according to William; and it was while he was in the latter mood that he had that awful automobile accident and broke his arm—and almost his neck. He was wildly delirious, and called continually for Billy.

"Well, it seems Billy didn't know all this; but a week ago she came home, and in some way found out about it, I think through Pete—William's old butler, you know. Just exactly what happened I can't say, but I do know that she dragged poor old Aunt Hannah down to Bertram's at some unearthly hour, and in the rain; and Aunt Hannah couldn't do a thing with her. All Billy would say, was, 'Bertram wants me.' And Aunt Hannah told me that if I could have seen Billy's face I'd have known that she'd have gone to Bertram then if he'd been at the top of the Himalaya Mountains, or at the bottom of the China Sea. So perhaps it's just as well—for Aunt Hannah's sake, at least—that he was in no worse place than on his own couch at home. Anyhow, she went, and in half an hour they blandly informed Aunt Hannah that they were going to be married to-day.

"Aunt Hannah said she tried to stop that, and get them to put it off till October (the original date, you know), but Bertram was obdurate. And when he declared he'd marry her the next day if it wasn't for the new license law, Aunt Hannah said she gave up for fear he'd get a special dispensation, or go to the Governor or the President, or do some other dreadful thing. (What a funny old soul Aunt Hannah is!) Bertram told *me* that he should never feel safe till Billy was really his; that she'd read something, or hear something, or think something, or get a letter from me (as if anything *I* could say would do any good-or harm!), and so break the engagement again.

"Well, she's his now, so I suppose he's satisfied; though, for my part, I haven't changed my mind at all. I still say that they are not one bit suited to each other, and that matrimony will simply ruin his career. Bertram never has loved and never will love any girl long—except to paint. But if he simply *would* get married, why couldn't he have taken a nice, sensible domestic girl that would have kept him fed and mended?

"Not but that I'm very fond of Billy, as you know, dear; but imagine Billy as a wife—worse yet, a mother! Billy's a dear girl, but she knows about as much of real life and its problems as—as our little Kate. A more impulsive, irresponsible, regardless-of-consequences young woman I never saw. She can play divinely, and write delightful songs, I'll acknowledge; but what is that when a man is hungry, or has lost a button?

"Billy has had her own way, and had everything she wanted for years now—a rather dangerous preparation for marriage, especially marriage to a fellow like Bertram who has had *his* own way and everything *he's* wanted for years. Pray, what's going to happen when those ways conflict, and neither one gets the thing wanted?

"And think of her ignorance of cooking—but, there! What's the use? They're married now, and it can't be helped.

"Mercy, what a letter I've written! But I, had to talk to some one; besides, I'd promised I to let you know how matters stood as soon as I could. As you see, though, my trip East has been practically useless. I saw the wedding, to be sure, but I didn't prevent it, or even postpone it—though I meant to do one or the other, else I should never have made that tiresome journey half across the continent at two hours' notice.

"However, we shall see what we shall see. As for me, I'm dead tired. Good night.

"Affectionately yours,

"KATE."

Quite naturally, Mrs. Kate Hartwell was not the only one who was thinking that evening of the wedding. In the home of Bertram's brother Cyril, Cyril himself was at the piano, but where his thoughts were was plain to be seen—or rather, heard; for from under his fingers there came the Lohengrin wedding march until all the room seemed filled with the scent of orange blossoms, the mistiness of floating veils, and the echoing peals of far-away organs heralding the "Fair Bride and Groom."

Over by the table in the glowing circle of the shaded lamp, sat Marie, Cyril's wife, a dainty sewing-basket by her side. Her hands, however, lay idly across the stocking in her lap.

As the music ceased, she drew a long sigh.

What a perfectly beautiful wedding that was! she breathed.

Cyril whirled about on the piano stool.

"It was a very sensible wedding," he said with emphasis.

"They looked so happy—both of them," went on Marie, dreamily; "so—so sort of above and beyond everything about them, as if nothing ever, ever could trouble them—*now*."

Cyril lifted his eyebrows.

"Humph! Well, as I said before, it was a very *sensible* wedding," he declared.

This time Marie noticed the emphasis. She laughed, though her eyes looked a little troubled.

"I know, dear, of course, what you mean. *I* thought our wedding was beautiful; but I would have made it simpler if I'd realized in time how you—you—"

"How I abhorred pink teas and purple pageants," he finished for her, with a frowning smile. "Oh, well, I stood it—for the sake of what it brought me." His face showed now only the smile; the frown had vanished. For a man known for years to his friends as a "hater of women and all other confusion," Cyril Henshaw was looking remarkably well-pleased with himself.

His wife of less than a year colored as she met his gaze. Hurriedly she picked up her needle.

The man laughed happily at her confusion.

"What are you doing? Is that my stocking?" he demanded.

A look, half pain, half reproach, crossed her face.

"Why, Cyril, of course not! You—you told me not to, long ago. You said my darns made—bunches.

"Ho! I meant I didn't want to *wear* them," retorted the man, upon whom the tragic wretchedness of that half-sobbed "bunches" had been quite lost. "I love to see you *mending* them," he finished, with an approving glance at the pretty little picture of domesticity before him.

A peculiar expression came to Marie's eyes.

"Why, Cyril, you mean you *like* to have me mend them just for—for the sake of seeing me do it, when you *know* you won't ever wear them?"

"Sure!" nodded the man, imperturbably. Then, with a sudden laugh, he asked: "I wonder now, does Billy love to mend socks?"

Marie smiled, but she sighed, too, and shook her head.

"I'm afraid not, Cyril."

"Nor cook?"

Marie laughed outright this time. The vaguely troubled look had fled from her eyes

"Oh, Billy's helped me beat eggs and butter sometimes, but I never knew her to cook a thing or want to cook a thing, but once; then she spent nearly two weeks trying to learn to make puddings—for you."

"For *me!*"

Marie puckered her lips queerly.

"Well, I supposed they were for you at the time. At all events she was trying to make them for some one of you boys; probably it was really for Bertram, though."

"Humph!" grunted Cyril. Then, after a minute, he observed: "I judge Kate thinks Billy'll never make them—for anybody. I'm afraid Sister Kate isn't pleased."

"Oh, but Mrs. Hartwell was—was disappointed in the wedding," apologized Marie, quickly. "You know she wanted it put off anyway, and she didn't like such a simple one.

"Hm-m; as usual Sister Kate forgot it wasn't her funeral—I mean, her wedding," retorted Cyril, dryly. "Kate is never happy, you know, unless she's managing things."

"Yes, I know," nodded Marie, with a frowning smile of recollection at certain features of her own wedding.

"She doesn't approve of Billy's taste in guests, either," remarked Cyril, after a moment's silence.

"I thought her guests were lovely," spoke up Marie, in quick defense. "Of course, most of her social friends are away—in July; but Billy is never a society girl, you know, in spite of the way Society is always trying to lionize her and Bertram."

"Oh, of course Kate knows that; but she says it seems as if Billy needn't have gone out and gathered in the lame and the halt and the blind."

"Nonsense!" cried Marie, with unusual sharpness for her. "I suppose she said that just because of Mrs. Greggory's and Tommy Dunn's crutches."

"Well, they didn't make a real festive-looking wedding party, you must admit," laughed Cyril; "what with the bridegroom's own arm in a sling, too! But who were they all, anyway?"

"Why, you knew Mrs. Greggory and Alice, of course—and Pete," smiled Marie. "And wasn't Pete happy? Billy says she'd have had Pete if she had no one else; that there wouldn't have been any wedding, anyway, if it hadn't been for his telephoning Aunt Hannah that night."

"Yes; Will told me."

"As for Tommy and the others—most of them were those people that Billy had at her home last summer for a two weeks' vacation—people, you know, too poor to give themselves one, and too proud to accept one from ordinary charity. Billy's been following them up and doing little things for them ever since—sugarplums and frosting on their cake, she calls it; and they adore her, of course. I think it was lovely of her to have them, and they did have such a good time! You should have seen Tommy when you played that wedding march for Billy to enter the room. His poor little face was so transfigured with joy that I almost cried, just to look at him. Billy says he loves music—poor little fellow!"

"Well, I hope they'll be happy, in spite of Kate's doleful prophecies. Certainly they looked happy enough to-day," declared Cyril, patting a yawn as he rose to his feet. "I fancy Will and Aunt Hannah are lonesome, though, about now," he added.

"Yes," smiled Marie, mistily, as she gathered up her work. "I know what Aunt Hannah's doing. She's helping Rosa put the house to rights, and she's stopping to cry over every slipper and handkerchief of Billy's she finds. And she'll do that until that funny clock of hers strikes twelve, then she'll say 'Oh, my grief and conscience—midnight!' But the next minute she'll remember that it's only half-past eleven, after all, and she'll send Rosa to bed and sit patting Billy's slipper in her lap till it really is midnight by all the other clocks."

Cyril laughed appreciatively.

"Well, I know what Will is doing," he declared.

"Will is in Bertram's den dozing before the fireplace with Spunkie curled up in his lap."

As it happened, both these surmises were not far from right. In the Strata, the Henshaws' old Beacon Street home, William was sitting before the fireplace with the cat in his lap, but he was not dozing. He was talking.

"Spunkie," he was saying, "your master, Bertram, got married to-day—and to Miss Billy. He'll be bringing her home one of these days—your new mistress. And such a mistress! Never did cat or house have a better!

"Just think; for the first time in years this old place is to know the touch of a woman's hand—and that's what it hasn't known for almost twenty years, except for those few short months six years ago when a dark-eyed girl and a little gray kitten (that was Spunk, your predecessor, you know) blew in and blew out again before we scarcely knew they were here. That girl was Miss Billy, and she was a dear then, just as she is now, only now she's coming here to stay. She's coming home, Spunkie; and she'll make it a home for you, for me, and for all of us. Up to now, you know, it hasn't really been a home, for years—just us men, so. It'll be very different, Spunkie, as you'll soon find out. Now mind, madam! We must show that we appreciate all this: no tempers, no tantrums, no showing of claws, no leaving our coats—either yours or mine—on the drawing-room chairs, no tracking in of mud on clean rugs and floors! For we're going to have a home, Spunkie—a home!"

At Hillside, Aunt Hannah was, indeed, helping Rosa to put the house to rights, as Marie had said. She was crying, too, over a glove she had found on Billy's piano; but she was crying over something else, also. Not only had she lost Billy, but she had lost her home.

To be sure, nothing had been said during that nightmare of a week of hurry and confusion about Aunt Hannah's future; but Aunt Hannah knew very well how it must be. This dear little house on the side of Corey Hill was Billy's home, and Billy would not need it any longer. It would be sold, of course; and she, Aunt Hannah, would go back to a "second-story front" and loneliness in some Back Bay boarding-house; and a second story front and loneliness would not be easy now, after these years of home—and Billy.

No wonder, indeed, that Aunt Hannah sat crying and patting the little white glove in her hand. No wonder, too, that—being Aunt Hannah—she reached for the shawl near by and put it on, shiveringly. Even July, to-night, was cold—to Aunt Hannah.

In yet another home that evening was the wedding of Billy Neilson and Bertram Henshaw uppermost in thought and speech. In a certain little South-End flat where, in two rented rooms, lived Alice Greggory and her crippled mother, Alice was talking to Mr. M. J. Arkwright, commonly known to his friends as "Mary Jane," owing to the mystery in which he had for so long shrouded his name.

Arkwright to-night was plainly moody and ill at ease.

"You're not listening. You're not listening at all," complained Alice Greggory at last, reproachfully.

With a visible effort the man roused himself.

"Indeed I am," he maintained.

"I thought you'd be interested in the wedding. You used to be friends—you and Billy." The girl's voice still vibrated with reproach.

There was a moment's silence; then, a little harshly, the man said:

"Perhaps—because I wanted to be more than—a friend—is why you're not satisfied with my interest now."

A look that was almost terror came to Alice Greggory's eyes. She flushed painfully, then grew very white.

"You mean—"

"Yes," he nodded dully, without looking up. "I cared too much for her. I supposed Henshaw was just a friend—till too late."

There was a breathless hush before, a little unsteadily, the girl stammered:

"Oh, I'm so sorry—so very sorry! I—I didn't know."

"No, of course you didn't. I've almost told you, though, lots of times; you've been so good to me all these weeks." He raised his head now, and looked at her, frank comradeship in his eyes.

The girl stirred restlessly. Her eyes swerved a little under his level gaze.

"Oh, but I've done nothing—n-nothing," she stammered. Then, at the light tap of crutches on a bare floor she turned in obvious relief. "Oh, here's mother. She's been in visiting with Mrs. Delano, our landlady. Mother, Mr. Arkwright is here."

Meanwhile, speeding north as fast as steam could carry them, were the bride and groom. The wondrousness of the first hour of their journey side by side had become a joyous certitude that always it was to be like this now.

"Bertram," began the bride, after a long minute of eloquent silence.

"Yes, love."

"You know our wedding was very different from most weddings."

"Of course it was!"

"Yes, but *really* it was. Now listen." The bride's voice grew tenderly earnest. "I think our marriage is going to be different, too."

"Different?"

"Yes." Billy's tone was emphatic. "There are so many common, everyday marriages where—where—Why, Bertram, as if you could ever be to me like—like Mr. Carleton is, for instance!"

"Like Mr. Carleton is—to you?" Bertram's voice was frankly puzzled.

"No, no! As Mr. Carleton is to Mrs. Carleton, I mean."

"Oh!" Bertram subsided in relief.

"And the Grahams and Whartons, and the Freddie Agnews, and—and a lot of others. Why, Bertram, I've seen the Grahams and the Whartons not even speak to each other a whole evening, when they've been at a dinner, or something; and I've seen Mrs. Carleton not even seem to know her husband came into the room. I don't mean quarrel, dear. Of course we'd never *quarrel!* But I mean I'm sure we shall never get used to—to you being you, and I being I."

"Indeed we sha'n't," agreed Bertram, rapturously.

"Ours is going to be such a beautiful marriage!"

"Of course it will be."

"And we'll be so happy!"

"I shall be, and I shall try to make you so."

"As if I could be anything else," sighed Billy, blissfully. "And now we *can't* have any misunderstandings, you see."

"Of course not. Er—what's that?"

"Why, I mean that—that we can't ever repeat hose miserable weeks of misunderstanding. Everything is all explained up. I *know*, now, that you don't love Miss Winthrop, or just girls—any girl—to paint. You love me. Not the tilt of my chin, nor the turn of my head; but *me.*"

"I do—just you." Bertram's eyes gave the caress his lips would have given had it not been for the presence of the man in the seat across the aisle of the sleeping-car.

"And you—you know now that I love you—just you?"

"Not even Arkwright?"

"Not even Arkwright," smiled Billy.

There was the briefest of hesitations; then, a little constrainedly, Bertram asked:

"And you said you—you never *had* cared for Arkwright, didn't you?"

For the second time in her life Billy was thankful that Bertram's question had turned upon *her* love for Arkwright, not Arkwright's love for her. In Billy's opinion, a man's unrequited love for a girl was his secret, not hers, and was certainly one that the girl had no right to tell. Once before Bertram had asked her if she had ever cared for Arkwright, and then she had answered emphatically, as she did now:

"Never, dear."

"I thought you said so," murmured Bertram, relaxing a little.

"I did; besides, didn't I tell you?" she went on airily, "I think he'll marry Alice Greggory. Alice wrote me all the time I was away, and—oh, she didn't say anything definite, I'll admit," confessed Billy, with an arch smile; "but she spoke of his being there lots, and they used to know each other years ago, you see. There was almost a romance there, I think, before the Greggorys lost their money and moved away from all their friends."

"Well, he may have her. She's a nice girl—a mighty nice girl," answered Bertram, with the unmistakably satisfied air of the man who knows he himself possesses the nicest girl of them all.

Billy, reading unerringly the triumph in his voice, grew suddenly grave. She regarded her husband with a thoughtful frown; then she drew a profound sigh.

"Whew!" laughed Bertram, whimsically. "So soon as this?"

"Bertram!" Billy's voice was tragic.

"Yes, my love." The bridegroom pulled his face into sobriety; then Billy spoke, with solemn impressiveness.

"Bertram, I don't know a thing about—cooking—except what I've been learning in Rosa's cook-book this last week."

Bertram laughed so loud that the man across the aisle glanced over the top of his paper surreptitiously.

"Rosa's cook-book! Is that what you were doing all this week?"

"Yes; that is—I tried so hard to learn something," stammered Billy. "But I'm afraid I didn't—much; there were so many things for me to think of, you know, with only a week. I believe I *could* make peach fritters, though. They were the last thing I studied."

Bertram laughed again, uproariously; but, at Billy's unchangingly tragic face, he grew suddenly very grave and tender.

"Billy, dear, I didn't marry you to—to get a cook," he said gently.

Billy shook her head.

"I know; but Aunt Hannah said that even if I never expected to cook, myself, I ought to know how it was done, so to properly oversee it. She said that—that no woman, who didn't know how to cook and keep house properly, had any business to be a wife. And, Bertram, I did try, honestly, all this week. I tried so hard to remember when you sponged bread and when you kneaded it."

"I don't ever need—*yours*," cut in Bertram, shamelessly; but he got only a deservedly stern glance in return.

"And I repeated over and over again how many cupfuls of flour and pinches of salt and spoonfuls of baking-powder went into things; but, Bertram, I simply could not keep my mind on it. Everything, everywhere was singing to me. And how do you suppose I could remember how many pinches of flour and spoonfuls of salt and cupfuls of baking-powder went into a loaf of cake when all the while the very teakettle on the stove was singing: 'It's all right—Bertram loves me—I'm going to marry Bertram!'?"

"You darling!" (In spite of the man across the aisle Bertram did almost kiss her this time.) "As if anybody cared how many cupfuls of baking-powder went anywhere—with that in your heart!"

"Aunt Hannah says you will—when you're hungry. And Kate said—"

Bertram uttered a sharp word behind his teeth.

"Billy, for heaven's sake don't tell me what Kate said, if you want me to stay sane, and not attempt to fight somebody—broken arm, and all. Kate *thinks* she's kind, and I suppose she means well; but—well, she's made trouble enough between us already. I've got you now, sweetheart. You're mine—all mine—" his voice shook, and dropped to a tender whisper—"'till death us do part.'"

"Yes; 'till death us do part,'" breathed Billy.

And then, for a time, they fell silent.

"'I, Bertram, take thee, Billy,'" sang the whirring wheels beneath them, to one.

"'I, Billy, take thee, Bertram,'" sang the whirring wheels beneath them, to the other. While straight ahead before them both, stretched fair and beautiful in their eyes, the wondrous path of life which they were to tread together.

CHAPTER II
FOR WILLIAM—A HOME

On the first Sunday after the wedding Pete came up-stairs to tell his master, William, that Mrs. Stetson wanted to see him in the drawing-room.

William went down at once.

"Well, Aunt Hannah," he began, reaching out a cordial hand. "Why, what's the matter?" he broke off concernedly, as he caught a clearer view of the little old lady's drawn face and troubled eyes.

"William, it's silly, of course," cried Aunt Hannah, tremulously, "but I simply had to go to some one. I—I feel so nervous and unsettled! Did—did Billy say anything to you—what she was going to do?"

"What she was going to do? About what? What do you mean?"

"About the house—selling it," faltered Aunt Hannah, sinking wearily back into her chair.

William frowned thoughtfully.

"Why, no," he answered. "It was all so hurried at the last, you know. There was really very little chance to make plans for anything—except the wedding," he finished, with a smile.

"Yes, I know," sighed Aunt Hannah. "Everything was in such confusion! Still, I didn't know but she might have said something—to you."

"No, she didn't. But I imagine it won't be hard to guess what she'll do. When they get back from their trip I fancy she won't lose much time in having what things she wants brought down here. Then she'll sell the rest and put the house on the market."

"Yes, of—of course," stammered Aunt Hannah, pulling herself hastily to a more erect position. "That's what I thought, too. Then don't you think we'd better dismiss Rosa and close the house at once?"

"Why—yes, perhaps so. Why not? Then you'd be all settled here when she comes home. I'm sure, the sooner you come, the better I'll be pleased," he smiled.

Aunt Hannah turned sharply.

"Here!" she ejaculated. "William Henshaw, you didn't suppose I was coming *here* to live, did you?"

It was William's turn to look amazed.

"Why, of course you're coming here! Where else should you go, pray?"

"Where I was before—before Billy came—to you," returned Aunt Hannah a little tremulously, but with a certain dignity. "I shall take a room in some quiet boarding-house, of course."

"Nonsense, Aunt Hannah! As if Billy would listen to that! You came before; why not come now?"

Aunt Hannah lifted her chin the fraction of an inch.

"You forget. I was needed before. Billy is a married woman now. She needs no chaperon."

"Nonsense!" scowled William, again. "Billy will always need you."

Aunt Hannah shook her head mournfully.

"I like to think—she wants me, William, but I know, in my heart, it isn't best."

"Why not?"

There was a moment's pause; then, decisively came the answer.

"Because I think young married folks should not have outsiders in the home."

William laughed relievedly.

"Oh, so that's it! Well, Aunt Hannah, you're no outsider. Come, run right along home and pack your trunk."

Aunt Hannah was plainly almost crying; but she held her ground.

"William, I can't," she reiterated.

"But—Billy is such a child, and—"

For once in her circumspect life Aunt Hannah was guilty of an interruption.

"Pardon me, William, she is not a child. She is a woman now, and she has a woman's problems to meet."

"Well, then, why don't you help her meet them?" retorted William, still with a whimsical smile.

But Aunt Hannah did not smile. For a minute she did not speak; then, with her eyes studiously averted, she said:

"William, the first four years of my married life were—were spoiled by an outsider in our home. I don't mean to spoil Billy's."

William relaxed visibly. The smile fled from his face.

"Why—Aunt—Hannah!" he exclaimed.

The little old lady turned with a weary sigh.

"Yes, I know. You are shocked, of course. I shouldn't have told you. Still, it is all past long ago, and—I wanted to make you understand why I can't come. He was my husband's eldest brother—a bachelor. He was good and kind, and meant well, I suppose; but—he interfered with everything. I was young, and probably headstrong. At all events, there was constant friction. He went away once and stayed two whole months. I shall never forget the utter freedom and happiness of those months for us, with the whole house to ourselves. No, William, I can't come." She rose abruptly and turned toward the door. Her eyes were wistful, and her face was still drawn with suffering; but her whole frail little self quivered plainly with high resolve. "John has Peggy outside. I must go."

"But—but, Aunt Hannah," began William, helplessly.

She lifted a protesting hand.

"No, don't urge me, please. I can't come here. But—I believe I won't close the house till Billy gets home, after all," she declared. The next moment she was gone, and William, dazedly, from the doorway, was watching John help her into Billy's automobile, called by Billy and half her friends, "Peggy," short for "Pegasus."

Still dazedly William turned back into the house and dropped himself into the nearest chair.

What a curious call it had been! Aunt Hannah had not acted like herself at all. Not once had she said "Oh, my grief and conscience!" while the things she *had* said—! Someway, he had never thought of Aunt Hannah as being young, and a bride. Still, of course she must have been—once. And the reason she gave for not coming there to live—the pitiful story of that outsider in her home! But she was no outsider! She was no interfering brother of Billy's—

William caught his breath suddenly, and held it suspended. Then he gave a low ejaculation and half sprang from his chair.

Spunkie, disturbed from her doze by the fire, uttered a purring "me-o-ow," and looked up inquiringly.

For a long minute William gazed dumbly into the cat's yellow, sleepily contented eyes; then he said with tragic distinctness:

"Spunkie, it's true: Aunt Hannah isn't Billy's husband's brother, but—I am! Do you hear? I *am!*"

"Pur-r-me-ow!" commented Spunkie; and curled herself for another nap.

There was no peace for William after that. In vain he told himself that he was no "interfering" brother, and that this was his home and had been all his life; in vain did he declare emphatically that he could not go, he would not go; that Billy would not wish him to go: always before his eyes was the vision of that little bride of years long gone; always in his ears was the echo of Aunt Hannah's "I shall never forget the utter freedom and happiness of those months for us, with the whole house to ourselves." Nor, turn which way he would, could he find anything to comfort him. Simply because he was so fearfully looking for it, he found it—the thing that had for its theme the wretchedness that might be expected from the presence of a third person in the new home.

Poor William! Everywhere he met it—the hint, the word, the story, the song, even; and always it added its mite to the woeful whole. Even the hoariest of mother-in-law jokes had its sting for him; and, to make his cup quite full, he chanced to remember one day what Marie had said when he had suggested that she and Cyril come to the Strata to live: "No; I think young folks should begin by themselves."

Unhappy, indeed, were these days for William. Like a lost spirit he wandered from room to room, touching this, fingering that. For long minutes he would stand before some picture, or some treasured bit of old mahogany, as if to stamp indelibly upon his mind a thing that was soon to be no more. At other times, like a man without a home, he would go out into the Common or the Public Garden and sit for hours on some bench— thinking.

All this could have but one ending, of course. Before the middle of August William summoned Pete to his rooms.

"Oh, Pete, I'm going to move next week," he began nonchalantly. His voice sounded as if moving were a pleasurable circumstance that occurred in his life regularly once a month. "I'd like you to begin to pack up these things, please, to-morrow."

The old servant's mouth fell open.

"You're goin' to—to what, sir?" he stammered.

"Move—*move*, I said." William spoke with unusual harshness.

Pete wet his lips.

"You mean you've sold the old place, sir?—that we—we ain't goin' to live here no longer?"

"Sold? Of course not! *I'm* going to move away; not you."

If Pete could have known what caused the sharpness in his master's voice, he would not have been so grieved—or, rather, he would have been grieved for a different reason. As it was he could only falter miserably:

"*You* are goin' to move away from here!"

"Yes, yes, man! Why, Pete, what ails you? One would think a body never moved before."

"They didn't—not you, sir."

William turned abruptly, so that his face could not be seen. With stern deliberation he picked up an elaborately decorated teapot; but the valuable bit of Lowestoft shook so in his hand that he set it down at once. It clicked sharply against its neighbor, betraying his nervous hand.

Pete stirred.

"But, Mr. William," he stammered thickly; "how are you—what'll you do without—There doesn't nobody but me know so well about your tea, and the two lumps in your coffee; and there's your flannels that you never put on till I get 'em out, and the woolen socks that you'd wear all summer if I didn't hide 'em. And—and who's goin' to take care of these?" he finished, with a glance that encompassed the overflowing cabinets and shelves of curios all about him.

His master smiled sadly. An affection that had its inception in his boyhood days shone in his eyes. The hand in which the Lowestoft had shaken rested now heavily on an old man's bent shoulder—a shoulder that straightened itself in unconscious loyalty under the touch.

"Pete, you have spoiled me, and no mistake. I don't expect to find another like you. But maybe if I wear the woolen socks too late you'll come and hunt up the others for me. Eh?" And, with a smile that was meant to be quizzical, William turned and began to shift the teapots about again.

"But, Mr. William, why—that is, what will Mr. Bertram and Miss Billy do—without you?" ventured the old man.

There was a sudden tinkling crash. On the floor lay the fragments of a silver-luster teapot.

The servant exclaimed aloud in dismay, but his master did not even glance toward his once treasured possession on the floor.

"Nonsense, Pete!" he was saying in a particularly cheery voice. "Have you lived all these years and not found out that newly-married folks don't *need* any one else around? Come, do you suppose we could begin to pack these teapots to-night?" he added, a little feverishly. "Aren't there some boxes down cellar?"

"I'll see, sir," said Pete, respectfully; but the expression on his face as he turned away showed that he was not thinking of teapots—nor of boxes in which to pack them.

CHAPTER III
BILLY SPEAKS HER MIND

Mr. and Mrs. Bertram Henshaw were expected home the first of September. By the thirty-first of August the old Beacon Street homestead facing the Public Garden was in spick-and-span order, with Dong Ling in the basement hovering over a well-stocked larder, and Pete searching the rest of the house for a chair awry, or a bit of dust undiscovered.

Twice before had the Strata—as Bertram long ago dubbed the home of his boyhood—been prepared for the coming of Billy, William's namesake: once, when it had been decorated with guns and fishing-rods to welcome the "boy" who turned out to be a girl; and again when with pink roses and sewing-baskets the three brothers got joyously ready for a feminine Billy who did not even come at all.

The house had been very different then. It had been, indeed, a "strata," with its distinctive layers of fads and pursuits as represented by Bertram and his painting on one floor, William and his curios on another, and Cyril with his music on a third. Cyril was gone now. Only Pete and his humble belongings occupied the top floor. The floor below, too, was silent now, and almost empty save for a rug or two, and a few pieces of heavy furniture that William had not cared to take with him to his new quarters on top of Beacon Hill. Below this, however, came Billy's old rooms, and on these Pete had lavished all his skill and devotion.

Freshly laundered curtains were at the windows, dustless rugs were on the floor. The old work-basket had been brought down from the top-floor storeroom, and the long-closed piano stood invitingly open. In a conspicuous place, also, sat the little green god, upon whose exquisitely carved shoulders was supposed to rest the "heap plenty velly good luckee" of Dong Ling's prophecy.

On the first floor Bertram's old rooms and the drawing-room came in for their share of the general overhauling. Even Spunkie did not escape, but had to submit to the ignominy of a bath. And then dawned fair and clear the first day of September, bringing at five o'clock the bride and groom.

Respectfully lined up in the hall to meet them were Pete and Dong Ling: Pete with his wrinkled old face alight with joy and excitement; Dong Ling grinning and kotowing, and chanting in a high-pitched treble:

"Miss Billee, Miss Billee—plenty much welcome, Miss Billee!"

"Yes, welcome home, Mrs. *Henshaw!*" bowed Bertram, turning at the door, with an elaborate flourish that did not in the least hide his tender pride in his new wife.

Billy laughed and colored a pretty pink.

"Thank you—all of you," she cried a little unsteadily. "And how good, good everything does look to me! Why, where's Uncle William?" she broke off, casting hurriedly anxious eyes about her.

"Well, I should say so," echoed Bertram. "Where is he, Pete? He isn't sick, is he?"

A quick change crossed the old servant's face. He shook his head dumbly.

Billy gave a gleeful laugh.

"I know—he's asleep!" she caroled, skipping to the bottom of the stairway and looking up.

"Ho, Uncle William! Better wake up, sir. The folks have come!"

Pete cleared his throat.

"Mr. William isn't here, Miss—ma'am," he corrected miserably.

Billy smiled, but she frowned, too.

"Not here! Well, I like that," she pouted; "—and when I've brought him the most beautiful pair of mirror knobs he ever saw, and all the way in my bag, too, so I could give them to him the very first thing," she added, darting over to the small bag she had brought in with her. "I'm glad I did, too, for our trunks didn't come," she continued laughingly. "Still, if he isn't here to receive them—There, Pete, aren't they beautiful?" she cried, carefully taking from their wrappings two exquisitely decorated porcelain discs mounted on two long spikes. "They're Batterseas—the real article. I know enough for that; and they're finer than anything he's got. Won't he be pleased?"

"Yes, Miss—ma'am, I mean," stammered the old man.

"These new titles come hard, don't they, Pete?" laughed Bertram.

Pete smiled faintly.

"Never mind, Pete," soothed his new mistress. "You shall call me 'Miss Billy' all your life if you want to. Bertram," she added, turning to her husband, "I'm going to just run up-stairs and put these in Uncle William's rooms so they'll be there when he comes in. We'll see how soon he discovers them!"

Before Pete could stop her she was half-way up the first flight of stairs. Even then he tried to speak to his young master, to explain that Mr. William was not living there; but the words refused to come. He could only stand dumbly waiting.

In a minute it came—Billy's sharp, startled cry.

"Bertram! Bertram!"

Bertram sprang for the stairway, but he had not reached the top when he met his wife coming down. She was white-faced and trembling.

"Bertram—those rooms—there's not so much as a teapot there! Uncle William's—gone!"

"Gone!" Bertram wheeled sharply. "Pete, what is the meaning of this? Where is my brother?" To hear him, one would think he suspected the old servant of having hidden his master.

Pete lifted a shaking hand and fumbled with his collar.

"He's moved, sir."

"Moved! Oh, you mean to other rooms—to Cyril's." Bertram relaxed visibly. "He's upstairs, maybe."

Pete shook his head.

"No, sir. He's moved away—out of the house, sir."

For a brief moment Bertram stared as if he could not believe what his ears had heard. Then, step by step, he began to descend the stairs.

"Do you mean—to say—that my brother—has moved-gone away—left—his *home?*" he demanded.

"Yes, sir."

Billy gave a low cry.

"But why—why?" she choked, almost stumbling headlong down the stairway in her effort to reach the two men at the bottom. "Pete, why did he go?"

There was no answer.

"Pete,"—Bertram's voice was very sharp—"what is the meaning of this? Do you know why my brother left his home?"

The old man wet his lips and swallowed chokingly, but he did not speak.

"I'm waiting, Pete."

Billy laid one hand on the old servant's arm—in the other hand she still tightly clutched the mirror knobs.

"Pete, if you do know, won't you tell us, please?" she begged.

Pete looked down at the hand, then up at the troubled young face with the beseeching eyes. His own features worked convulsively. With a visible effort he cleared his throat.

"I know—what he said," he stammered, his eyes averted.

"What was it?"

There was no answer.

"Look here, Pete, you'll have to tell us, you know," cut in Bertram, decisively, "so you might as well do it now as ever."

Once more Pete cleared his throat. This time the words came in a burst of desperation.

"Yes, sir. I understand, sir. It was only that he said—he said as how young folks didn't *need* any one else around. So he was goin'."

"Didn't *need* any one else!" exclaimed Bertram, plainly not comprehending.

"Yes, sir. You two bein' married so, now." Pete's eyes were still averted.

Billy gave a low cry.

"You mean—because I came?" she demanded.

"Why, yes, Miss—no—that is—" Pete stopped with an appealing glance at Bertram.

"Then it was—it *was*—on account of *me*," choked Billy.

Pete looked still more distressed

"No, no!" he faltered. "It was only that he thought you wouldn't want him here now."

"Want him here!" ejaculated Bertram.

"Want him here!" echoed Billy, with a sob.

"Pete, where is he?" As she asked the question she dropped the mirror knobs into her open bag, and reached for her coat and gloves—she had not removed her hat.

Pete gave the address.

"It's just down the street a bit and up the hill," he added excitedly, divining her purpose. "It's a sort of a boarding-house, I reckon."

"A *boarding-house*—for Uncle William!" scorned Billy, her eyes ablaze. "Come, Bertram, we'll see about that."

Bertram reached out a detaining hand.

"But, dearest, you're so tired," he demurred. "Hadn't we better wait till after dinner, or till to-morrow?"

"After dinner! To-morrow!" Billy's eyes blazed anew. "Why, Bertram Henshaw, do you think I'd leave that dear man even one minute longer, if I could help it, with a notion in his blessed old head that we didn't *want* him?"

"But you said a little while ago you had a headache, dear," still objected Bertram. "If you'd just eat your dinner!"

"Dinner!" choked Billy. "I wonder if you think I could eat any dinner with Uncle William turned out of his home! I'm going to find Uncle William." And she stumbled blindly toward the door.

Bertram reached for his hat. He threw a despairing glance into Pete's eyes.

"We'll be back—when we can," he said, with a frown.

"Yes, sir," answered Pete, respectfully. Then, as if impelled by some hidden force, he touched his master's arm. "It was that way she looked, sir, when she came to *you*—that night last July—with her eyes all shining," he whispered.

A tender smile curved Bertram's lips. The frown vanished from his face.

"Bless you, Pete—and bless her, too!" he whispered back. The next moment he had hurried after his wife.

The house that bore the number Pete had given proved to have a pretentious doorway, and a landlady who, in response to the summons of the neat maid, appeared with a most impressive rustle of black silk and jet bugles.

No, Mr. William Henshaw was not in his rooms. In fact, he was very seldom there. His business, she believed, called him to State Street through the day. Outside of that, she had been told, he spent much time sitting on a bench in the Common. Doubtless, if they cared to search, they could find him there now.

"A bench in the Common, indeed!" stormed Billy, as she and Bertram hurried down the wide stone steps. "Uncle William—on a bench!"

"But surely now, dear," ventured her husband, "you'll come home and get your dinner!"

Billy turned indignantly.

"And leave Uncle William on a bench in the Common? Indeed, no! Why, Bertram, you wouldn't, either," she cried, as she turned resolutely toward one of the entrances to the Common.

And Bertram, with the "eyes all shining" still before him, could only murmur: "No, of course not, dear!" and follow obediently where she led.

Under ordinary circumstances it would have been a delightful hour for a walk. The sun had almost set, and the shadows lay long across the grass. The air was cool and unusually bracing for a day so early in September. But all this was lost on Bertram. Bertram did not wish to take a walk. He was hungry. He wanted his dinner; and he wanted, too, his old home with his new wife flitting about the rooms as he had pictured this first evening together. He wanted William, of course. Certainly he wanted William; but if William would insist on running away and sitting on park benches in this ridiculous fashion, he ought to take the consequences—until to-morrow.

Five, ten, fifteen minutes passed. Up one path and down another trudged the anxious-eyed Billy and her increasingly impatient husband. Then when the fifteen weary minutes had become a still more weary half-hour, the bonds Bertram had set on his temper snapped.

"Billy," he remonstrated despairingly, "do, please, come home! Don't you see how highly improbable it is that we should happen on William if we walked like this all night? He might move—change his seat—go home, even. He probably has gone home. And surely never before did a bride insist on spending the first evening after her return tramping up and down a public park for hour after hour like this, looking for any man. *Won't* you come home?"

But Billy had not even heard. With a glad little cry she had darted to the side of the humped-up figure of a man alone on a park bench just ahead of them.

"Uncle William! Oh, Uncle William, how could you?" she cried, dropping herself on to one end of the seat and catching the man's arm in both her hands.

"Yes, how could you?" demanded Bertram, with just a touch of irritation, dropping himself on to the other end of the seat, and catching the man's other arm in his one usable hand.

The bent shoulders and bowed head straightened up with a jerk.

"Well, well, bless my soul! If it isn't our little bride," cried Uncle William, fondly. "And the happy bridegroom, too. When did you get home?"

"We haven't got home," retorted Bertram, promptly, before his wife could speak. "Oh, we looked in at the door an hour or so back; but we didn't stay. We've been hunting for you ever since."

"Nonsense, children!" Uncle William spoke with gay cheeriness; but he refused to meet either Billy's or Bertram's eyes.

"Uncle William, how could you do it?" reproached Billy, again.

"Do what?" Uncle William was plainly fencing for time.

"Leave the house like that?"

"Ho! I wanted a change."

"As if we'd believe that!" scoffed Billy.

"All right; let's call it you've had the change, then," laughed Bertram, "and we'll send over for your things to-morrow. Come—now let's go home to dinner."

William shook his head. He essayed a gay smile.

"Why, I've only just begun. I'm going to stay—oh, I don't know how long I'm going to stay," he finished blithely.

Billy lifted her chin a little.

"Uncle William, you aren't playing square. Pete told us what you said when you left."

"Eh? What?" William looked up with startled eyes.

"About—about our not *needing* you. So we know, now, why you left; and we *sha'n't stand* it."

"Pete? That? Oh, that—that's nonsense I—I'll settle with Pete."

Billy laughed softly.

"Poor Pete! Don't. We simply dragged it out of him. And now we're here to tell you that we *do* want you, and that you *must* come back."

Again William shook his head. A swift shadow crossed his face.

"Thank you, no, children," he said dully.

"You're very kind, but you don't need me. I should be just an interfering elder brother. I should spoil your young married life." (William's voice now sounded as if he were reciting a well-learned lesson.) "If I went away and stayed two months, you'd never forget the utter freedom and joy of those two whole months with the house all to yourselves."

"Uncle William," gasped Billy, "what *are* you talking about?"

"About—about my not going back, of course."

"But you are coming back," cut in Bertram, almost angrily. "Oh, come, Will, this is utter nonsense, and you know it! Come, let's go home to dinner."

A stern look came to the corners of William's mouth—a look that Bertram understood well.

"All right, I'll go to dinner, of course; but I sha'n't stay," said William, firmly. "I've thought it all out. I know I'm right. Come, we'll go to dinner now, and say no more about it," he finished with a cheery smile, as he rose to his feet. Then, to the bride, he added: "Did you have a nice trip, little girl?"

Billy, too, had risen, now, but she did not seem to have heard his question. In the fast falling twilight her face looked a little white.

"Uncle William," she began very quietly, "do you think for a minute that just because I married your brother I am going to live in that house and turn you out of the home you've lived in all your life?"

"Nonsense, dear! I'm not turned out. I just go," corrected Uncle William, gayly.

With superb disdain Billy brushed this aside.

"Oh, no, you won't," she declared; "but—*I shall.*"

"Billy!" gasped Bertram.

"My—my dear!" expostulated William, faintly.

"Uncle William! Bertram! Listen," panted Billy. "I never told you much before, but I'm going to, now. Long ago, when I went away with Aunt Hannah, your sister Kate showed me how dear the old home was to you—how much you thought of it. And she said—she said that I had upset everything." (Bertram interjected a sharp word, but Billy paid no attention.) "That's why I went; and *I shall go again*—if you don't come home to-morrow to stay, Uncle William. Come, now let's go to dinner, please. Bertram's hungry," she finished, with a bright smile.

There was a tense moment of silence. William glanced at Bertram; Bertram returned the glance—with interest.

"Er—ah—yes; well, we might go to dinner," stammered William, after a minute.

"Er—yes," agreed Bertram. And the three fell into step together.

CHAPTER IV
"JUST LIKE BILLY"

Billy did not leave the Strata this time. Before twenty-four hours had passed, the last cherished fragment of Mr. William Henshaw's possessions had been carefully carried down the imposing steps of the Beacon Hill boarding-house under the disapproving eyes of its bugle-adorned mistress, who found herself now with a month's advance rent and two vacant "parlors" on her hands. Before another twenty-four hours had passed her quondam boarder, with a tired sigh, sank into his favorite morris chair in his old familiar rooms, and looked about him with contented eyes. Every treasure was in place, from the traditional four small stones of his babyhood days to the Batterseas Billy had just brought him. Pete, as of yore, was hovering near with a dust-cloth. Bertram's gay whistle sounded from the floor below. William Henshaw was at home again.

This much accomplished, Billy went to see Aunt Hannah.

Aunt Hannah greeted her affectionately, though with tearfully troubled eyes. She was wearing a gray shawl to-day topped with a black one—sure sign of unrest, either physical or mental, as all her friends knew.

"I'd begun to think you'd forgotten—me," she faltered, with a poor attempt at gayety.

"You've been home three whole days."

"I know, dearie," smiled Billy; "and 'twas a shame. But I have been so busy! My trunks came at last, and I've been helping Uncle William get settled, too."

Aunt Hannah looked puzzled.

"Uncle William get settled? You mean—he's changed his room?"

Billy laughed oddly, and threw a swift glance into Aunt Hannah's face.

"Well, yes, he did change," she murmured; "but he's moved back now into the old quarters. Er—you haven't heard from Uncle William then, lately, I take it."

"No." Aunt Hannah shook her head abstractedly. "I did see him once, several weeks ago; but I haven't, since. We had quite a talk, then; and, Billy, I've been wanting to speak to you," she hurried on, a little feverishly. "I didn't like to leave, of course, till you did come home, as long as you'd said nothing about your plans; but—"

"Leave!" interposed Billy, dazedly. "Leave where? What do you mean?"

"Why, leave here, of course, dear. I mean. I didn't like to get my room while you were away; but I shall now, of course, at once."

"Nonsense, Aunt Hannah! As if I'd let you do that," laughed Billy.

Aunt Hannah stiffened perceptibly. Her lips looked suddenly thin and determined. Even the soft little curls above her ears seemed actually to bristle with resolution.

"Billy," she began firmly, "we might as well understand each other at once. I know your good heart, and I appreciate your kindness. But I can not come to live with you. I shall not. It wouldn't be best. I should be like an interfering elder brother in your home. I should spoil your young married life; and if I went away for two months you'd never forget the utter joy and freedom of those two months with the whole house ali to yourselves."

At the beginning of this speech Billy's eyes had still carried their dancing smile, but as the peroration progressed on to the end, a dawning surprise, which soon became a puzzled questioning, drove the smile away. Then Billy sat suddenly erect.

"Why, Aunt Hannah, that's exactly what Uncle William—" Billy stopped, and regarded Aunt Hannah with quick suspicion. The next moment she burst into gleeful laughter.

Aunt Hannah looked grieved, and not a little surprised; but Billy did not seem to notice this.

"Oh, oh, Aunt Hannah—you, too! How perfectly funny!" she gurgled. "To think you two old blesseds should get your heads together like this!"

Aunt Hannah stirred restively, and pulled the black shawl more closely about her.

"Indeed, Billy, I don't know what you mean by that," she sighed, with a visible effort at self-control; "but I do know that I can not go to live with you."

"Bless your heart, dear, I don't want you to," soothed Billy, with gay promptness.

"Oh! O-h-h," stammered Aunt Hannah, surprise, mortification, dismay, and a grieved hurt bringing a flood of color to her face. It is one thing to refuse a home, and quite another to have a home refused you.

"Oh! O-h-h, Aunt Hannah," cried Billy, turning very red in her turn. "Please, *please* don't look like that. I didn't mean it that way. I do want you, dear, only—I want you somewhere else more. I want you—here."

"Here!" Aunt Hannah looked relieved, but unconvinced.

"Yes. Don't you like it here?"

"Like it! Why, I love it, dear. You know I do. But you don't need this house now, Billy."

"Oh, yes, I do," retorted Billy, airily. "I'm going to keep it up, and I want you here.

"Fiddlededee, Billy! As if I'd let you keep up this house just for me," scorned Aunt Hannah.

"'Tisn't just for you. It's for—for lots of folks."

"My grief and conscience, Billy! What are you talking about?"

Billy laughed, and settled herself more comfortably on the hassock at Aunt Hannah's feet.

"Well, I'll tell you. Just now I want it for Tommy Dunn, and the Greggorys if I can get them, and maybe one or two others. There'll always be somebody. You see, I had thought I'd have them at the Strata."

"Tommy Dunn—at the Strata!"

Billy laughed again ruefully.

"O dear! You sound just like Bertram," she pouted. "He didn't want Tommy, either, nor any of the rest of them."

"The rest of them!"

"Well, I could have had a lot more, you know, the Strata is so big, especially now that Cyril has gone, and left all those empty rooms. *I* got real enthusiastic, but Bertram didn't. He just laughed and said 'nonsense!' until he found I was really in earnest; then he—well, he said 'nonsense,' then, too—only he didn't laugh," finished Billy, with a sigh.

Aunt Hannah regarded her with fond, though slightly exasperated eyes.

"Billy, you are, indeed, a most extraordinary young woman—at times. Surely, with you, a body never knows what to expect—except the unexpected."

"Why, Aunt Hannah!—and from you, too!" reproached Billy, mischievously; but Aunt Hannah had yet more to say.

"Of course Bertram thought it was nonsense. The idea of you, a bride, filling up your house with—with people like that! Tommy Dunn, indeed!"

"Oh, Bertram said he liked Tommy all right," sighed Billy; "but he said that that didn't mean he wanted him for three meals a day. One would think poor Tommy was a breakfast food! So that is when I thought of keeping up this house, you see, and that's why I want you here—to take charge of it. And you'll do that—for me, won't you?"

Aunt Hannah fell back in her chair.

"Why, y-yes, Billy, of course, if—if you want it. But what an extraordinary idea, child!"

Billy shook her head. A deeper color came to her cheeks, and a softer glow to her eyes.

"I don't think so, Aunt Hannah. It's only that I'm so happy that some of it has just got to overflow somewhere, and this is going to be the overflow house—a sort of safety valve for me, you see. I'm going to call it the Annex— it will be an annex to our home. And I want to keep it full, always, of people who—who can make the best use of all that extra happiness that I can't possibly use myself," she finished a little tremulously. "Don't you see?"

"Oh, yes, I see," replied Aunt Hannah, with a fond shake of the head.

"But, really, listen—it's sensible," urged Billy. "First, there's Tommy. His mother died last month. He's at a neighbor's now, but they're going to send him to a Home for Crippled Children; and he's grieving his heart out over it. I'm going to bring him here to a real home—the kind that doesn't begin with a capital letter. He adores music, and he's got real talent, I think. Then there's the Greggorys."

Aunt Hannah looked dubious.

"You can't get the Greggorys to—to use any of that happiness, Billy. They're too proud."

Billy smiled radiantly.

"I know I can't get them to *use* it, Aunt Hannah, but I believe I can get them to *give* it," she declared triumphantly. "I shall ask Alice Greggory to teach Tommy music, and I shall ask Mrs. Greggory to teach him books; and I shall tell them both that I positively need them to keep you company."

"Oh, but Billy," bridled Aunt Hannah, with prompt objection.

"Tut, tut!—I know you'll be willing to be thrown as a little bit of a sop to the Greggorys' pride," coaxed Billy. "You just wait till I get the Overflow Annex in running order. Why, Aunt Hannah, you don't know how busy you're going to be handing out all that extra happiness that I can't use!"

"You dear child!" Aunt Hannah smiled mistily. The black shawl had fallen unheeded to the floor now. "As if anybody ever had any more happiness than one's self could use!"

"I have," avowed Billy, promptly, "and it's going to keep growing and growing, I know."

"Oh, my grief and conscience, Billy, don't!" exclaimed Aunt Hannah, lifting shocked hands of remonstrance. "Rap on wood—do! How can you boast like that?"

Billy dimpled roguishly and sprang to her feet.

"Why, Aunt Hannah, I'm ashamed of you! To be superstitious like that—you, a good Presbyterian!"

Aunt Hannah subsided shamefacedly.

"Yes, I know, Billy, it is silly; but I just can't help it."

"Oh, but it's worse than silly, Aunt Hannah," teased Billy, with a remorseless chuckle. "It's really *heathen!* Bertram told me once that it dates 'way back to the time of the Druids—appealing to the god of trees, or something like that—when you rap on wood, you know."

"Ugh!" shuddered Aunt Hannah. "As if I would, Billy! How is Bertram, by the by?"

A swift shadow crossed Billy's bright face.

"He's lovely—only his arm."

"His arm! But I thought that was better."

"Oh, it is," drooped Billy, "but it gets along so slowly, and it frets him dreadfully. You know he never can do anything with his left hand, he says, and he just hates to have things done for him—though Pete and Dong Ling are quarreling with each other all the time to do things for him, and I'm quarreling with both of them to do them for him myself! By the way, Dong Ling is going to leave us next week. Did you know it?"

"Dong Ling—leave!"

"Yes. Oh, he told Bertram long ago he should go when we were married; that he had plenty much money, and was going back to China, and not be Melican man any longer. But I don't think Bertram thought he'd do it.

William says Dong Ling went to Pete, however, after we left, and told him he wanted to go; that he liked the little Missee plenty well, but that there'd be too much hen-talk when she got back, and—"

"Why, the impudent creature!"

Billy laughed merrily.

"Yes; Pete was furious, William says, but Dong Ling didn't mean any disrespect, I'm sure. He just wasn't used to having petticoats around, and didn't want to take orders from them; that's all."

"But, Billy, what will you do?"

"Oh, Pete's fixed all that lovely," returned Billy, nonchalantly. "You know his niece lives over in South Boston, and it seems she's got a daughter who's a fine cook and will be glad to come. Mercy! Look at the time," she broke off, glancing at the clock. "I shall be late to dinner, and Dong Ling loathes anybody who's late to his meals—as I found out to my sorrow the night we got home. Good-by, dear. I'll be out soon again and fix it all up— about the Annex, you know." And with a bright smile she was gone.

"Dear me," sighed Aunt Hannah, stooping to pick up the black shawl; "dear me! Of course everything will be all right—there's a girl coming, even if Dong Ling is going. But—but—Oh, my grief and conscience, what an extraordinary child Billy is, to be sure—but what a dear one!" she added, wiping a quick tear from her eye. "An Overflow Annex, indeed, for her 'extra happiness'! Now isn't that just like Billy?"

CHAPTER V
TIGER SKINS

September passed and October came, bringing with it cool days and clear, crisp evenings royally ruled over by a gorgeous harvest moon. According to Billy everything was just perfect—except, of course, poor Bertram's arm; and even the fact that that gained so slowly was not without its advantage (again according to Billy), for it gave Bertram more time to be with her.

"You see, dear, as long as you *can't* paint," she told him earnestly, one day, "why, I'm not really hindering you by keeping you with me so much."

"You certainly are not," he retorted, with a smile.

"Then I may be just as happy as I like over it," settled Billy, comfortably.

"As if you ever could hinder me," he ridiculed.

"Oh, yes, I could," nodded Billy, emphatically. "You forget, sir. That was what worried me so. Everybody, even the newspapers and magazines, said I *would* do it, too. They said I'd slay your Art, stifle your Ambition, destroy your Inspiration, and be a nuisance generally. And Kate said—"

"Yes. Well, never mind what Kate said," interrupted the man, savagely.

Billy laughed, and gave his ear a playful tweak.

"All right; but I'm not going to do it, you know—spoil your career, sir. You just wait," she continued dramatically. "The minute your arm gets so you can paint, I myself shall conduct you to your studio, thrust the brushes into your hand, fill your palette with all the colors of the rainbow, and order you to paint, my lord, paint! But—until then I'm going to have you all I like," she finished, with a complete change of manner, nestling into the ready curve of his good left arm.

"You witch!" laughed the man, fondly. "Why, Billy, you couldn't hinder me. You'll *be* my inspiration, dear, instead of slaying it. You'll see. *This* time Marguerite Winthrop's portrait is going to be a success."

Billy turned quickly.

"Then you are—that is, you haven't—I mean, you're going to—paint it?"

"I just am," avowed the artist. "And this time it'll be a success, too, with you to help."

Billy drew in her breath tremulously.

"I didn't know but you'd already started it," she faltered.

He shook his head.

"No. After the other one failed, and Mr. Winthrop asked me to try again, I couldn't *then*. I was so troubled over you. That's the time you did hinder me," he smiled. "Then came your note breaking the engagement. Of course I knew too much to attempt a thing like that portrait then. But now—*now*—!" The pause and the emphasis were eloquent.

"Of course, *now*," nodded Billy, brightly, but a little feverishly. "And when do you begin?"

"Not till January. Miss Winthrop won't be back till then. I saw J. G. last week, and I told him I'd accept his offer to try again."

"What did he say?"

"He gave my left hand a big grip and said: 'Good!—and you'll win out this time.'"

"Of course you will," nodded Billy, again, though still a little feverishly. "And this time I sha'n't mind a bit if you do stay to luncheon, and break engagements with me, sir," she went on, tilting her chin archly, "for I shall know it's the portrait and not the sitter that's really keeping you. Oh, you'll see what a fine artist's wife I'll make!"

"The very best," declared Bertram so ardently that Billy blushed, and shook her head in reproof.

"Nonsense! I wasn't fishing. I didn't mean it that way," she protested. Then, as he tried to catch her, she laughed and danced teasingly out of his reach.

Because Bertram could not paint, therefore, Billy had him quite to herself these October days; nor did she hesitate to appropriate him. Neither, on his part, was Bertram loath to be appropriated. Like two lovers they read and walked and talked together, and like two children, sometimes, they romped through the stately old rooms with Spunkie, or with Tommy Dunn, who was a frequent guest. Spunkie, be it known, was renewing her kittenhood, so potent was the influence of the dangling strings and rolling balls that she encountered everywhere; and Tommy Dunn, with Billy's help, was learning that not even a pair of crutches need keep a lonely little lad from a frolic. Even William, roused from his after-dinner doze by peals of laughter, was sometimes inveigled into activities that left him breathless, but curiously aglow. While Pete, polishing silver in the dining-room down-stairs, smiled indulgently at the merry clatter above—and forgot the teasing pain in his side.

But it was not all nonsense with Billy, nor gay laughter. More often it was a tender glow in the eyes, a softness in the voice, a radiant something like an aura of joy all about her, that told how happy indeed were these days for her. There was proof by word of mouth, too—long talks with Bertram in the dancing firelight when they laid dear plans for the future, and when she tried so hard to make her husband understand what a good, good wife she intended to be, and how she meant never to let anything come between them.

It was so earnest and serious a Billy by this time that Bertram would turn startled, dismayed eyes on his young wife; whereupon, with a very Billy-like change of mood, she would give him one of her rare caresses, and perhaps sigh:

"Goosey—it's only because I'm so happy, happy, happy! Why, Bertram, if it weren't for that Overflow Annex I believe I—I just couldn't live!"

It was Bertram who sighed then, and who prayed fervently in his heart that never might he see a real shadow cloud that dear face.

Thus far, certainly, the cares of matrimony had rested anything but heavily upon the shapely young shoulders of the new wife. Domestic affairs at the Strata moved like a piece of well-oiled machinery. Dong Ling, to be sure, was not there; but in his place reigned Pete's grandniece, a fresh-faced, capable young woman who (Bertram declared) cooked like an angel and minded her own business like a man. Pete, as of yore, had full charge of the house; and a casual eye would see few changes. Even the brothers themselves saw few, for that matter.

True, at the very first, Billy had donned a ruffled apron and a bewitching dust-cap, and had traversed the house from cellar to garret with a prettily important air of "managing things," as she suggested changes right and left. She had summoned Pete, too, for three mornings in succession, and with great dignity had ordered the meals for the day. But when Bertram was discovered one evening tugging back his favorite chair, and when William had asked if Billy were through using his pipe-tray, the young wife had concluded to let things remain about as they were. And when William ate no breakfast one morning, and Bertram aggrievedly refused dessert that night at dinner, Billy—learning through an apologetic Pete that Master William always had to have eggs for breakfast no matter what else there was, and that Master Bertram never ate boiled rice—gave up planning the meals. True, for three more mornings she summoned Pete for "orders," but the orders were nothing more nor less than a blithe "Well, Pete, what are we going to have for dinner to-day?" By the end of a week even this ceremony was given up, and before a month had passed, Billy was little more than a guest in her own home, so far as responsibility was concerned.

Billy was not idle, however; far from it. First, there were the delightful hours with Bertram. Then there was her music: Billy was writing a new song—the best she had ever written, Billy declared.

"Why, Bertram, it can't help being that," she said to her husband, one day. "The words just sang themselves to me right out of my heart; and the melody just dropped down from the sky. And now, everywhere, I'm hearing the most wonderful harmonies. The whole universe is singing to me. If only now I can put it on paper what I hear! Then I can make the whole universe sing to some one else!"

Even music, however, had to step one side for the wedding calls which were beginning to be received, and which must be returned, in spite of the occasional rebellion of the young husband. There were the more intimate friends to be seen, also, and Cyril and Marie to be visited. And always there was the Annex.

The Annex was in fine running order now, and was a source of infinite satisfaction to its founder and great happiness to its beneficiaries. Tommy Dunn was there, learning wonderful things from books and still more wonderful things from the piano in the living-room. Alice Greggory and her mother were there, too—the result of much persuasion. Indeed, according to Bertram, Billy had been able to fill the Annex only by telling each prospective resident that he or she was absolutely necessary to the welfare and happiness of every other resident. Not that the house was full, either. There were still two unoccupied rooms.

"But then, I'm glad there are," Billy had declared, "for there's sure to be some one that I'll want to send there."

"Some *one*, did you say?" Bertram had retorted, meaningly; but his wife had disdained to answer this.

Billy herself was frequently at the Annex. She told Aunt Hannah that she had to come often to bring the happiness—it accumulated so fast. Certainly she always found plenty to do there, whenever she came. There was Aunt Hannah to be read to, Mrs. Greggory to be sung to, and Tommy Dunn to be listened to; for Tommy Dunn was always quivering with eagerness to play her his latest "piece."

Billy knew that some day at the Annex she would meet Mr. M. J. Arkwright; and she told herself that she hoped she should.

Billy had not seen Arkwright (except on the stage of the Boston Opera House) since the day he had left her presence in white-faced, stony-eyed misery after declaring his love for her, and learning of her engagement to Bertram. Since then, she knew, he had been much with his old friend, Alice Greggory. She did not believe, should she see him now, that he would be either white-faced, or stony-eyed. His heart, she was sure, had gone where it ought to have gone in the first place—to Alice. Such being, in her opinion, the case, she longed to get the embarrassment of a first meeting between themselves over with, for, after that, she was sure, their old friendship could be renewed, and she would be in a position to further this pretty love affair between him and Alice. Very decidedly, therefore, Billy wished to meet Arkwright. Very pleased, consequently, was she when, one day, coming into the living-room at the Annex, she found the man sitting by the fire.

Arkwright was on his feet at once.

"Miss—Mrs. H—Henshaw," he stammered

"Oh, Mr. Arkwright," she cried, with just a shade of nervousness in her voice as she advanced, her hand outstretched. "I'm glad to see you."

"Thank you. I wanted to see Miss Greggory," he murmured. Then, as the unconscious rudeness of his reply dawned on him, he made matters infinitely worse by an attempted apology. "That is, I mean—I didn't mean— " he began to stammer miserably.

Some girls might have tossed the floundering man a straw in the shape of a light laugh intended to turn aside all embarrassment—but not Billy. Billy held out a frankly helping hand that was meant to set the man squarely on his feet at her side.

"Mr. Arkwright, don't, please," she begged earnestly. "You and I don't need to beat about the bush. I *am* glad to see you, and I hope you're glad to see me. We're going to be the best of friends from now on, I'm sure; and some day, soon, you're going to bring Alice to see me, and we'll have some music. I left her up-stairs. She'll be down at once, I dare say—I met Rosa going up with your card. Good-by," she finished with a bright smile, as she turned and walked rapidly from the room.

Outside, on the steps, Billy drew a long breath.

"There," she whispered; "that's over—and well over!" The next minute she frowned vexedly. She had missed her glove. "Never mind! I sha'n't go back in there for it now, anyway," she decided.

In the living-room, five minutes later, Alice Greggory found only a hastily scrawled note waiting for her.

"If you'll forgive the unforgivable," she read "you'll forgive me for not being here when you come down. 'Circumstances over which I have no control have called me away.' May we let it go at that?

"M. J. ARKWRIGHT."

As Alice Greggory's amazed, questioning eyes left the note they fell upon the long white glove on the floor by the door. Half mechanically she crossed the room and picked it up; but almost at once she dropped it with a low cry.

"Billy! He—saw—Billy!" Then a flood of understanding dyed her face scarlet as she turned and fled to the blessedly unseeing walls of her own room.

Not ten minutes later Rosa tapped at her door with a note.

"It's from Mr. Arkwright, Miss. He's downstairs." Rosa's eyes were puzzled, and a bit startled.

"Mr. Arkwright!"

"Yes, Miss. He's come again. That is, I didn't know he'd went—but he must have, for he's come again now. He wrote something in a little book; then he tore it out and gave it to me. He said he'd wait, please, for an answer."

"Oh, very well, Rosa."

Miss Greggory took the note and spoke with an elaborate air of indifference that was meant to express a calm ignoring of the puzzled questioning in the other's eyes. The next moment she read this in Arkwright's peculiar scrawl:

"If you've already forgiven the unforgivable, you'll do it again, I know, and come down-stairs. Won't you, please? I want to see you."

Miss Greggory lifted her head with a jerk. Her face was a painful red.

"Tell Mr. Arkwright I can't possibly—" She came to an abrupt pause. Her eyes had encountered Rosa's, and in Rosa's eyes the puzzled questioning was plainly fast becoming a shrewd suspicion.

There was the briefest of hesitations; then, lightly, Miss Greggory tossed the note aside.

"Tell Mr. Arkwright I'll be down at once, please," she directed carelessly, as she turned back into the room.

But she was not down at once. She was not down until she had taken time to bathe her red eyes, powder her telltale nose, smoothe her ruffled hair, and whip herself into the calm, steady-eyed, self-controlled young woman that Arkwright finally rose to meet when she came into the room.

"I thought it was only women who were privileged to change their mind," she began brightly; but Arkwright ignored her attempt to conventionalize the situation.

"Thank you for coming down," he said, with a weariness that instantly drove the forced smile from the girl's lips. "I—I wanted to—to talk to you."

"Yes?" She seated herself and motioned him to a chair near her. He took the seat, and then fell silent, his eyes out the window.

"I thought you said you—you wanted to talk, she reminded him nervously, after a minute.

"I did." He turned with disconcerting abruptness. "Alice, I'm going to tell you a story."

"I shall be glad to listen. People always like stories, don't they?"

"Do they?" The somber pain in Arkwright's eyes deepened. Alice Greggory did not know it, but he was thinking of another story he had once told in that same room. Billy was his listener then, while now—A little precipitately he began to speak.

"When I was a very small boy I went to visit my uncle, who, in his young days, had been quite a hunter. Before the fireplace in his library was a huge tiger skin with a particularly lifelike head. The first time I saw it I screamed, and ran and hid. I refused then even to go into the room again. My cousins urged, scolded, pleaded, and laughed at me by turns, but I was obdurate. I would not go where I could see the fearsome thing again, even though it was, as they said, 'nothing but a dead old rug!'

"Finally, one day, my uncle took a hand in the matter. By sheer willpower he forced me to go with him straight up to the dreaded creature, and stand by its side. He laid one of my shrinking hands on the beast's smooth head, and thrust the other one quite into the open red mouth with its gleaming teeth.

"'You see,' he said, 'there's absolutely nothing to fear. He can't possibly hurt you. Just as if you weren't bigger and finer and stronger in every way than that dead thing on the floor!'

"Then, when he had got me to the point where of my own free will I would walk up and touch the thing, he drew a lesson for me.

"'Now remember,' he charged me. 'Never run and hide again. Only cowards do that. Walk straight up and face the thing. Ten to one you'll find it's nothing but a dead skin masquerading as the real thing. Even if it isn't if it's alive—face it. Find a weapon and fight it. Know that you are going to conquer it and you'll conquer. Never run. Be a man. Men don't run, my boy!'"

Arkwright paused, and drew a long breath. He did not look at the girl in the opposite chair. If he had looked he would have seen a face transfigured.

"Well," he resumed, "I never forgot that tiger skin, nor what it stood for, after that day when Uncle Ben thrust my hand into its hideous, but harmless, red mouth. Even as a kid I began, then, to try—not to run. I've tried ever since But to-day—I did run."

Arkwright's voice had been getting lower and lower. The last three words would have been almost inaudible to ears less sensitively alert than were Alice Greggory's. For a moment after the words were uttered, only the clock's ticking broke the silence; then, with an obvious effort, the man roused himself, as if breaking away from some benumbing force that held him.

"Alice, I don't need to tell you, after what I said the other night, that I loved Billy Neilson. That was bad enough, for I found she was pledged to another man. But to-day I discovered something worse: I discovered that I loved Billy *Henshaw*—another man's wife. And—I ran. But I've come back. I'm going to face the thing. Oh, I'm not deceiving myself! This love of mine is no dead tiger skin. It's a beast, alive and alert—God pity me!—to destroy my very soul. But I'm going to fight it; and—I want you to help me."

The girl gave a half-smothered cry. The man turned, but he could not see her face distinctly. Twilight had come, and the room was full of shadows. He hesitated, then went on, a little more quietly.

"That's why I've told you all this—so you would help me. And you will, won't you?"

There was no answer. Once again he tried to see her face, but it was turned now quite away from him.

"You've been a big help already, little girl. Your friendship, your comradeship—they've been everything to me. You're not going to make me do without them—now?"

"No—oh, no!" The answer was low and a little breathless; but he heard it.

"Thank you. I knew you wouldn't." He paused, then rose to his feet. When he spoke again his voice carried a note of whimsical lightness that was a little forced. "But I must go—else you *will* take them from me, and with good reason. And please don't let your kind heart grieve too much—over me. I'm no deep-dyed villain in a melodrama, nor wicked lover in a ten-penny novel, you know. I'm just an everyday man in real life; and we're going to fight this thing out in everyday living. That's where your help is coming in. We'll go together to see Mrs. Bertram Henshaw. She's asked us to, and you'll do it, I know. We'll have music and everyday talk. We'll see Mrs. Bertram Henshaw in her own home with her husband, where she belongs; and—I'm not going to run again. But—I'm counting on your help, you know," he smiled a little wistfully, as he held out his hand in good-by.

One minute later Alice Greggory, alone, was hurrying up-stairs.

"I can't—I can't—I know I can't," she was whispering wildly. Then, in her own room, she faced herself in the mirror. "Yes—you—can, Alice Greggory," she asserted, with swift change of voice and manner. "This is *your* tiger skin, and you're going to fight it. Do you understand?—fight it! And you're going to win, too. Do you want that man to know you—*care*?"

CHAPTER VI
"THE PAINTING LOOK"

It was toward the last of October that Billy began to notice her husband's growing restlessness. Twice, when she had been playing to him, she turned to find him testing the suppleness of his injured arm. Several times, failing to receive an answer to her questions, she had looked up to discover him gazing abstractedly at nothing in particular.

They read and walked and talked together, to be sure, and Bertram's devotion to her lightest wish was beyond question; but more and more frequently these days Billy found him hovering over his sketches in his studio; and once, when he failed to respond to the dinner-bell, search revealed him buried in a profound treatise on "The Art of Foreshortening."

Then came the day when Billy, after an hour's vain effort to imprison within notes a tantalizing melody, captured the truant and rain down to the studio to tell Bertram of her victory.

But Bertram did not seem even to hear her. True, he leaped to his feet and hurried to meet her, his face radiantly aglow; but she had not ceased to speak before he himself was talking.

"Billy, Billy, I've been sketching," he cried. "My hand is almost steady. See, some of those lines are all right! I just picked up a crayon and—" He stopped abruptly, his eyes on Billy's face. A vaguely troubled shadow crossed his own. "Did—did you—were you saying anything in—in particular, when you came in?" he stammered.

For a short half-minute Billy looked at her husband without speaking. Then, a little queerly, she laughed.

"Oh, no, nothing at all in *particular*," she retorted airily. The next moment, with one of her unexpected changes of manner, she darted across the room, picked up a palette, and a handful of brushes from the long box near it. Advancing toward her husband she held them out dramatically. "And now paint, my lord, paint!" she commanded him, with stern insistence, as she thrust them into his hands.

Bertram laughed shamefacedly.

"Oh, I say, Billy," he began; but Billy had gone.

Out in the hall Billy was speeding up-stairs, talking fiercely to herself.

"We'll, Billy Neilson Henshaw, it's come! Now behave yourself. *That was the painting look!* You know what that means. Remember, he belongs to his Art before he does to you. Kate and everybody says so. And you—you expected him to tend to you and your silly little songs. Do you want to ruin his career? As if now he could spend all his time and give all his thoughts to you! But I—I just hate that Art!"

"What did you say, Billy?" asked William, in mild surprise, coming around the turn of the balustrade in the hall above. "Were you speaking to me, my dear?"

Billy looked up. Her face cleared suddenly, and she laughed—though a little ruefully.

"No, Uncle William, I wasn't talking to you," she sighed. "I was just—just administering first aid to the injured," she finished, as she whisked into her own room.

"Well, well, bless the child! What can she mean by that?" puzzled Uncle William, turning to go down the stairway.

Bertram began to paint a very little the next day. He painted still more the next, and yet more again the day following. He was like a bird let out of a cage, so joyously alive was he. The old sparkle came back to his eye, the old gay smile to his lips. Now that they had come back Billy realized what she had not been conscious of before: that for several weeks past they had not been there; and she wondered which hurt the more—that they had not been there before, or that they were there now. Then she scolded herself roundly for asking the question at all.

They were not easy—those days for Billy, though always to Bertram she managed to show a cheerfully serene face. To Uncle William, also, and to Aunt Hannah she showed a smiling countenance; and because she could not talk to anybody else of her feelings, she talked to herself. This, however, was no new thing for Billy to do From earliest childhood she had fought things out in like manner.

"But it's so absurd of you, Billy Henshaw," she berated herself one day, when Bertram had become so absorbed in his work that he had forgotten to keep his appointment with her for a walk. "Just because you have had his constant attention almost every hour since you were married is no reason why you should have it every hour now, when his arm is better! Besides, it's exactly what you said you wouldn't do—object—to his giving proper time to his work."

"But I'm not objecting," stormed the other half of herself. "I'm *telling* him to do it. It's only that he's so—so *pleased* to do it. He doesn't seem to mind a bit being away from me. He's actually happy!"

"Well, don't you want him to be happy in his work? Fie! For shame! A fine artist's wife you are. It seems Kate was right, then; you *are* going to spoil his career!"

"Ho!" quoth Billy, and tossed her head. Forthwith she crossed the room to her piano and plumped herself down hard on to the stool. Then, from under her fingers there fell a rollicking melody that seemed to fill the room with little dancing feet. Faster and faster sped Billy's fingers; swifter and swifter twinkled the little dancing feet. Then a door was jerked open, and Bertram's voice called:

"Billy!"

The music stopped instantly. Billy sprang from her seat, her eyes eagerly seeking the direction from which had come the voice. Perhaps— *perhaps* Bertram wanted her. Perhaps he was not going to paint any longer that morning, after all. "Billy!" called the voice again. "Please, do you mind stopping that playing just for a little while? I'm a brute, I know, dear, but my brush *will* try to keep time with that crazy little tune of yours, and you know my hand is none too steady, anyhow, and when it tries to keep up with that jiggety, jig, jig, jiggety, jig, jig—! *Do* you mind, darling, just—just sewing, or doing something still for a while?"

All the light fled from Billy's face, but her voice, when she spoke, was the quintessence of cheery indifference.

"Why, no, of course not, dear."

"Thank you. I knew you wouldn't," sighed Bertram. Then the door shut.

For a long minute Billy stood motionless before she glanced at her watch and sped to the telephone.

"Is Miss Greggory there, Rosa?" she called when the operator's ring was answered.

"Mis' Greggory, the lame one?"

"No; *Miss* Greggory—Miss Alice."

"Oh! Yes'm."

"Then won't you ask her to come to the telephone, please."

There was a moment's wait, during which Billy's small, well-shod foot beat a nervous tattoo on the floor.

"Oh, is that you, Alice?" she called then. "Are you going to be home for an hour or two?"

"Why, y-yes; yes, indeed."

"Then I'm coming over. We'll play duets, sing—anything. I want some music."

"Do! And—Mr. Arkwright is here. He'll help."

"Mr. Arkwright? You say he's there? Then I won't—Yes, I will, too." Billy spoke with renewed firmness. "I'll be there right away. Good-by." And she hung up the receiver, and went to tell Pete to order John and Peggy at once.

"I suppose I ought to have left Alice and Mr. Arkwright alone together," muttered the young wife feverishly, as she hurriedly prepared for departure. "But I'll make it up to them later. I'm going to give them lots of chances. But to-day—to-day I just had to go—somewhere!"

At the Annex, with Alice Greggory and Arkwright, Billy sang duets and trios, and reveled in a sonorous wilderness of new music to her heart's content. Then, rested, refreshed, and at peace with all the world, she hurried home to dinner and to Bertram.

"There! I feel better," she sighed, as she took off her hat in her own room; "and now I'll go find Bertram. Bless his heart—of course he didn't want me to play when he was so busy!"

Billy went straight to the studio, but Bertram was not there. Neither was he in William's room, nor anywhere in the house. Down-stairs in the dining-room Pete was found looking rather white, leaning back in a chair. He struggled at once to his feet, however, as his mistress entered the room.

Billy hurried forward with a startled exclamation.

"Why, Pete, what is it? Are you sick?" she cried, her glance encompassing the half-set table.

"No, ma'am; oh, no, ma'am!" The old man stumbled forward and began to arrange the knives and forks. "It's just a pesky pain—beggin' yer pardon—in my side. But I ain't sick. No, Miss—ma'am."

Billy frowned and shook her head. Her eyes were on Pete's palpably trembling hands.

"But, Pete, you are sick," she protested. "Let Eliza do that."

Pete drew himself stiffly erect. The color had begun to come back to his face.

"There hain't no one set this table much but me for more'n fifty years, an' I've got a sort of notion that nobody can do it just ter suit me. Besides, I'm better now. It's gone—that pain."

"But, Pete, what is it? How long have you had it?"

"I hain't had it any time, steady. It's the comin' an' goin' kind. It seems silly ter mind it at all; only, when it does come, it sort o' takes the backbone right out o' my knees, and they double up so's I have ter set down. There, ye see? I'm pert as a sparrer, now!" And, with stiff celerity, Pete resumed his task.

His mistress still frowned.

"That isn't right, Pete," she demurred, with a slow shake of her head. "You should see a doctor."

The old man paled a little. He had seen a doctor, and he had not liked what the doctor had told him. In fact, he stubbornly refused to believe what the doctor had said. He straightened himself now a little aggressively.

"Humph! Beggin' yer pardon, Miss—ma'am, but I don't think much o' them doctor chaps."

Billy shook her head again as she smiled and turned away. Then, as if casually, she asked:

"Oh, did Mr. Bertram go out, Pete?"

"Yes, Miss; about five o'clock. He said he'd be back to dinner."

"Oh! All right."

From the hall the telephone jangled sharply.

"I'll go," said Pete's mistress, as she turned and hurried up-stairs.

It was Bertram's voice that answered her opening "Hullo."

"Oh, Billy, is that you, dear? Well, you're just the one I wanted. I wanted to say—that is, I wanted to ask you—" The speaker cleared his throat a little nervously, and began all over again. "The fact is, Billy, I've run across a couple of old classmates on from New York, and they are very anxious I should stay down to dinner with them. Would you mind—very much if I did?"

A cold hand seemed to clutch Billy's heart. She caught her breath with a little gasp and tried to speak; but she had to try twice before the words came.

"Why, no—no, of course not!" Billy's voice was very high-pitched and a little shaky, but it was surpassingly cheerful.

"You sure you won't be—lonesome?" Bertram's voice was vaguely troubled.

"Of course not!"

"You've only to say the word, little girl," came Bertram's anxious tones again, "and I won't stay."

Billy swallowed convulsively. If only, only he would *stop* and leave her to herself! As if she were going to own up that *she* was lonesome for *him*— if *he* was not lonesome for *her!*

"Nonsense! of course you'll stay," called Billy, still in that high-pitched, shaky treble. Then, before Bertram could answer, she uttered a gay "Good-by!" and hung up the receiver.

Billy had ten whole minutes in which to cry before Pete's gong sounded for dinner; but she had only one minute in which to try to efface the woefully visible effects of those ten minutes before William tapped at her door, and called:

"Gone to sleep, my dear? Dinner's ready. Didn't you hear the gong?"

"Yes, I'm coming, Uncle William." Billy spoke with breezy gayety, and threw open the door; but she did not meet Uncle William's eyes. Her head was turned away. Her hands were fussing with the hang of her skirt.

"Bertram's dining out, Pete tells me," observed William, with cheerful nonchalance, as they went down-stairs together.

Billy bit her lip and looked up sharply. She had been bracing herself to meet with disdainful indifference this man's pity—the pity due a poor neglected wife whose husband *preferred* to dine with old classmates rather than with herself. Now she found in William's face, not pity, but a calm, even jovial, acceptance of the situation as a matter of course. She had known she was going to hate that pity; but now, curiously enough, she was conscious only of anger that the pity was not there—that she might hate it.

She tossed her head a little. So even William—Uncle William—regarded this monstrous thing as an insignificant matter of everyday experience. Maybe he expected it to occur frequently—every night, or so. Doubtless he did expect it to occur every night, or so. Indeed! Very well. As if she were going to show *now* that she cared whether Bertram were there or not! They should see.

So with head held high and eyes asparkle, Billy marched into the dining-room and took her accustomed place.

CHAPTER VII
THE BIG BAD QUARREL

It was a brilliant dinner—because Billy made it so. At first William met her sallies of wit with mild surprise; but it was not long before he rose gallantly to the occasion, and gave back full measure of retort. Even Pete twice had to turn his back to hide a smile, and once his hand shook so that the tea he was carrying almost spilled. This threatened catastrophe, however, seemed to frighten him so much that his face was very grave throughout the rest of the dinner.

Still laughing and talking gayly, Billy and Uncle William, after the meal was over, ascended to the drawing-room. There, however, the man, in spite of the young woman's gay badinage, fell to dozing in the big chair before the fire, leaving Billy with only Spunkie for company—Spunkie, who, disdaining every effort to entice her into a romp, only winked and blinked stupid eyes, and finally curled herself on the rug for a nap.

Billy, left to her own devices, glanced at her watch.

Half-past seven! Time, almost, for Bertram to be coming. He had said "dinner"; and, of course, after dinner was over he would be coming home—to her. Very well; she would show him that she had at least got along without him as well as he had without her. At all events he would not find her forlornly sitting with her nose pressed against the window-pane! And forthwith Billy established herself in a big chair (with its back carefully turned toward the door by which Bertram would enter), and opened a book.

Five, ten, fifteen minutes passed. Billy fidgeted in her chair, twisted her neck to look out into the hall—and dropped her book with a bang.

Uncle William jerked himself awake, and Spunkie opened sleepy eyes. Then both settled themselves for another nap. Billy sighed, picked up her book, and flounced back into her chair. But she did not read. Disconsolately she sat staring straight ahead—until a quick step on the sidewalk outside stirred her into instant action. Assuming a look of absorbed interest she twitched the book open and held it before her face.... But the step passed by the door: and Billy saw then that her book was upside down.

Five, ten, fifteen more minutes passed. Billy still sat, apparently reading, though she had not turned a page. The book now, however, was right side up. One by one other minutes passed till the great clock in the hall struck nine long strokes.

"Well, well, bless my soul!" mumbled Uncle William, resolutely forcing himself to wake up. "What time was that?"

"Nine o'clock." Billy spoke with tragic distinctness, yet very cheerfully.

"Eh? Only nine?" blinked Uncle William. "I thought it must be ten. Well, anyhow, I believe I'll go up-stairs. I seem to be unusually sleepy."

Billy said nothing. "'Only nine,' indeed!" she was thinking wrathfully.

At the door Uncle William turned.

"You're not going to sit up, my dear, of course," he remarked.

For the second time that evening a cold hand seemed to clutch Billy's heart.

Sit up! Had it come already to that? Was she even now a wife who had need to *sit up* for her husband?

"I really wouldn't, my dear," advised Uncle William again. "Good night."

"Oh, but I'm not sleepy at all, yet," Billy managed to declare brightly. "Good night."

Then Uncle William went up-stairs.

Billy turned to her book, which happened to be one of William's on "Fake Antiques."

"'To collect anything, these days, requires expert knowledge, and the utmost care and discrimination,'" read Billy's eyes. "So Uncle William *expected* Bertram was going to spend the whole evening as well as stay to dinner!" ran Billy's thoughts. "'The enormous quantity of bijouterie, Dresden and Battersea enamel ware that is now flooding the market, is made on the Continent—and made chiefly for the American trade,'" continued the book.

"Well, who cares if it is," snapped Billy, springing to her feet and tossing the volume aside. "Spunkie, come here! You've simply got to play with me. Do you hear? I want to be gay—*gay*—GAY! He's gay. He's down there with those men, where he wants to be. Where he'd *rather* be than be with me! Do you think I want him to come home and find me moping over a stupid old book? Not much! I'm going to have him find me gay, too. Now, come,

Spunkie; hurry—wake up! He'll be here right away, I'm sure." And Billy shook a pair of worsted reins, hung with little soft balls, full in Spunkie's face.

But Spunkie would not wake up, and Spunkie would not play. She pretended to. She bit at the reins, and sank her sharp claws into the dangling balls. For a fleeting instant, even, something like mischief gleamed in her big yellow eyes. Then the jaws relaxed, the paws turned to velvet, and Spunkie's sleek gray head settled slowly back into lazy comfort. Spunkie was asleep.

Billy gazed at the cat with reproachful eyes.

"And you, too, Spunkie," she murmured. Then she got to her feet and went back to her chair. This time she picked up a magazine and began to turn the leaves very fast, one after another.

Half-past nine came, then ten. Pete appeared at the door to get Spunkie, and to see that everything was all right for the night.

"Mr. Bertram is not in yet?" he began doubtfully.

Billy shook her head with a bright smile.

"No, Pete. Go to bed. I expect him every minute. Good night."

"Thank you, ma'am. Good night."

The old man picked up the sleepy cat and went down-stairs. A little later Billy heard his quiet steps coming back through the hall and ascending the stairs. She listened until from away at the top of the house she heard his door close. Then she drew a long breath.

Ten o'clock—after ten o'clock, and Bertram not there yet! And was this what he called dinner? Did one eat, then, till ten o'clock, when one dined with one's friends?

Billy was angry now—very angry. She was too angry to be reasonable. This thing that her husband had done seemed monstrous to her, smarting, as she was, under the sting of hurt pride and grieved loneliness—the state of mind into which she had worked herself. No longer now did she wish to be gay when her husband came. No longer did she even pretend to assume indifference. Bertram had done wrong. He had been unkind, cruel, thoughtless, inconsiderate of her comfort and happiness. Furthermore he *did not* love her as well as she did him or he never, never could have done it! She would let him see, when he came, just how hurt and grieved she was—and how disappointed, too.

Billy was walking the floor now, back and forth, back and forth.

Half-past ten came, then eleven. As the eleven long strokes reverberated through the silent house Billy drew in her breath and held it suspended. A new look came to her eyes. A growing terror crept into them and culminated in a frightened stare at the clock.

Billy ran then to the great outer door and pulled it open. A cold wind stung her face, and caused her to shut the door quickly. Back and forth she began to pace the floor again; but in five minutes she had run to the door once more. This time she wore a heavy coat of Bertram's which she caught up as she passed the hall-rack.

Out on to the broad top step Billy hurried, and peered down the street. As far as she could see not a person was in sight. Across the street in the Public Garden the wind stirred the gray tree-branches and set them to casting weird shadows on the bare, frozen ground. A warning something behind her sent Billy scurrying into the house just in time to prevent the heavy door's closing and shutting her out, keyless, in the cold.

Half-past eleven came, and again Billy ran to the door. This time she put the floor-mat against the casing so that the door could not close. Once more she peered wildly up and down the street, and across into the deserted, wind-swept Garden.

There was only terror now in Billy's face. The anger was all gone. In Billy's mind there was not a shadow of doubt—something had happened to Bertram.

Bertram was ill—hurt—dead! And he was so good, so kind, so noble; such a dear, dear husband! If only she could see him once. If only she could ask his forgiveness for those wicked, unkind, accusing thoughts. If only she could tell him again that she did love him. If only—

Far down the street a step rang sharply on the frosty air. A masculine figure was hurrying toward the house. Retreating well into the shadow of the doorway, Billy watched it, her heart pounding against her side in great suffocating throbs. Nearer and nearer strode the approaching figure until Billy had almost sprung to meet it with a glad cry—almost, but not quite; for the figure neither turned nor paused, but marched straight on—and Billy saw then, under the arc light, a brown-bearded man who was not Bertram at all.

Three times during the next few minutes did the waiting little bride on the doorstep watch with palpitating yearning a shadowy form appear, approach—and pass by. At the third heart-breaking disappointment, Billy wrung her hands helplessly.

"I don't see how there can be—so many—utterly *useless* people in the world!" she choked. Then, thoroughly chilled and sick at heart, she went into the house and closed the door.

Once again, back and forth, back and forth, Billy took up her weary vigil. She still wore the heavy coat. She had forgotten to take it off. Her face was pitifully white and drawn. Her eyes were wild. One of her hands was nervously caressing the rough sleeve of the coat as it hung from her shoulder.

One—two—three—

Billy gave a sharp cry and ran into the hall.

Yes, it was twelve o'clock. And now, always, all the rest of the dreary, useless hours that that clock would tick away through an endless existence, she would have to live—without Bertram. If only she could see him once more! But she could not. He was dead. He must be dead, now. Here it was twelve o'clock, and—

There came a quick step, the click of a key in the lock, then the door swung back and Bertram, big, strong, and merry-eyed, stood before her.

"Well, well, hullo," he called jovially. "Why, Billy, what's the matter?" he broke off, in quite a different tone of voice.

And then a curious thing happened. Billy, who, a minute before, had been seeing only a dear, noble, adorable, *lost* Bertram, saw now suddenly only the man that had stayed *happily* till midnight with two friends, while she—she—

"Matter! Matter!" exclaimed Billy sharply, then. "Is this what you call staying to dinner, Bertram Henshaw?"

Bertram stared. A slow red stole to his forehead. It was his first experience of coming home to meet angry eyes that questioned his behavior—and he did not like it. He had been, perhaps, a little conscience-smitten when he saw how late he had stayed; and he had intended to say he was sorry, of course. But to be thus sharply called to account for a perfectly innocent good time with a couple of friends—! To come home and find Billy making a ridiculous scene like this—! He—he would not stand for it! He—

Bertram's lips snapped open. The angry retort was almost spoken when something in the piteously quivering chin and white, drawn face opposite stopped it just in time.

"Why, Billy—darling!" he murmured instead.

It was Billy's turn to change. All the anger melted away before the dismayed tenderness in those dear eyes and the grieved hurt in that dear voice.

"Well, you—you—I—" Billy began to cry.

It was all right then, of course, for the next minute she was crying on Bertram's big, broad shoulder; and in the midst of broken words, kisses, gentle pats, and inarticulate croonings, the Big, Bad Quarrel, that had been all ready to materialize, faded quite away into nothingness.

"I didn't have such an awfully good time, anyhow," avowed Bertram, when speech became rational. "I'd rather have been home with you."

"Nonsense!" blinked Billy, valiantly. "Of course you had a good time; and it was perfectly right you should have it, too! And I—I hope you'll have it again."

"I sha'n't," emphasized Bertram, promptly, "—not and leave you!"

Billy regarded him with adoring eyes.

"I'll tell you; we'll have 'em come here," she proposed gayly.

"Sure we will," agreed Bertram.

"Yes; sure we will," echoed Billy, with a contented sigh. Then, a little breathlessly, she added: "Anyhow, I'll know—where you are. I won't think you're—dead!"

"You—blessed—little-goose!" scolded Bertram, punctuating each word with a kiss.

Billy drew a long sigh.

"If this is a quarrel I'm going to have them often," she announced placidly.

"Billy!" The young husband was plainly aghast.

"Well, I am—because I like the making-up," dimpled Billy, with a mischievous twinkle as she broke from his clasp and skipped ahead up the stairway.

CHAPTER VIII
BILLY CULTIVATES A "COMFORTABLE INDIFFERENCE"

The next morning, under the uncompromising challenge of a bright sun, Billy began to be uneasily suspicious that she had been just a bit unreasonable and exacting the night before. To make matters worse she chanced to run across a newspaper criticism of a new book bearing the ominous title: "When the Honeymoon Wanes A Talk to Young Wives."

Such a title, of course, attracted her supersensitive attention at once; and, with a curiously faint feeling, she picked up the paper and began to read.

As the most of the criticism was taken up with quotations from the book, it was such sentences as these that met her startled eyes:

"Perhaps the first test comes when the young wife awakes to the realization that while her husband loves her very much, he can still make plans with his old friends which do not include herself.... Then is when the foolish wife lets her husband see how hurt she is that he can want to be with any one but herself.... Then is when the husband—used all his life to independence, perhaps—begins to chafe under these new bonds that hold him so fast.... No man likes to be held up at the end of a threatened scene and made to give an account of himself.... Before a woman has learned to cultivate a comfortable indifference to her husband's comings and goings, she is apt to be tyrannical and exacting."

"'Comfortable indifference,' indeed!" stormed Billy to herself. "As if I ever could be comfortably indifferent to anything Bertram did!"

She dropped the paper; but there were still other quotations from the book there, she knew; and in a moment she was back at the table reading them.

"No man, however fondly he loves his wife, likes to feel that she is everlastingly peering into the recesses of his mind, and weighing his every act to find out if he does or does not love her to-day as well as he did yesterday at this time.... Then, when spontaneity is dead, she is the chief mourner at its funeral.... A few couples never leave the Garden of Eden. They grow old hand in hand. They are the ones who bear and forbear; who have learned to adjust themselves to the intimate relationship of living together.... A certain amount of liberty, both of action and thought, must be allowed on each side.... The family shut in upon itself grows so narrow that all interest in the outside world is lost.... No two people are ever fitted to fill each other's lives entirely. They ought not to try to do it. If they do try, the process is belittling to each, and the result, if it is successful, is nothing less than a tragedy; for it could not mean the highest ideals, nor the truest devotion.... Brushing up against other interests and other personalities is good for both husband and wife. Then to each other they bring the best of what they have found, and each to the other continues to be new and interesting.... The young wife, however, is apt to be jealous of everything that turns her husband's attention for one moment away from herself. She is jealous of his thoughts, his words, his friends, even his business.... But the wife who has learned to be the clinging vine when her husband wishes her to cling, and to be the sturdy oak when clinging vines would be tiresome, has solved a tremendous problem."

At this point Billy dropped the paper. She flung it down, indeed, a bit angrily. There were still a few more words in the criticism, mostly the critic's own opinion of the book; but Billy did not care for this. She had read quite enough—too much, in fact. All that sort of talk might be very well, even necessary, perhaps (she told herself), for ordinary husbands and wives! but for her and Bertram—

Then vividly before her rose those initial quoted words:

"Perhaps the first test comes when the young wife awakes to the realization that while her husband loves her very much, he can still make plans with his old friends which do not include herself."

Billy frowned, and put her finger to her lips. Was that then, last night, a "test"? Had she been "tyrannical and exacting"? Was she "everlastingly peering into the recesses" of Bertram's mind and "weighing his every act"? Was Bertram already beginning to "chafe" under these new bonds that held him?

No, no, never that! She could not believe that. But what if he should sometime begin to chafe? What if they two should, in days to come, degenerate into just the ordinary, everyday married folk, whom she saw about her everywhere, and for whom just such horrid books as this must be written? It was unbelievable, unthinkable. And yet, that man had said—

With a despairing sigh Billy picked up the paper once more and read carefully every word again. When she had finished she stood soberly thoughtful, her eyes out of the window.

After all, it was nothing but the same old story. She was exacting. She did want her husband's every thought. She *gloried* in peering into every last recess of his mind if she had half a chance. She was jealous of his work. She had almost hated his painting—at times. She had held him up with a threatened scene only the night before and demanded that he should give an account of himself. She had, very likely, been the clinging vine when she should have been the sturdy oak.

Very well, then. (Billy lifted her head and threw back her shoulders.) He should have no further cause for complaint. She would be an oak. She would cultivate that comfortable indifference to his comings and goings. She would brush up against other interests and personalities so as to be "new" and "interesting" to her husband. She would not be tyrannical, exacting, or jealous. She would not threaten scenes, nor peer into recesses. Whatever happened, she would not let Bertram begin to chafe against those bonds!

Having arrived at this heroic and (to her) eminently satisfactory state of mind, Billy turned from the window and fell to work on a piece of manuscript music.

"'Brush up against other interests,'" she admonished herself sternly, as she reached for her pen.

Theoretically it was beautiful; but practically—

Billy began at once to be that oak. Not an hour after she had first seen the fateful notice of "When the Honeymoon Wanes," Bertram's ring sounded at the door down-stairs.

Bertram always let himself in with his latchkey; but, from the first of Billy's being there, he had given a peculiar ring at the bell which would bring his wife flying to welcome him if she were anywhere in the house. To-day, when the bell sounded, Billy sprang as usual to her feet, with a joyous "There's Bertram!" But the next moment she fell back.

"Tut, tut, Billy Neilson Henshaw! Learn to cultivate a comfortable indifference to your husband's comings and goings," she whispered fiercely. Then she sat down and fell to work again.

A moment later she heard her husband's voice talking to some one— Pete, she surmised. "Here? You say she's here?" Then she heard Bertram's quick step on the stairs. The next minute, very quietly, he came to her door.

"Ho!" he ejaculated gayly, as she rose to receive his kiss. "I thought I'd find you asleep, when you didn't hear my ring."

Billy reddened a little.

"Oh, no, I wasn't asleep."

"But you didn't hear—" Bertram stopped abruptly, an odd look in his eyes. "Maybe you did hear it, though," he corrected.

Billy colored more confusedly. The fact that she looked so distressed did not tend to clear Bertram's face.

"Why, of course, Billy, I didn't mean to insist on your coming to meet me," he began a little stiffly; but Billy interrupted him.

"Why, Bertram, I just love to go to meet you," she maintained indignantly. Then, remembering just in time, she amended: "That is, I did love to meet you, until—" With a sudden realization that she certainly had not helped matters any, she came to an embarrassed pause.

A puzzled frown showed on Bertram's face.

"You did love to meet me until—" he repeated after her; then his face changed. "Billy, you aren't—you *can't* be laying up last night against me!" he reproached her a little irritably.

"Last night? Why, of course not," retorted Billy, in a panic at the bare mention of the "test" which—according to "When the Honeymoon Wanes"—was at the root of all her misery. Already she thought she detected in Bertram's voice signs that he was beginning to chafe against those "bonds." "It is a matter of—of the utmost indifference to me what time you come home at night, my dear," she finished airily, as she sat down to her work again.

Bertram stared; then he frowned, turned on his heel and left the room. Bertram, who knew nothing of the "Talk to Young Wives" in the newspaper at Billy's feet, was surprised, puzzled, and just a bit angry.

Billy, left alone, jabbed her pen with such force against her paper that the note she was making became an unsightly blot.

"Well, if this is what that man calls being 'comfortably indifferent,' I'd hate to try the *un*comfortable kind," she muttered with emphasis.

CHAPTER IX
THE DINNER BILLY TRIED TO GET

Notwithstanding what Billy was disposed to regard as the non-success of her first attempt to profit by the "Talk to Young Wives;" she still frantically tried to avert the waning of her honeymoon. Assiduously she cultivated the prescribed "indifference," and with at least apparent enthusiasm she sought the much-to-be-desired "outside interests." That is, she did all this when she thought of it when something reminded her of the sword of destruction hanging over her happiness. At other times, when she was just being happy without question, she was her old self impulsive, affectionate, and altogether adorable.

Naturally, under these circumstances, her conduct was somewhat erratic. For three days, perhaps, she would fly to the door at her husband's ring, and hang upon his every movement. Then, for the next three, she would be a veritable will-o'-the-wisp for elusiveness, caring, apparently, not one whit whether her husband came or went until poor Bertram, at his wit's end, scourged himself with a merciless catechism as to what he had done to vex her. Then, perhaps, just when he had nerved himself almost to the point of asking her what was the trouble, there would come another change, bringing back to him the old Billy, joyous, winsome, and devoted, plainly caring nothing for anybody or anything but himself. Scarcely, however, would he become sure that it was his Billy back again before she was off once more, quite beyond his reach, singing with Arkwright and Alice Greggory, playing with Tommy Dunn, plunging into some club or church work—anything but being with him.

That all this was puzzling and disquieting to Bertram, Billy not once suspected. Billy, so far as she was concerned, was but cultivating a comfortable indifference, brushing up against outside interests, and being an oak.

December passed, and January came, bringing Miss Marguerite Winthrop to her Boston home. Bertram's arm was "as good as ever" now, according to its owner; and the sittings for the new portrait began at once. This left Billy even more to her own devices, for Bertram entered into his new work with an enthusiasm born of a glad relief from forced idleness, and a consuming eagerness to prove that even though he had failed the first time, he could paint a portrait of Marguerite Winthrop that would be a credit to himself, a conclusive retort to his critics, and a source of pride to his once mortified friends. With his whole heart, therefore, he threw himself into the work before him, staying sometimes well into the afternoon on the days Miss Winthrop could find time between her social engagements to give him a sitting.

It was on such a day, toward the middle of the month, that Billy was called to the telephone at half-past twelve o'clock to speak to her husband.

"Billy, dear," began Bertram at once, "if you don't mind I'm staying to luncheon at Miss Winthrop's kind request. We've changed the pose—neither of us was satisfied, you know—but we haven't quite settled on the new one. Miss Winthrop has two whole hours this afternoon that she can give me if I'll stay; and, of course, under the circumstances, I want to do it."

"Of course," echoed Billy. Billy's voice was indomitably cheerful.

"Thank you, dear. I knew you'd understand," sighed Bertram, contentedly. "You see, really, two whole hours, so—it's a chance I can't afford to lose."

"Of course you can't," echoed Billy, again.

"All right then. Good-by till to-night," called the man.

"Good-by," answered Billy, still cheerfully. As she turned away, however, she tossed her head. "A new pose, indeed!" she muttered, with some asperity. "Just as if there could be a *new* pose after all those she tried last year!"

Immediately after luncheon Pete and Eliza started for South Boston to pay a visit to Eliza's mother, and it was soon after they left the house that Bertram called his wife up again.

"Say, dearie, I forgot to tell you," he began, "but I met an old friend in the subway this morning, and I—well, I remembered what you said about bringing 'em home to dinner next time, so I asked him for to-night. Do you mind? It's—"

"Mind? Of course not! I'm glad you did," plunged in Billy, with feverish eagerness. (Even now, just the bare mention of anything connected with that awful "test" night was enough to set Billy's nerves to tingling.) "I want you to always bring them home, Bertram."

"All right, dear. We'll be there at six o'clock then. It's—it's Calderwell, this time. You remember Calderwell, of course."

"Not—*Hugh* Calderwell?" Billy's question was a little faint.

"Sure!" Bertram laughed oddly, and lowered his voice. "I suspect *once* I wouldn't have brought him home to you. I was too jealous. But now—well, now maybe I want him to see what he's lost."

"*Bertram!*"

But Bertram only laughed mischievously, and called a gay "Good-by till to-night, then!"

Billy, at her end of the wires, hung up the receiver and backed against the wall a little palpitatingly.

Calderwell! To dinner—Calderwell! Did she remember Calderwell? Did she, indeed! As if one could easily forget the man that, for a year or two, had proposed marriage as regularly (and almost as lightly!) as he had torn a monthly leaf from his calendar! Besides, was it not he, too, who had said that Bertram would never love any girl, *really*; that it would be only the tilt of her chin or the turn of her head that he loved—to paint? And now he was coming to dinner—and with Bertram.

Very well, he should see! He should see that Bertram *did* love her; *her*—not the tilt of her chin nor the turn of her head. He should see how happy they were, what a good wife she made, and how devoted and *satisfied* Bertram was in his home. He should see! And forthwith Billy picked up her skirts and tripped up-stairs to select her very prettiest house-gown to do honor to the occasion. Up-stairs, however, one thing and another delayed her, so that it was four o'clock when she turned her attention to her toilet; and it was while she was hesitating whether to be stately and impressive in royally sumptuous blue velvet and ermine, or cozy and tantalizingly homy{sic} in bronze-gold crêpe de Chine and swan's-down, that the telephone bell rang again.

Eliza and Pete had not yet returned; so, as before, Billy answered it. This time Eliza's shaking voice came to her.

"Is that you, ma'am?"

"Why, yes, Eliza?"

"Yes'm, it's me, ma'am. It's about Uncle Pete. He's give us a turn that's 'most scared us out of our wits."

"Pete! You mean he's sick?"

"Yes, ma'am, he was. That is, he is, too—only he's better, now, thank goodness," panted Eliza. "But he ain't hisself yet. He's that white and shaky!

Would you—could you—that is, would you mind if we didn't come back till into the evenin', maybe?"

"Why, of course not," cried Pete's mistress, quickly. "Don't come a minute before he's able, Eliza. Don't come until to-morrow."

Eliza gave a trembling little laugh.

"Thank you, ma'am; but there wouldn't be no keepin' of Uncle Pete here till then. If he could take five steps alone he'd start now. But he can't. He says he'll be all right pretty quick, though. He's had 'em before—these spells—but never quite so bad as this, I guess; an' he's worryin' somethin' turrible 'cause he can't start for home right away."

"Nonsense!" cut in Mrs. Bertram Henshaw.

"Yes'm. I knew you'd feel that way," stammered Eliza, gratefully. "You see, I couldn't leave him to come alone, and besides, anyhow, I'd have to stay, for mother ain't no more use than a wet dish-rag at such times, she's that scared herself. And she ain't very well, too. So if—if you *could* get along—"

"Of course we can! And tell Pete not to worry one bit. I'm so sorry he's sick!"

"Thank you, ma'am. Then we'll be there some time this evenin'," sighed Eliza.

From the telephone Billy turned away with a troubled face.

"Pete *is* ill," she was saying to herself. "I don't like the looks of it; and he's so faithful he'd come if—" With a little cry Billy stopped short. Then, tremblingly, she sank into the nearest chair. "Calderwell—and he's coming to *dinner!*" she moaned.

For two benumbed minutes Billy sat staring at nothing. Then she ran to the telephone and called the Annex.

Aunt Hannah answered.

"Aunt Hannah, for heaven's sake, if you love me," pleaded Billy, "send Rosa down instanter! Pete is sick over to South Boston, and Eliza is with him; and Bertram is bringing Hugh Calderwell home to dinner. *Can* you spare Rosa?"

"Oh, my grief and conscience, Billy! Of course I can—I mean I could— but Rosa isn't here, dear child! It's her day out, you know."

"O dear, of course it is! I might have known, if I'd thought; but Pete and Eliza have spoiled me. They never take days out at meal time—both together, I mean—until to-night."

"But, my dear child, what will you do?"

"I don't know. I've got to think. I *must* do something!"

"Of course you must! I'd come over myself if it wasn't for my cold."

"As if I'd let you!"

"There isn't anybody here, only Tommy. Even Alice is gone. Oh, Billy, Billy, this only goes to prove what I've always said, that *no* woman *ought* to be a wife until she's an efficient housekeeper; and—"

"Yes, yes, Aunt Hannah, I know," moaned Billy, frenziedly. "But I am a wife, and I'm not an efficient housekeeper; and Hugh Calderwell won't wait for me to learn. He's coming to-night. *To-night!* And I've got to do something. Never mind. I'll fix it some way. Good-by!"

"But, Billy, Billy! Oh, my grief and conscience," fluttered Aunt Hannah's voice across the wires as Billy snapped the receiver into place.

For the second time that day Billy backed palpitatingly against the wall. Her eyes sought the clock fearfully.

Fifteen minutes past four. She had an hour and three quarters. She could, of course, telephone Bertram to dine Calderwell at a club or some hotel. But to do this now, the very first time, when it had been her own suggestion that he "bring them home"—no, no, she could not do that! Anything but that! Besides, very likely she could not reach Bertram, anyway. Doubtless he had left the Winthrops' by this time.

There was Marie. She could telephone Marie. But Marie could not very well come just now, she knew; and then, too, there was Cyril to be taken into consideration. How Cyril would gibe at the wife who had to call in all the neighbors just because her husband was bringing home a friend to dinner! How he would—Well, he shouldn't! He should not have the chance. So, there!

With a jerk Mrs. Bertram Henshaw pulled herself away from the wall and stood erect. Her eyes snapped, and the very poise of her chin spelled determination.

Very well, she would show them. Was not Bertram bringing this man home because he was proud of her? Mighty proud he would be if she had to call in half of Boston to get his dinner for him! Nonsense! She would get it herself. Was not this the time, if ever, to be an oak? A vine, doubtless, would lean and cling and telephone, and whine "I can't!" But not an oak. An oak would hold up its head and say "I can!" An oak would go ahead and get that dinner. She would be an oak. She would get that dinner.

What if she didn't know how to cook bread and cake and pies and things? One did not have to cook bread and cake and pies just to get a dinner—meat and potatoes and vegetables! Besides, she *could* make peach fritters. She knew she could. She would show them!

And with actually a bit of song on her lips, Billy skipped up-stairs for her ruffled apron and dust-cap—two necessary accompaniments to this dinner-getting, in her opinion.

Billy found the apron and dust-cap with no difficulty; but it took fully ten of her precious minutes to unearth from its obscure hiding-place the blue-and-gold "Bride's Helper" cookbook, one of Aunt Hannah's wedding gifts.

On the way to the kitchen, Billy planned her dinner. As was natural, perhaps, she chose the things she herself would like to eat.

"I won't attempt anything very elaborate," she said to herself. "It would be wiser to have something simple, like chicken pie, perhaps. I love chicken pie! And I'll have oyster stew first—that is, after the grapefruit. Just oysters boiled in milk must be easier than soup to make. I'll begin with grapefruit with a cherry in it, like Pete fixes it. Those don't have to be cooked, anyhow. I'll have fish—Bertram loves the fish course. Let me see, halibut, I guess, with egg sauce. I won't have any roast; nothing but the chicken pie. And I'll have squash and onions. I can have a salad, easy—just lettuce and stuff. That doesn't have to be cooked. Oh, and the peach fritters, if I get time to make them. For dessert—well, maybe I can find a new pie or pudding in the cookbook. I want to use that cookbook for something, after hunting all this time for it!"

In the kitchen Billy found exquisite neatness, and silence. The first brought an approving light to her eyes; but the second, for some unapparent reason, filled her heart with vague misgiving. This feeling, however, Billy resolutely cast from her as she crossed the room, dropped her book on to the table, and turned toward the shining black stove.

There was an excellent fire. Glowing points of light showed that only a good draft was needed to make the whole mass of coal red-hot. Billy, however, did not know this. Her experience of fires was confined to burning wood in open grates—and wood in open grates had to be poked to make it red and glowing. With confident alacrity now, therefore, Billy caught up the poker, thrust it into the mass of coals and gave them a fine stirring up. Then she set back the lid of the stove and went to hunt up the ingredients for her dinner.

By the time Billy had searched five minutes and found no chicken, no oysters, and no halibut, it occurred to her that her larder was not, after all, an open market, and that one's provisions must be especially ordered to fit one's needs. As to ordering them now—Billy glanced at the clock and shook her head.

"It's almost five, already, and they'd never get here in time," she sighed regretfully. "I'll have to have something else."

Billy looked now, not for what she wanted, but for what she could find. And she found: some cold roast lamb, at which she turned up her nose; an uncooked beefsteak, which she appropriated doubtfully; a raw turnip and a head of lettuce, which she hailed with glee; and some beets, potatoes, onions, and grapefruit, from all of which she took a generous supply. Thus laden she went back to the kitchen.

Spread upon the table they made a brave show.

"Oh, well, I'll have quite a dinner, after all," she triumphed, cocking her head happily. "And now for the dessert," she finished, pouncing on the cookbook.

It was while she was turning the leaves to find the pies and puddings that she ran across the vegetables and found the word "beets" staring her in the face. Mechanically she read the line below.

"Winter beets will require three hours to cook. Use hot water."

Billy's startled eyes sought the clock.

Three hours—and it was five, now!

Frenziedly, then, she ran her finger down the page.

"Onions, one and one-half hours. Use hot water. Turnips require a long time, but if cut thin they will cook in an hour and a quarter."

"An hour and a quarter, indeed!" she moaned.

"Isn't there anything anywhere that doesn't take forever to cook?"

"Early peas—... green corn—... summer squash—..." mumbled Billy's dry lips. "But what do folks eat in January—*January*?"

It was the apparently inoffensive sentence, "New potatoes will boil in thirty minutes," that brought fresh terror to Billy's soul, and set her to fluttering the cookbook leaves with renewed haste. If it took *new* potatoes thirty minutes to cook, how long did it take old ones? In vain she searched for the answer. There were plenty of potatoes. They were mashed, whipped, scalloped, creamed, fried, and broiled; they were made into puffs, croquettes, potato border, and potato snow. For many of these they were boiled first—"until tender," one rule said.

"But that doesn't tell me how long it takes to get 'em tender," fumed Billy, despairingly. "I suppose they think anybody ought to know that—but I don't!" Suddenly her eyes fell once more on the instructions for boiling turnips, and her face cleared. "If it helps to cut turnips thin, why not potatoes?" she cried. "I *can* do that, anyhow; and I will," she finished, with a sigh of relief, as she caught up half a dozen potatoes and hurried into the pantry for a knife. A few minutes later, the potatoes, peeled, and cut almost to wafer thinness, were dumped into a basin of cold water.

"There! now I guess you'll cook," nodded Billy to the dish in her hand as she hurried to the stove.

Chilled by an ominous unresponsiveness, Billy lifted the stove lid and peered inside. Only a mass of black and graying coals greeted her. The fire was out.

"To think that even you had to go back on me like this!" upbraided Billy, eyeing the dismal mass with reproachful gaze.

This disaster, however, as Billy knew, was not so great as it seemed, for there was still the gas stove. In the old days, under Dong Ling's rule, there had been no gas stove. Dong Ling disapproved of "devil stoves" that had "no coalee, no woodee, but burned like hellee." Eliza, however, did approve of them; and not long after her arrival, a fine one had been put in for her use. So now Billy soon had her potatoes with a brisk blaze under them.

In frantic earnest, then, Billy went to work. Brushing the discarded onions, turnip, and beets into a pail under the table, she was still confronted with the beefsteak, lettuce, and grapefruit. All but the beefsteak she pushed to one side with gentle pats.

"You're all right," she nodded to them. "I can use you. You don't have to be cooked, bless your hearts! But *you*—!" Billy scowled at the beefsteak and ran her finger down the index of the "Bride's Helper"—Billy knew how to handle that book now.

"No, you don't—not for me!" she muttered, after a minute, shaking her finger at the tenderloin on the table. "I haven't got any 'hot coals,' and I thought a 'gridiron' was where they played football; though it seems it's some sort of a dish to cook you in, here—but I shouldn't know it from a teaspoon, probably, if I should see it. No, sir! It's back to the refrigerator for you, and a nice cold sensible roast leg of lamb for me, that doesn't have to be cooked. Understand? *Cooked*," she finished, as she carried the beefsteak away and took possession of the hitherto despised cold lamb.

Once more Billy made a mad search through cupboards and shelves. This time she bore back in triumph a can of corn, another of tomatoes, and a glass jar of preserved peaches. In the kitchen a cheery bubbling from the potatoes on the stove greeted her. Billy's spirits rose with the steam.

"There, Spunkie," she said gayly to the cat, who had just uncurled from a nap behind the stove. "Tell me I can't get up a dinner! And maybe we'll have the peach fritters, too," she chirped. "I've got the peach-part, anyway."

But Billy did not have the peach fritters, after all. She got out the sugar and the flour, to be sure, and she made a great ado looking up the rule; but a hurried glance at the clock sent her into the dining-room to set the table, and all thought of the peach fritters was given up.

CHAPTER X
THE DINNER BILLY GOT

At five minutes of six Bertram and Calderwell came. Bertram gave his peculiar ring and let himself in with his latchkey; but Billy did not meet him in the hall, nor in the drawing-room. Excusing himself, Bertram hurried up-stairs. Billy was not in her room, nor anywhere on that floor. She was not in William's room. Coming down-stairs to the hall again, Bertram confronted William, who had just come in.

"Where's Billy?" demanded the young husband, with just a touch of irritation, as if he suspected William of having Billy in his pocket.

William stared slightly.

"Why, I don't know. Isn't she here?"

"I'll ask Pete," frowned Bertram.

In the dining-room Bertram found no one, though the table was prettily set, and showed half a grapefruit at each place. In the kitchen—in the kitchen Bertram found a din of rattling tin, an odor of burned food—, a confusion of scattered pots and pans, a frightened cat who peered at him from under a littered stove, and a flushed, disheveled young woman in a blue dust-cap and ruffled apron, whom he finally recognized as his wife.

"Why, Billy!" he gasped.

Billy, who was struggling with something at the sink, turned sharply.

"Bertram Henshaw," she panted, "I used to think you were wonderful because you could paint a picture. I even used to think I was a little wonderful because I could write a song. Well, I don't any more! But I'll tell you who *is* wonderful. It's Eliza and Rosa, and all the rest of those women who can get a meal on to the table all at once, so it's fit to eat!"

"Why, Billy!" gasped Bertram again, falling back to the door he had closed behind him. "What in the world does this mean?"

"Mean? It means I'm getting dinner," choked Billy. "Can't you see?"

"But—Pete! Eliza!"

"They're sick—I mean he's sick; and I said I'd do it. I'd be an oak. But how did I know there wasn't anything in the house except stuff that took hours to cook—only potatoes? And how did I know that *they* cooked in no time, and then got all smushy and wet staying in the water? And how did I know that everything else would stick on and burn on till you'd used every dish there was in the house to cook 'em in?"

"Why, Billy!" gasped Bertram, for the third time. And then, because he had been married only six months instead of six years, he made the mistake of trying to argue with a woman whose nerves were already at the snapping point. "But, dear, it was so foolish of you to do all this! Why didn't you telephone? Why didn't you get somebody?"

Like an irate little tigress, Billy turned at bay.

"Bertram Henshaw," she flamed angrily, "if you don't go up-stairs and tend to that man up there, I shall *scream*. Now go! I'll be up when I can."

And Bertram went.

It was not so very long, after all, before Billy came in to greet her guest. She was not stately and imposing in royally sumptuous blue velvet and ermine; nor yet was she cozy and homy in bronze-gold crêpe de Chine and swan's-down. She was just herself in a pretty little morning house gown of blue gingham. She was minus the dust-cap and the ruffled apron, but she had a dab of flour on the left cheek, and a smutch of crock on her forehead. She had, too, a cut finger on her right hand, and a burned thumb on her left. But she was Billy—and being Billy, she advanced with a bright smile and held out a cordial hand—not even wincing when the cut finger came under Calderwell's hearty clasp.

"I'm glad to see you," she welcomed him. "You'll excuse my not appearing sooner, I'm sure, for—didn't Bertram tell you?—I'm playing Bridget to-night. But dinner is ready now, and we'll go down, please," she smiled, as she laid a light hand on her guest's arm.

Behind her, Bertram, remembering the scene in the kitchen, stared in sheer amazement. Bertram, it might be mentioned again, had been married six months, not six years.

What Billy had intended to serve for a "simple dinner" that night was: grapefruit with cherries, oyster stew, boiled halibut with egg sauce, chicken pie, squash, onions, and potatoes, peach fritters, a "lettuce and stuff" salad, and some new pie or pudding. What she did serve was: grapefruit (without the cherries), cold roast lamb, potatoes (a mush of sogginess), tomatoes (canned, and slightly burned), corn (canned, and very much burned), lettuce (plain); and for dessert, preserved peaches and cake (the latter rather dry and stale). Such was Billy's dinner.

The grapefruit everybody ate. The cold lamb too, met with a hearty reception, especially after the potatoes, corn, and tomatoes were served—and tasted. Outwardly, through it all, Billy was gayety itself. Inwardly she was burning up with anger and mortification. And because she was all this, there was, apparently, no limit to her laughter and sparkling repartee as she talked with Calderwell, her guest—the guest who, according to her original plans, was to be shown how happy she and Bertram were, what a good wife she made, and how devoted and *satisfied* Bertram was in his home.

William, picking at his dinner—as only a hungry man can pick at a dinner that is uneatable—watched Billy with a puzzled, uneasy frown. Bertram, choking over the few mouthfuls he ate, marked his wife's animated face and Calderwell's absorbed attention, and settled into gloomy silence.

But it could not continue forever. The preserved peaches were eaten at last, and the stale cake left. (Billy had forgotten the coffee—which was just as well, perhaps.) Then the four trailed up-stairs to the drawing-room.

At nine o'clock an anxious Eliza and a remorseful, apologetic Pete came home and descended to the horror the once orderly kitchen and dining-room had become. At ten, Calderwell, with very evident reluctance, tore himself away from Billy's gay badinage, and said good night. At two minutes past ten, an exhausted, nerve-racked Billy was trying to cry on the shoulders of both Uncle William and Bertram at once.

"There, there, child, don't! It went off all right," patted Uncle William.

"Billy, darling," pleaded Bertram, "please don't cry so! As if I'd ever let you step foot in that kitchen again!"

At this Billy raised a tear-wet face, aflame with indignant determination.

"As if I'd ever let you keep me *from* it, Bertram Henshaw, after this!" she contested. "I'm not going to do another thing in all my life but *cook!* When I think of the stuff we had to eat, after all the time I took to get it, I'm simply crazy! Do you think I'd run the risk of such a thing as this ever happening again?"

CHAPTER XI
CALDERWELL DOES SOME QUESTIONING

On the day after his dinner with Mr. and Mrs. Bertram Henshaw, Hugh Calderwell left Boston and did not return until more than a month had passed. One of his first acts, when he did come, was to look up Mr. M. J. Arkwright at the address which Billy had given him.

Calderwell had not seen Arkwright since they parted in Paris some two years before, after a six-months tramp through Europe together. Calderwell liked Arkwright then, greatly, and he lost no time now in renewing the acquaintance.

The address, as given by Billy, proved to be an attractive but modest apartment hotel near the Conservatory of Music; and Calderwell was delighted to find Arkwright at home in his comfortable little bachelor suite.

Arkwright greeted him most cordially.

"Well, well," he cried, "if it isn't Calderwell! And how's Mont Blanc? Or is it the Killarney Lakes this time, or maybe the Sphinx that I should inquire for, eh?"

"Guess again," laughed Calderwell, throwing off his heavy coat and settling himself comfortably in the inviting-looking morris chair his friend pulled forward.

"Sha'n't do it," retorted Arkwright, with a smile. "I never gamble on palpable uncertainties, except for a chance throw or two, as I gave a minute ago. Your movements are altogether too erratic, and too far-reaching, for ordinary mortals to keep track of."

"Well, maybe you're right," grinned Calderwell, appreciatively. "Anyhow, you would have lost this time, sure thing, for I've been working."

"Seen the doctor yet?" queried Arkwright, coolly, pushing the cigars across the table.

"Thanks—for both," sniffed Calderwell, with a reproachful glance, helping himself. "Your good judgment in some matters is still unimpaired, I see," he observed, tapping the little gilded band which had told him the cigar was an old favorite. "As to other matters, however,—you're wrong again, my friend, in your surmise. I am not sick, and I have been working."

"So? Well, I'm told they have very good specialists here. Some one of them ought to hit your case. Still—how long has it been running?" Arkwright's face showed only grave concern.

"Oh, come, let up, Arkwright," snapped Calderwell, striking his match alight with a vigorous jerk. "I'll admit I haven't ever given any *special* indication of an absorbing passion for work. But what can you expect of a fellow born with a whole dozen silver spoons in his mouth? And that's what I was, according to Bertram Henshaw. According to him again, it's a wonder I ever tried to feed myself; and perhaps he's right—with my mouth already so full."

"I should say so," laughed Arkwright.

"Well, be that as it may. I'm going to feed myself, and I'm going to earn my feed, too. I haven't climbed a mountain or paddled a canoe, for a year. I've been in Chicago cultivating the acquaintance of John Doe and Richard Roe."

"You mean—law?"

"Sure. I studied it here for a while, before that bout of ours a couple of years ago. Billy drove me away, then."

"Billy!—er—Mrs. Henshaw?"

"Yes. I thought I told you. She turned down my tenth-dozen proposal so emphatically that I lost all interest in Boston and took to the tall timber again. But I've come back. A friend of my father's wrote me to come on and consider a good opening there was in his law office. I came on a month ago, and considered. Then I went back to pack up. Now I've come for good, and here I am. You have my history to date. Now tell me of yourself. You're looking as fit as a penny from the mint, even though you have discarded that 'lovely' brown beard. Was that a concession to—er—*Mary Jane*?"

Arkwright lifted a quick hand of protest.

"'Michael Jeremiah,' please. There is no 'Mary Jane,' now," he said a bit stiffly.

The other stared a little. Then he gave a low chuckle.

"'Michael Jeremiah,'" he repeated musingly, eyeing the glowing tip of his cigar. "And to think how that mysterious 'M. J.' used to tantalize me! Do you mean," he added, turning slowly, "that no one calls you 'Mary Jane' now?"

"Not if they know what is best for them."

"Oh!" Calderwell noted the smouldering fire in the other's eyes a little curiously. "Very well. I'll take the hint—Michael Jeremiah."

"Thanks." Arkwright relaxed a little. "To tell the truth, I've had quite enough now—of Mary Jane."

"Very good. So be it," nodded the other, still regarding his friend thoughtfully. "But tell me—what of yourself?"

Arkwright shrugged his shoulders.

"There's nothing to tell. You've seen. I'm here."

"Humph! Very pretty," scoffed Calderwell. "Then if *you* won't tell, I *will*. I saw Billy a month ago, you see. It seems you've hit the trail for Grand Opera, as you threatened to that night in Paris; but you *haven't* brought up in vaudeville, as you prophesied you would do—though, for that matter, judging from the plums some of the stars are picking on the vaudeville stage, nowadays, that isn't to be sneezed at. But Billy says you've made two or three appearances already on the sacred boards themselves—one of them a subscription performance—and that you created no end of a sensation."

"Nonsense! I'm merely a student at the Opera School here," scowled Arkwright.

"Oh, yes, Billy said you were that, but she also said you wouldn't be, long. That you'd already had one good offer—I'm not speaking of marriage—and that you were going abroad next summer, and that they were all insufferably proud of you."

"Nonsense!" scowled Arkwright, again, coloring like a girl. "That is only some of—of Mrs. Henshaw's kind flattery."

Calderwell jerked the cigar from between his lips, and sat suddenly forward in his chair.

"Arkwright, tell me about them. How are they making it go?"

Arkwright frowned.

"Who? Make what go?" he asked.

"The Henshaws. Is she happy? Is he—on the square?"

Arkwright's face darkened.

"Well, really," he began; but Calderwell interrupted.

"Oh, come; don't be squeamish. You think I'm butting into what doesn't concern me; but I'm not. What concerns Billy does concern me. And if he doesn't make her happy, I'll—I'll kill him."

In spite of himself Arkwright laughed. The vehemence of the other's words, and the fierceness with which he puffed at his cigar as he fell back in his chair were most expressive.

"Well, I don't think you need to load revolvers nor sharpen daggers, just yet," he observed grimly.

Calderwell laughed this time, though without much mirth.

"Oh, I'm not in love with Billy, now," he explained. "Please don't think I am. I shouldn't see her if I was, of course."

Arkwright changed his position suddenly, bringing his face into the shadow. Calderwell talked on without pausing.

"No, I'm not in love with Billy. But Billy's a trump. You know that."

"I do." The words were low, but steadily spoken.

"Of course you do! We all do. And we want her happy. But as for her marrying Bertram—you could have bowled me over with a soap bubble when I heard she'd done it. Now understand: Bertram is a good fellow, and I like him. I've known him all his life, and he's all right. Oh, six or eight years ago, to be sure, he got in with a set of fellows—Bob Seaver and his clique—that were no good. Went in for Bohemianism, and all that rot. It wasn't good for Bertram. He's got the confounded temperament that goes with his talent, I suppose—though why a man can't paint a picture, or sing a song, and keep his temper and a level head I don't see!"

"He can," cut in Arkwright, with curt emphasis.

"Humph! Well, that's what I think. But, about this marriage business. Bertram admires a pretty face wherever he sees it—to paint, and always has. Not but that he's straight as a string with women—I don't mean that; but girls are always just so many pictures to be picked up on his brushes and transferred to his canvases. And as for his settling down and marrying anybody for keeps, right along—Great Scott! imagine Bertram Henshaw as a domestic man!"

Arkwright stirred restlessly as he spoke up in quick defense:

"Oh, but he is, I assure you. I—I've seen them in their home together—many times. I think they are—very happy." Arkwright spoke with decision, though still a little diffidently.

Calderwell was silent. He had picked up the little gilt band he had torn from his cigar and was fingering it musingly.

"Yes; I've seen them—once," he said, after a minute. "I took dinner with them when I was on, a month ago."

"I heard you did."

At something in Arkwright's voice, Calderwell turned quickly.

"What do you mean? Why do you say it like that?"

Arkwright laughed. The constraint fled from his manner.

"Well, I may as well tell you. You'll hear of it. It's no secret. Mrs. Henshaw herself tells of it everywhere. It was her friend, Alice Greggory, who told me of it first, however. It seems the cook was gone, and the mistress had to get the dinner herself."

"Yes, I know that."

"But you should hear Mrs. Henshaw tell the story now, or Bertram. It seems she knew nothing whatever about cooking, and her trials and tribulations in getting that dinner on to the table were only one degree worse than the dinner itself, according to her story. Didn't you—er—notice anything?"

"Notice anything!" exploded Calderwell. "I noticed that Billy was so brilliant she fairly radiated sparks; and I noticed that Bertram was so glum he—he almost radiated thunderclaps. Then I saw that Billy's high spirits were all assumed to cover a threatened burst of tears, and I laid it all to him. I thought he'd said something to hurt her; and I could have punched him. Great Scott! Was *that* what ailed them?"

"I reckon it was. Alice says that since then Mrs. Henshaw has fairly haunted the kitchen, begging Eliza to teach her everything, *every single thing* she knows!"

Calderwell chuckled.

"If that isn't just like Billy! She never does anything by halves. By George, but she was game over that dinner! I can see it all now."

"Alice says she's really learning to cook, in spite of old Pete's horror, and Eliza's pleadings not to spoil her pretty hands."

"Then Pete is back all right? What a faithful old soul he is!"

Arkwright frowned slightly.

"Yes, he's faithful, but he isn't all right, by any means. I think he's a sick man, myself."

"What makes Billy let him work, then?"

"Let him!" sniffed Arkwright. "I'd like to see you try to stop him! Mrs. Henshaw begs and pleads with him to stop, but he scouts the idea. Pete is thoroughly and unalterably convinced that the family would starve to death if it weren't for him; and Mrs. Henshaw says that she'll admit he has some grounds for his opinion when one remembers the condition of the kitchen and dining-room the night she presided over them."

"Poor Billy!" chuckled Calderwell. "I'd have gone down into the kitchen myself if I'd suspected what was going on."

Arkwright raised his eyebrows.

"Perhaps it's well you didn't—if Bertram's picture of what he found there when he went down is a true one. Mrs. Henshaw acknowledges that even the cat sought refuge under the stove."

"As if the veriest worm that crawls ever needed to seek refuge from Billy!" scoffed Calderwell. "By the way, what's this Annex I hear of? Bertram mentioned it, but I couldn't get either of them to tell what it was. Billy wouldn't, and Bertram said he couldn't—not with Billy shaking her head at him like that. So I had my suspicions. One of Billy's pet charities?"

"She doesn't call it that." Arkwright's face and voice softened. "It is Hillside. She still keeps it open. She calls it the Annex to her home. She's filled it with a crippled woman, a poor little music teacher, a lame boy, and Aunt Hannah."

"But how—extraordinary!"

"She doesn't think so. She says it's just an overflow house for the extra happiness she can't use."

There was a moment's silence. Calderwell laid down his cigar, pulled out his handkerchief, and blew his nose furiously. Then he got to his feet and walked to the fireplace. After a minute he turned.

"Well, if she isn't the beat 'em!" he spluttered. "And I had the gall to ask you if Henshaw made her—happy! Overflow house, indeed!"

"The best of it is, the way she does it," smiled Arkwright. "They're all the sort of people ordinary charity could never reach; and the only way she got them there at all was to make each one think that he or she was absolutely necessary to the rest of them. Even as it is, they all pay a little something toward the running expenses of the house. They insisted on that, and Mrs. Henshaw had to let them. I believe her chief difficulty now is that she has not less than six people whom she wishes to put into the two extra rooms still unoccupied, and she can't make up her mind which to take. Her husband says he expects to hear any day of an Annexette to the Annex."

"Humph!" grunted Calderwell, as he turned and began to walk up and down the room. "Bertram is still painting, I suppose."

"Oh, yes."

"What's he doing now?"

"Several things. He's up to his eyes in work. As you probably have heard, he met with a severe accident last summer, and lost the use of his right arm for many months. I believe they thought at one time he had lost it forever. But it's all right now, and he has several commissions for portraits. Alice says he's doing ideal heads again, too."

"Same old 'Face of a Girl'?"

"I suppose so, though Alice didn't say. Of course his special work just now is painting the portrait of Miss Marguerite Winthrop. You may have heard that he tried it last year and—and didn't make quite a success of it."

"Yes. My sister Belle told me. She hears from Billy once in a while. Will it be a go, this time?"

"We'll hope so—for everybody's sake. I imagine no one has seen it yet—it's not finished; but Alice says—"

Calderwell turned abruptly, a quizzical smile on his face.

"See here, my son," he interposed, "it strikes me that this Alice is saying a good deal—to you! Who is she?"

Arkwright gave a light laugh.

"Why, I told you. She is Miss Alice Greggory, Mrs. Henshaw's friend— and mine. I have known her for years."

"Hm-m; what is she like?"

"Like? Why, she's like—like herself, of course. You'll have to know Alice. She's the salt of the earth—Alice is," smiled Arkwright, rising to his feet with a remonstrative gesture, as he saw Calderwell pick up his coat. "What's your hurry?"

"Hm-m," commented Calderwell again, ignoring the question. "And when, may I ask, do you intend to appropriate this—er—salt—to—er—ah, season your own life with, as I might say—eh?"

Arkwright laughed. There was not the slightest trace of embarrassment in his face.

"Never. *You're* on the wrong track, this time. Alice and I are good friends—always have been, and always will be, I hope."

"Nothing more?"

"Nothing more. I see her frequently. She is musical, and the Henshaws are good enough to ask us there often together. You will meet her, doubtless, now, yourself. She is frequently at the Henshaw home."

"Hm-m." Calderwell still eyed his host shrewdly. "Then you'll give me a clear field, eh?"

"Certainly." Arkwright's eyes met his friend's gaze without swerving.

"All right. However, I suppose you'll tell me, as I did you, once, that a right of way in such a case doesn't mean a thoroughfare for the party interested. If my memory serves me, I gave you right of way in Paris to win the affections of a certain elusive Miss Billy here in Boston, if you could. But I see you didn't seem to improve your opportunities," he finished teasingly.

Arkwright stooped, of a sudden, to pick up a bit of paper from the floor.

"No," he said quietly. "I didn't seem to improve my opportunities." This time he did not meet Calderwell's eyes.

The good-byes had been said when Calderwell turned abruptly at the door.

"Oh, I say, I suppose you're going to that devil's carnival at Jordan Hall to-morrow night."

"Devil's carnival! You don't mean—Cyril Henshaw's piano recital!"

"Sure I do," grinned Calderwell, unabashed. "And I'll warrant it'll be a devil's carnival, too. Isn't Mr. Cyril Henshaw going to play his own music? Oh, I know I'm hopeless, from your standpoint, but I can't help it. I like mine with some go in it, and a tune that you can find without hunting for it. And I don't like lost spirits gone mad that wail and shriek through ten perfectly good minutes, and then die with a gasping moan whose home is the tombs. However, you're going, I take it."

"Of course I am," laughed the other. "You couldn't hire Alice to miss one shriek of those spirits. Besides, I rather like them myself, you know."

"Yes, I suppose you do. You're brought up on it—in your business. But me for the 'Merry Widow' and even the hoary 'Jingle Bells' every time! However, I'm going to be there—out of respect to the poor fellow's family. And, by the way, that's another thing that bowled me over—Cyril's marriage. Why, Cyril hates women!"

"Not all women—we'll hope," smiled Arkwright. "Do you know his wife?"

"Not much. I used to see her a little at Billy's. Music teacher, wasn't she? Then she's the same sort, I suppose."

"But she isn't," laughed Arkwright. "Oh, she taught music, but that was only because of necessity, I take it. She's domestic through and through, with an overwhelming passion for making puddings and darning socks, I hear. Alice says she believes Mrs. Cyril knows every dish and spoon by its Christian name, and that there's never so much as a spool of thread out of order in the house."

"But how does Cyril stand it—the trials and tribulations of domestic life? Bertram used to declare that the whole Strata was aquiver with fear when Cyril was composing, and I remember him as a perfect bear if anybody so much as whispered when he was in one of his moods. I never forgot the night Bertram and I were up in William's room trying to sing 'When Johnnie comes marching home,' to the accompaniment of a banjo in Bertram's hands, and a guitar in mine. Gorry! it was Hugh that went marching home that night."

"Oh, well, from reports I reckon Mrs. Cyril doesn't play either a banjo or a guitar," smiled Arkwright. "Alice says she wears rubber heels on her shoes, and has put hushers on all the chair-legs, and felt-mats between all the plates and saucers. Anyhow, Cyril is building a new house, and he looks as if he were in a pretty healthy condition, as you'll see to-morrow night."

"Humph! I wish he'd make his music healthy, then," grumbled Calderwell, as he opened the door.

CHAPTER XII
FOR BILLY—SOME ADVICE

February brought busy days. The public opening of the Bohemian Ten Club Exhibition was to take place the sixth of March, with a private view for invited guests the night before; and it was at this exhibition that Bertram planned to show his portrait of Marguerite Winthrop. He also, if possible, wished to enter two or three other canvases, upon which he was spending all the time he could get.

Bertram felt that he was doing very good work now. The portrait of Marguerite Winthrop was coming on finely. The spoiled idol of society had at last found a pose and a costume that suited her, and she was graciously pleased to give the artist almost as many sittings as he wanted. The "elusive something" in her face, which had previously been so baffling, was now already caught and held bewitchingly on his canvas. He was confident that the portrait would be a success. He was also much interested in another piece of work which he intended to show called "The Rose." The model for this was a beautiful young girl he had found selling flowers with her father in a street booth at the North End.

On the whole, Bertram was very happy these days. He could not, to be sure, spend quite so much time with Billy as he wished; but she understood, of course, as did he, that his work must come first. He knew that she tried to show him that she understood it. At the same time, he could not help thinking, occasionally, that Billy did sometimes mind his necessary absorption in his painting.

To himself Bertram owned that Billy was, in some ways, a puzzle to him. Her conduct was still erratic at times. One day he would seem to be everything to her; the next—almost nothing, judging by the ease with which she relinquished his society and substituted that of some one else: Arkwright, or Calderwell, for instance.

And that was another thing. Bertram was ashamed to hint even to himself that he was jealous of either of those men. Surely, after what had happened, after Billy's emphatic assertion that she had never loved any one but himself, it would seem not only absurd, but disloyal, that he should doubt for an instant Billy's entire devotion to him, and yet—there were times when he wished he *could* come home and not always find Alice Greggory, Calderwell, Arkwright, or all three of them strumming the piano in the drawing-room! At such times, always, though, if he did feel impatient, he immediately demanded of himself: "Are you, then, the kind of husband that begrudges your wife young companions of her own age and tastes to help her while away the hours that you cannot possibly spend with her yourself?"

This question, and the answer that his better self always gave to it, were usually sufficient to send him into some florists for a bunch of violets for Billy, or into a candy shop on a like atoning errand.

As to Billy—Billy, too, was busy these days chief of her concerns being, perhaps, attention to that honeymoon of hers, to see that it did not wane. At least, the most of her thoughts, and many of her actions, centered about that object.

Billy had the book, now—the "Talk to Young Wives." For a time she had worked with only the newspaper criticism to guide her; but, coming at last to the conclusion that if a little was good, more must be better, she had shyly gone into a bookstore one day and, with a pink blush, had asked for the book. Since bringing it home she had studied assiduously (though never if Bertram was near), keeping it well-hidden, when not in use, in a remote corner of her desk.

There was a good deal in the book that Billy did not like, and there were some statements that worried her; but yet there was much that she tried earnestly to follow. She was still striving to be the oak, and she was still eagerly endeavoring to brush up against those necessary outside interests. She was so thankful, in this connection, for Alice Greggory, and for Arkwright and Hugh Calderwell. It was such a help that she had them! They were not only very pleasant and entertaining outside interests, but one or another of them was almost always conveniently within reach.

Then, too, it pleased her to think that she was furthering the pretty love story between Alice and Mr. Arkwright. And she *was* furthering it. She was sure of that. Already she could see how dependent the man was on Alice, how he looked to her for approbation, and appealed to her on all occasions, exactly as if there was not a move that he wanted to make without her presence near him. Billy was very sure, now, of Arkwright. She only wished she were as much so of Alice. But Alice troubled her. Not but that Alice was kindness itself to the man, either. It was only a peculiar something almost like fear, or constraint, that Billy thought she saw in Alice's eyes, sometimes, when Arkwright made a particularly intimate appeal. There was Calderwell, too. He, also, worried Billy. She feared he was going to complicate matters still more by falling in love with Alice, himself; and this, certainly, Billy did not want at all. As this phase of the matter presented itself, indeed, Billy determined to appropriate Calderwell a little more exclusively to herself, when the four were together, thus leaving Alice for Arkwright. After all, it was rather entertaining—this playing at Cupid's assistant. If she *could* not have Bertram all the time, it was fortunate that these outside interests were so pleasurable.

Most of the mornings Billy spent in the kitchen, despite the remonstrances of both Pete and Eliza. Almost every meal, now, was graced with a palatable cake, pudding, or muffin that Billy would proudly claim as her handiwork. Pete still served at table, and made strenuous efforts to keep up all his old duties; but he was obviously growing weaker, and really serious blunders were beginning to be noticeable. Bertram even hinted once or twice that perhaps it would be just as well to insist on his going; but to this Billy would not give her consent. Even when one night his poor old trembling hands spilled half the contents of a soup plate over a new and costly evening gown of Billy's own, she still refused to have him dismissed.

"Why, Bertram, I wouldn't do it," she declared hotly; "and you wouldn't, either. He's been here more than fifty years. It would break his heart. He's really too ill to work, and I wish he would go of his own accord, of course; but I sha'n't ever tell him to go—not if he spills soup on every dress I've got. I'll buy more—and more, if it's necessary. Bless his dear old heart! He thinks he's really serving us—and he is, too."

"Oh, yes, you're right, he *is!*" sighed Bertram, with meaning emphasis, as he abandoned the argument.

In addition to her "Talk to Young Wives," Billy found herself encountering advice and comment on the marriage question from still other quarters—from her acquaintances (mostly the feminine ones) right and left. Continually she was hearing such words as these:

"Oh, well, what can you expect, Billy? You're an old married woman, now."

"Never mind, you'll find he's like all the rest of the husbands. You just wait and see!"

"Better begin with a high hand, Billy. Don't let him fool you!"

"Mercy! If I had a husband whose business it was to look at women's beautiful eyes, peachy cheeks, and luxurious tresses, I should go crazy! It's hard enough to keep a man's eyes on yourself when his daily interests are supposed to be just lumps of coal and chunks of ice, without flinging him into the very jaws of temptation like asking him to paint a pretty girl's picture!"

In response to all this, of course, Billy could but laugh, and blush, and toss back some gay reply, with a careless unconcern. But in her heart she did not like it. Sometimes she told herself that if there were not any advice or comment from anybody—either book or woman—if there were not anybody but just Bertram and herself, life would be just one long honeymoon forever and forever.

Once or twice Billy was tempted to go to Marie with this honeymoon question; but Marie was very busy these days, and very preoccupied. The new house that Cyril was building on Corey Hill, not far from the Annex, was almost finished, and Marie was immersed in the subject of house-furnishings and interior decoration. She was, too, still more deeply engrossed in the fashioning of tiny garments of the softest linen, lace, and woolen; and there was on her face such a look of beatific wonder and joy that Billy did not like to so much as hint that there was in the world such a book as "When the Honeymoon Wanes: A Talk to Young Wives."

Billy tried valiantly these days not to mind that Bertram's work was so absorbing. She tried not to mind that his business dealt, not with lumps of coal and chunks of ice, but with beautiful women like Marguerite Winthrop who asked him to luncheon, and lovely girls like his model for "The Rose" who came freely to his studio and spent hours in the beloved presence, being studied for what Bertram declared was absolutely the most wonderful poise of head and shoulders that he had ever seen.

Billy tried, also, these days, to so conduct herself that not by any chance could Calderwell suspect that sometimes she was jealous of Bertram's art. Not for worlds would she have had Calderwell begin to get the notion into his head that his old-time prophecy concerning Bertram's caring only for the turn of a girl's head or the tilt of her chin—to paint, was being fulfilled. Hence, particularly gay and cheerful was Billy when Calderwell was near. Nor could it be said that Billy was really unhappy at any time. It was only that, on occasion, the very depth of her happiness in Bertram's love frightened her, lest it bring disaster to herself or Bertram.

Billy still went frequently to the Annex. There were yet two unfilled rooms in the house. Billy was hesitating which two of six new friends of hers to choose as occupants; and it was one day early in March, after she had been talking the matter over with Aunt Hannah, that Aunt Hannah said:

"Dear me, Billy, if you had your way I believe you'd open another whole house!"

"Do you know?—that's just what I'm thinking of," retorted Billy, gravely. Then she laughed at Aunt Hannah's shocked gesture of protest. "Oh, well, I don't expect to," she added. "I haven't lived very long, but I've lived long enough to know that you can't always do what you want to."

"Just as if there were anything *you* wanted to do that you don't do, my dear," reproved Aunt Hannah, mildly.

"Yes, I know." Billy drew in her breath with a little catch. "I have so much that is lovely; and that's why I need this house, you know, for the overflow," she nodded brightly. Then, with a characteristic change of subject, she added: "My, but you should have tasted of the popovers I made for breakfast this morning!"

"I should like to," smiled Aunt Hannah. "William says you're getting to be quite a cook."

"Well, maybe," conceded Billy, doubtfully. "Oh, I can do some things all right; but just wait till Pete and Eliza go away again, and Bertram brings home a friend to dinner. That'll tell the tale. I think now I could have something besides potato-mush and burned corn—but maybe I wouldn't, when the time came. If only I could buy everything I needed to cook with, I'd be all right. But I can't, I find."

"Can't buy what you need! What do you mean?"

Billy laughed ruefully.

"Well, every other question I ask Eliza, she says: 'Why, I don't know; you have to use your judgment.' Just as if I had any judgment about how much salt to use, or what dish to take! Dear me, Aunt Hannah, the man that will grow judgment and can it as you would a mess of peas, has got his fortune made!"

"What an absurd child you are, Billy," laughed Aunt Hannah. "I used to tell Marie—By the way, how is Marie? Have you seen her lately?"

"Oh, yes, I saw her yesterday," twinkled Billy. "She had a book of wall-paper samples spread over the back of a chair, two bunches of samples of different colored damasks on the table before her, a 'Young Mother's Guide' propped open in another chair, and a pair of baby's socks in her lap with a roll each of pink, and white, and blue ribbon. She spent most of the time, after I had helped her choose the ribbon, in asking me if I thought she ought to let the baby cry and bother Cyril, or stop its crying and hurt the baby, because her 'Mother's Guide' says a certain amount of crying is needed to develop a baby's lungs."

Aunt Hannah laughed, but she frowned, too.

"The idea! I guess Cyril can stand proper crying—and laughing, too—from his own child!" she said then, crisply.

"Oh, but Marie is afraid he can't," smiled Billy. "And that's the trouble. She says that's the only thing that worries her—Cyril."

"Nonsense!" ejaculated Aunt Hannah.

"Oh, but it isn't nonsense to Marie," retorted Billy. "You should see the preparations she's made and the precautions she's taken. Actually, when I saw those baby's socks in her lap, I didn't know but she was going to put rubber heels on them! They've built the new house with deadening felt in all the walls, and Marie's planned the nursery and Cyril's den at opposite ends of the house; and she says she shall keep the baby there *all* the time—the nursery, I mean, not the den. She says she's going to teach it to be a quiet baby and hate noise. She says she thinks she can do it, too."

"Humph!" sniffed Aunt Hannah, scornfully.

"You should have seen Marie's disgust the other day," went on Billy, a bit mischievously. "Her Cousin Jane sent on a rattle she'd made herself, all soft worsted, with bells inside. It was a dear; but Marie was horror-stricken. 'My baby have a rattle?' she cried. 'Why, what would Cyril say? As if he could stand a rattle in the house!' And if she didn't give that rattle to the janitor's wife that very day, while I was there!"

"Humph!" sniffed Aunt Hannah again, as Billy rose to go. "Well, I'm thinking Marie has still some things to learn in this world—and Cyril, too, for that matter."

"I wouldn't wonder," laughed Billy, giving Aunt Hannah a good-by kiss.

CHAPTER XIII
PETE

Bertram Henshaw had no disquieting forebodings this time concerning his portrait of Marguerite Winthrop when the doors of the Bohemian Ten Club Exhibition were thrown open to members and invited guests. Just how great a popular success it was destined to be, he could not know, of course, though he might have suspected it when he began to receive the admiring and hearty congratulations of his friends and fellow-artists on that first evening.

Nor was the Winthrop portrait the only jewel in his crown on that occasion. His marvelously exquisite "The Rose," and his smaller ideal picture, "Expectation," came in for scarcely less commendation. There was no doubt now. The originator of the famous "Face of a Girl" had come into his own again. On all sides this was the verdict, one long-haired critic of international fame even claiming openly that Henshaw had not only equaled his former best work, but had gone beyond it, in both artistry and technique.

It was a brilliant gathering. Society, as usual, in costly evening gowns and correct swallow-tails rubbed elbows with names famous in the world of Art and Letters. Everywhere were gay laughter and sparkling repartee. Even the austere-faced J. G. Winthrop unbent to the extent of grim smiles in response to the laudatory comments bestowed upon the pictured image of his idol, his beautiful daughter.

As to the great financier's own opinion of the work, no one heard him express it except, perhaps, the artist; and all that he got was a grip of the hand and a "Good! I knew you'd fetch it this time, my boy!" But that was enough. And, indeed, no one who knew the stern old man needed to more than look into his face that evening to know of his entire satisfaction in this portrait soon to be the most recent, and the most cherished addition to his far-famed art collection.

As to Bertram—Bertram was pleased and happy and gratified, of course, as was natural; but he was not one whit more so than was Bertram's wife. Billy fairly radiated happiness and proud joy. She told Bertram, indeed, that if he did anything to make her any prouder, it would take an Annex the size of the Boston Opera House to hold her extra happiness.

"Sh-h, Billy! Some one will hear you," protested Bertram, tragically; but, in spite of his horrified voice, he did not look displeased.

For the first time Billy met Marguerite Winthrop that evening. At the outset there was just a bit of shyness and constraint in the young wife's manner. Billy could not forget her old insane jealousy of this beautiful girl with the envied name of Marguerite. But it was for only a moment, and soon she was her natural, charming self.

Miss Winthrop was fascinated, and she made no pretense of hiding it. She even turned to Bertram at last, and cried:

"Surely, now, Mr. Henshaw, you need never go far for a model! Why don't you paint your wife?"

Billy colored. Bertram smiled.

"I have," he said. "I have painted her many times. In fact, I have painted her so often that she once declared it was only the tilt of her chin and the turn of her head that I loved—to paint," he said merrily, enjoying Billy's pretty confusion, and not realizing that his words really distressed her. "I have a whole studio full of 'Billys' at home."

"Oh, have you, really?" questioned Miss Winthrop, eagerly. "Then mayn't I see them? Mayn't I, please, Mrs. Henshaw? I'd so love to!"

"Why, of course you may," murmured both the artist and his wife.

"Thank you. Then I'm coming right away. May I? I'm going to Washington next week, you see. Will you let me come to-morrow at—at half-past three, then? Will it be quite convenient for you, Mrs. Henshaw?"

"Quite convenient. I shall be glad to see you," smiled Billy. And Bertram echoed his wife's cordial permission.

"Thank you. Then I'll be there at half-past three," nodded Miss Winthrop, with a smile, as she turned to give place to an admiring group, who were waiting to pay their respects to the artist and his wife.

There was, after all, that evening, one fly in Billy's ointment.

It fluttered in at the behest of an old acquaintance—one of the "advice women," as Billy termed some of her too interested friends.

"Well, they're lovely, perfectly lovely, of course, Mrs. Henshaw," said this lady, coming up to say good-night. "But, all the same, I'm glad my husband is just a plain lawyer. Look out, my dear, that while Mr. Henshaw is stealing all those pretty faces for his canvases—just look out that the fair ladies don't turn around and steal his heart before you know it. Dear me, but you must be so proud of him!"

"I am," smiled Billy, serenely; and only the jagged split that rent the glove on her hand, at that moment, told of the fierce anger behind that smile.

"As if I couldn't trust Bertram!" raged Billy passionately to herself, stealing a surreptitious glance at her ruined glove. "And as if there weren't ever any perfectly happy marriages—even if you don't ever hear of them, or read of them!"

Bertram was not home to luncheon on the day following the opening night of the Bohemian Ten Club. A matter of business called him away from the house early in the morning; but he told his wife that he surely would be on hand for Miss Winthrop's call at half-past three o'clock that afternoon.

"Yes, do," Billy had urged. "I think she's lovely, but you know her so much better than I do that I want you here. Besides, you needn't think *I'm* going to show her all those Billys of yours. I may be vain, but I'm not quite vain enough for that, sir!"

"Don't worry," her husband had laughed. "I'll be here."

As it chanced, however, something occurred an hour before half-past three o'clock that drove every thought of Miss Winthrop's call from Billy's head.

For three days, now, Pete had been at the home of his niece in South Boston. He had been forced, finally, to give up and go away. News from him the day before had been anything but reassuring, and to-day, Bertram being gone, Billy had suggested that Eliza serve a simple luncheon and go immediately afterward to South Boston to see how her uncle was. This suggestion Eliza had followed, leaving the house at one o'clock.

Shortly after two Calderwell had dropped in to bring Bertram, as he expressed it, a bunch of bouquets he had gathered at the picture show the night before. He was still in the drawing-room, chatting with Billy, when the telephone bell rang.

"If that's Bertram, tell him to come home; he's got company," laughed Calderwell, as Billy passed into the hall.

A moment later he heard Billy give a startled cry, followed by a few broken words at short intervals. Then, before he could surmise what had happened, she was back in the drawing-room again, her eyes full of tears.

"It's Pete," she choked. "Eliza says he can't live but a few minutes. He wants to see me once more. What shall I do? John's got Peggy out with Aunt Hannah and Mrs. Greggory. It was so nice to-day I made them go. But

I must get there some way—Pete is calling for me. Uncle William is going, and I told Eliza where she might reach Bertram; but what shall I do? How shall I go?"

Calderwell was on his feet at once.

"I'll get a taxi. Don't worry—we'll get there. Poor old soul—of course he wants to see you! Get on your things. I'll have it here in no time," he finished, hurrying to the telephone.

"Oh, Hugh, I'm so glad I've got *you* here," sobbed Billy, stumbling blindly toward the stairway. "I'll be ready in two minutes."

And she was; but neither then, nor a little later when she and Calderwell drove hurriedly away from the house, did Billy once remember that Miss Marguerite Winthrop was coming to call that afternoon to see Mrs. Bertram Henshaw and a roomful of Billy pictures.

Pete was still alive when Calderwell left Billy at the door of the modest little home where Eliza's mother lived.

"Yes, you're in time, ma'am," sobbed Eliza; "and, oh, I'm so glad you've come. He's been askin' and askin' for ye."

From Eliza Billy learned then that Mr. William was there, but not Mr. Bertram. They had not been able to reach Mr. Bertram, or Mr. Cyril.

Billy never forgot the look of reverent adoration that came into Pete's eyes as she entered the room where he lay.

"Miss Billy—my Miss Billy! You were so good-to come," he whispered faintly.

Billy choked back a sob.

"Of course I'd come, Pete," she said gently, taking one of the thin, worn hands into both her soft ones.

It was more than a few minutes that Pete lived. Four o'clock came, and five, and he was still with them. Often he opened his eyes and smiled. Sometimes he spoke a low word to William or Billy, or to one of the weeping women at the foot of the bed. That the presence of his beloved master and mistress meant much to him was plain to be seen.

"I'm so sorry," he faltered once, "about that pretty dress—I spoiled, Miss Billy. But you know—my hands—"

"I know, I know," soothed Billy; "but don't worry. It wasn't spoiled, Pete. It's all fixed now."

"Oh, I'm so glad," sighed the sick man. After another long interval of silence he turned to William.

"Them socks—the medium thin ones—you'd oughter be puttin' 'em on soon, sir, now. They're in the right-hand corner of the bottom drawer—you know."

"Yes, Pete; I'll attend to it," William managed to stammer, after he had cleared his throat.

Eliza's turn came next.

"Remember about the coffee," Pete said to her, "—the way Mr. William likes it. And always eggs, you know, for—for—" His voice trailed into an indistinct murmur, and his eyelids drooped wearily.

One by one the minutes passed. The doctor came and went: there was nothing he could do. At half-past five the thin old face became again alight with consciousness. There was a good-by message for Bertram, and one for Cyril. Aunt Hannah was remembered, and even little Tommy Dunn. Then, gradually, a gray shadow crept over the wasted features. The words came more brokenly. The mind, plainly, was wandering, for old Pete was young again, and around him were the lads he loved, William, Cyril, and Bertram. And then, very quietly, soon after the clock struck six, Pete fell into the beginning of his long sleep.

CHAPTER XIV
WHEN BERTRAM CAME HOME

It was a little after half-past three o'clock that afternoon when Bertram Henshaw hurried up Beacon Street toward his home. He had been delayed, and he feared that Miss Winthrop would already have reached the house. Mindful of what Billy had said that morning, he knew how his wife would fret if he were not there when the guest arrived. The sight of what he surmised to be Miss Winthrop's limousine before his door hastened his steps still more. But as he reached the house, he was surprised to find Miss Winthrop herself turning away from the door.

"Why, Miss Winthrop," he cried, "you're not going *now!* You can't have been here any—yet!"

"Well, no, I—I haven't," retorted the lady, with heightened color and a somewhat peculiar emphasis. "My ring wasn't answered."

"Wasn't answered!" Bertram reddened angrily. "Why, what can that mean? Where's the maid? Where's my wife? Mrs. Henshaw must be here! She was expecting you."

Bertram, in his annoyed amazement, spoke loudly, vehemently. Hence he was quite plainly heard by the group of small boys and girls who had been improving the mild weather for a frolic on the sidewalk, and who had been attracted to his door a moment before by the shining magnet of the Winthrop limousine with its resplendently liveried chauffeur. As Bertram spoke, one of the small girls, Bessie Bailey, stepped forward and piped up a shrill reply.

"She ain't, Mr. Henshaw! She ain't here. I saw her go away just a little while ago."

Bertram turned sharply.

"You saw her go away! What do you mean?"

Small Bessie swelled with importance. Bessie was thirteen, in spite of her diminutive height. Bessie's mother was dead, and Bessie's caretakers were gossiping nurses and servants, who frequently left in her way books that were much too old for Bessie to read—but she read them.

"I mean she ain't here—your wife, Mr. Henshaw. She went away. I saw her. I guess likely she's eloped, sir."

"Eloped!"

Bessie swelled still more importantly. To her experienced eyes the situation contained all the necessary elements for the customary flight of the heroine in her story-books, as here, now, was the irate, deserted husband.

"Sure! And 'twas just before you came—quite a while before. A big shiny black automobile like this drove up—only it wasn't quite such a nice one—an' Mrs. Henshaw an' a man came out of your house an' got in, an' drove right away *quick!* They just ran to get into it, too—didn't they?" She appealed to her young mates grouped about her.

A chorus of shrill exclamations brought Mr. Bertram Henshaw suddenly to his senses. By a desperate effort he hid his angry annoyance as he turned to the manifestly embarrassed young woman who was already descending the steps.

"My dear Miss Winthrop," he apologized contritely, "I'm sure you'll forgive this seeming great rudeness on the part of my wife. Notwithstanding the lurid tales of our young friends here, I suspect nothing more serious has happened than that my wife has been hastily summoned to Aunt Hannah, perhaps. Or, of course, she may not have understood that you were coming to-day at half-past three—though I thought she did. But I'm so sorry—when you were so kind as to come—" Miss Winthrop interrupted with a quick gesture.

"Say no more, I beg of you," she entreated. "Mrs. Henshaw is quite excusable, I'm sure. Please don't give it another thought," she finished, as with a hurried direction to the man who was holding open the door of her car, she stepped inside and bowed her good-byes.

Bertram, with stern self-control, forced himself to walk nonchalantly up his steps, leisurely take out his key, and open his door, under the interested eyes of Bessie Bailey and her friends; but once beyond their hateful stare, his demeanor underwent a complete change. Throwing aside his hat and coat, he strode to the telephone.

"Oh, is that you, Aunt Hannah?" he called crisply, a moment later. "Well, if Billy's there will you tell her I want to speak to her, please?"

"Billy?" answered Aunt Hannah's slow, gentle tones. "Why, my dear boy, Billy isn't here!"

"She isn't? Well, when did she leave? She's been there, hasn't she?"

"Why, I don't think so, but I'll see, if you like. Mrs. Greggory and I have just this minute come in from an automobile ride. We would have stayed longer, but it began to get chilly, and I forgot to take one of the shawls that I'd laid out."

"Yes; well, if you will see, please, if Billy has been there, and when she left," said Bertram, with grim self-control.

"All right. I'll see," murmured Aunt Hannah. In a few moments her voice again sounded across the wires. "Why, no, Bertram, Rosa says she hasn't been here since yesterday. Isn't she there somewhere about the house? Didn't you know where she was going?"

"Well, no, I didn't—else I shouldn't have been asking you," snapped the irate Bertram and hung up the receiver with most rude haste, thereby cutting off an astounded "Oh, my grief and conscience!" in the middle of it.

The next ten minutes Bertram spent in going through the whole house, from garret to basement. Needless to say, he found nothing to enlighten him, or to soothe his temper. Four o'clock came, then half-past, and five. At five Bertram began to look for Eliza, but in vain. At half-past five he watched for William; but William, too, did not come.

Bertram was pacing the floor now, nervously. He was a little frightened, but more mortified and angry. That Billy should have allowed Miss Winthrop to call by appointment only to find no hostess, no message, no maid, even, to answer her ring—it was inexcusable! Impulsiveness, unconventionality, and girlish irresponsibility were all very delightful, of course—at times; but not now, certainly. Billy was not a girl any longer. She was a married woman. *Something* was due to him, her husband! A pretty picture he must have made on those steps, trying to apologize for a truant wife, and to laugh off that absurd Bessie Bailey's preposterous assertion at the same time! What would Miss Winthrop think? What could she think? Bertram fairly ground his teeth with chagrin, at the situation in which he found himself.

Nor were matters helped any by the fact that Bertram was hungry. Bertram's luncheon had been meager and unsatisfying. That the kitchen down-stairs still remained in silent, spotless order instead of being astir with the sounds and smells of a good dinner (as it should have been) did not improve his temper. Where Billy was he could not imagine. He thought, once or twice, of calling up some of her friends; but something held him back from that—though he did try to get Marie, knowing very well that she was probably over to the new house and would not answer. He was not surprised, therefore, when he received no reply to his ring.

That there was the slightest truth in Bessie Bailey's absurd "elopement" idea, Bertram did not, of course, for an instant believe. The only thing that rankled about that was the fact that she had suggested such a thing, and that Miss Winthrop and those silly children had heard her. He recognized half of Bessie's friends as neighborhood youngsters, and he knew very well that there would be many a quiet laugh at his expense around various Beacon Street dinner-tables that night. At the thought of those dinner-tables, he scowled again. *He* had no dinner-table—at least, he had no dinner on it!

Who the man might be Bertram thought he could easily guess. It was either Arkwright or Calderwell, of course; and probably that tiresome Alice Greggory was mixed up in it somehow. He did wish Billy—

Six o'clock came, then half-past. Bertram was indeed frightened now, but he was more angry, and still more hungry. He had, in fact, reached that state of blind unreasonableness said to be peculiar to hungry males from time immemorial.

At ten minutes of seven a key clicked in the lock of the outer door, and William and Billy entered the hall.

It was almost dark. Bertram could not see their faces. He had not lighted the hall at all.

"Well," he began sharply, "is this the way you receive your callers, Billy? I came home and found Miss Winthrop just leaving—no one here to receive her! Where've you been? Where's Eliza? Where's my dinner? Of course I don't mean to scold, Billy, but there is a limit to even my patience— and it's reached now. I can't help suggesting that if you would tend to your husband and your home a little more, and go gallivanting off with

Calderwell and Arkwright and Alice Greggory a little less, that—Where is Eliza, anyway?" he finished irritably, switching on the lights with a snap.

There was a moment of dead silence. At Bertram's first words Billy and William had stopped short. Neither had moved since. Now William turned and began to speak, but Billy interrupted. She met her husband's gaze steadily.

"I will be down at once to get your dinner," she said quietly. "Eliza will not come to-night. Pete is dead."

Bertram started forward with a quick cry.

"Dead! Oh, Billy! Then you were—*there!* Billy!"

But his wife did not apparently hear him. She passed him without turning her head, and went on up the stairs, leaving him to meet the sorrowful, accusing eyes of William.

CHAPTER XV
AFTER THE STORM

The young husband's apologies were profuse and abject. Bertram was heartily ashamed of himself, and was man enough to acknowledge it. Almost on his knees he begged Billy to forgive him; and in a frenzy of self-denunciation he followed her down into the kitchen that night, piteously beseeching her to speak to him, to just *look* at him, even, so that he might know he was not utterly despised—though he did, indeed, deserve to be more than despised, he moaned.

At first Billy did not speak, or even vouchsafe a glance in his direction. Very quietly she went about her preparations for a simple meal, paying apparently no more attention to Bertram than as if he were not there. But that her ears were only seemingly, and not really deaf, was shown very clearly a little later, when, at a particularly abject wail on the part of the babbling shadow at her heels, Billy choked into a little gasp, half laughter, half sob. It was all over then. Bertram had her in his arms in a twinkling, while to the floor clattered and rolled a knife and a half-peeled baked potato.

Naturally, after that, there could be no more dignified silences on the part of the injured wife. There were, instead, half-smiles, tears, sobs, a tremulous telling of Pete's going and his messages, followed by a tearful listening to Bertram's story of the torture he had endured at the hands of Miss Winthrop, Bessie Bailey, and an empty, dinnerless house. And thus, in one corner of the kitchen, some time later, a hungry, desperate William found them, the half-peeled, cold baked potato still at their feet.

Torn between his craving for food and his desire not to interfere with any possible peace-making, William was obviously hesitating what to do, when Billy glanced up and saw him. She saw, too, at the same time, the empty, blazing gas-stove burner, and the pile of half-prepared potatoes, to warm which the burner had long since been lighted. With a little cry she broke away from her husband's arms.

"Mercy! and here's poor Uncle William, bless his heart, with not a thing to eat yet!"

They all got dinner then, together, with many a sigh and quick-coming tear as everywhere they met some sad reminder of the gentle old hands that would never again minister to their comfort.

It was a silent meal, and little, after all, was eaten, though brave attempts at cheerfulness and naturalness were made by all three. Bertram, especially, talked, and tried to make sure that the shadow on Billy's face was at least not the one his own conduct had brought there.

"For you do—you surely do forgive me, don't you?" he begged, as he followed her into the kitchen after the sorry meal was over.

"Why, yes, dear, yes," sighed Billy, trying to smile.

"And you'll forget?"

There was no answer.

"Billy! And you'll forget?" Bertram's voice was insistent, reproachful.

Billy changed color and bit her lip. She looked plainly distressed.

"Billy!" cried the man, still more reproachfully.

"But, Bertram, I can't forget—quite yet," faltered Billy.

Bertram frowned. For a minute he looked as if he were about to take up the matter seriously and argue it with her; but the next moment he smiled and tossed his head with jaunty playfulness—Bertram, to tell the truth, had now had quite enough of what he privately termed "scenes" and "heroics"; and, manlike, he was very ardently longing for the old easy-going friendliness, with all unpleasantness banished to oblivion.

"Oh, but you'll have to forget," he claimed, with cheery insistence, "for you've promised to forgive me—and one can't forgive without forgetting. So, there!" he finished, with a smilingly determined "now-everything-is-just-as-it-was-before" air.

Billy made no response. She turned hurriedly and began to busy herself with the dishes at the sink. In her heart she was wondering: could she ever forget what Bertram had said? Would anything ever blot out those awful words: "If you would tend to your husband and your home a little more, and go gallivanting off with Calderwell and Arkwright and Alice Greggory a little less—"? It seemed now that always, for evermore, they would ring in her ears; always, for evermore, they would burn deeper and deeper into her soul. And not once, in all Bertram's apologies, had he referred to them—those words he had uttered. He had not said he did not mean them. He had not said he was sorry he spoke them. He had ignored them; and he expected that now she, too, would ignore them. As if she could!" If you would tend to your husband and your home a little more, and go gallivanting off with Calderwell and Arkwright and Alice Greggory a little less—" Oh, if only she could, indeed,—forget!

When Billy went up-stairs that night she ran across her "Talk to Young Wives" in her desk. With a half-stifled cry she thrust it far back out of sight.

"I hate you, I hate you—with all your old talk about 'brushing up against outside interests'!" she whispered fiercely. "Well, I've 'brushed'—and now see what I've got for it!"

Later, however, after Bertram was asleep, Billy crept out of bed and got the book. Under the carefully shaded lamp in the adjoining room she turned the pages softly till she came to the sentence: "Perhaps it would be hard to find a more utterly unreasonable, irritable, irresponsible creature than a hungry man." With a long sigh she began to read; and not until some minutes later did she close the book, turn off the light, and steal back to bed.

During the next three days, until after the funeral at the shabby little South Boston house, Eliza spent only about half of each day at the Strata. This, much to her distress, left many of the household tasks for her young mistress to perform. Billy, however, attacked each new duty with a feverish eagerness that seemed to make the performance of it very like some glad penance done for past misdeeds. And when—on the day after they had laid the old servant in his last resting place—a despairing message came from Eliza to the effect that now her mother was very ill, and would need her care, Billy promptly told Eliza to stay as long as was necessary; that they could get along all right without her.

"But, Billy, what *are* we going to do?" Bertram demanded, when he heard the news. "We must have somebody!"

"*I'm* going to do it."

"Nonsense! As if you could!" scoffed Bertram.

Billy lifted her chin.

"Couldn't I, indeed," she retorted. "Do you realize, young man, how much I've done the last three days? How about those muffins you had this morning for breakfast, and that cake last night? And didn't you yourself say that you never ate a better pudding than that date puff yesterday noon?"

Bertram laughed and shrugged his shoulders.

"My dear love, I'm not questioning your *ability* to do it," he soothed quickly. "Still," he added, with a whimsical smile, "I must remind you that Eliza has been here half the time, and that muffins and date puffs, however delicious, aren't all there is to running a big house like this. Besides, just be sensible, Billy," he went on more seriously, as he noted the rebellious gleam coming into his young wife's eyes; "you'd know you couldn't do it, if you'd just stop to think. There's the Carletons coming to dinner Monday, and my studio Tea to-morrow, to say nothing of the Symphony and the opera, and the concerts you'd lose because you were too dead tired to go to them. You know how it was with that concert yesterday afternoon which Alice Greggory wanted you to go to with her."

"I didn't—want—to go," choked Billy, under her breath.

"And there's your music. You haven't done a thing with that for days, yet only last week you told me the publishers were hurrying you for that last song to complete the group."

"I haven't felt like—writing," stammered Billy, still half under her breath.

"Of course you haven't," triumphed Bertram. "You've been too dead tired. And that's just what I say. Billy, you *can't* do it all yourself!"

"But I want to. I want to—to tend to things," faltered Billy, with a half-fearful glance into her husband's face.

Billy was hearing very loudly now that accusing "If you'd tend to your husband and your home a little more—" Bertram, however, was not hearing it, evidently. Indeed, he seemed never to have heard it—much less to have spoken it.

"'Tend to things,'" he laughed lightly. "Well, you'll have enough to do to tend to the maid, I fancy. Anyhow, we're going to have one. I'll just step into one of those—what do you call 'em?—intelligence offices on my way down and send one up," he finished, as he gave his wife a good-by kiss.

An hour later Billy, struggling with the broom and the drawing-room carpet, was called to the telephone. It was her husband's voice that came to her.

"Billy, for heaven's sake, take pity on me. Won't you put on your duds and come and engage your maid yourself?"

"Why, Bertram, what's the matter?"

"Matter? Holy smoke! Well, I've been to three of those intelligence offices—though why they call them that I can't imagine. If ever there was a place utterly devoid of intelligence-but never mind! I've interviewed four fat ladies, two thin ones, and one medium with a wart. I've cheerfully divulged all our family secrets, promised every other half-hour out, and taken oath that our household numbers three adult members, and no more; but I simply *can't* remember how many handkerchiefs we have in the wash each week. Billy, will you come? Maybe you can do something with them. I'm sure you can!"

"Why, of course I'll come," chirped Billy. "Where shall I meet you?"

Bertram gave the street and number.

"Good! I'll be there," promised Billy, as she hung up the receiver.

Quite forgetting the broom in the middle of the drawing-room floor, Billy tripped up-stairs to change her dress. On her lips was a gay little song. In her heart was joy.

"I rather guess *now* I'm tending to my husband and my home!" she was crowing to herself.

Just as Billy was about to leave the house the telephone bell jangled again.

It was Alice Greggory.

"Billy, dear," she called, "can't you come out? Mr. Arkwright and Mr. Calderwell are here, and they've brought some new music. We want you. Will you come?"

"I can't, dear. Bertram wants me. He's sent for me. I've got some *housewifely* duties to perform to-day," returned Billy, in a voice so curiously triumphant that Alice, at her end of the wires, frowned in puzzled wonder as she turned away from the telephone.

CHAPTER XVI
INTO TRAINING FOR MARY ELLEN

Bertram told a friend afterwards that he never knew the meaning of the word "chaos" until he had seen the Strata during the weeks immediately following the laying away of his old servant.

"Every stratum was aquiver with apprehension," he declared; "and there was never any telling when the next grand upheaval would rock the whole structure to its foundations."

Nor was Bertram so far from being right. It was, indeed, a chaos, as none knew better than did Bertram's wife.

Poor Billy! Sorry indeed were these days for Billy; and, as if to make her cup of woe full to overflowing, there were Sister Kate's epistolary "I told you so," and Aunt Hannah's ever recurring lament: "If only, Billy, you were a practical housekeeper yourself, they wouldn't impose on you so!"

Aunt Hannah, to be sure, offered Rosa, and Kate, by letter, offered advice—plenty of it. But Billy, stung beyond all endurance, and fairly radiating hurt pride and dogged determination, disdained all assistance, and, with head held high, declared she was getting along very well, very well indeed!

And this was the way she "got along."

First came Nora. Nora was a blue-eyed, black-haired Irish girl, the sixth that the despairing Billy had interviewed on that fateful morning when Bertram had summoned her to his aid. Nora stayed two days. During her reign the entire Strata echoed to banged doors, dropped china, and slammed furniture. At her departure the Henshaws' possessions were less by four cups, two saucers, one plate, one salad bowl, two cut glass tumblers, and a teapot—the latter William's choicest bit of Lowestoft.

Olga came next. Olga was a Treasure. She was low-voiced, gentle-eyed, and a good cook. She stayed a week. By that time the growing frequency of the disappearance of sundry small articles of value and convenience led to Billy's making a reluctant search of Olga's room—and to Olga's departure; for the room was, indeed, a treasure house, the Treasure having gathered unto itself other treasures.

Following Olga came a period of what Bertram called "one night stands," so frequently were the dramatis personæ below stairs changed. Gretchen drank. Christine knew only four words of English: salt, good-by, no, and yes; and Billy found need occasionally of using other words. Mary was impertinent and lazy. Jennie could not even boil a potato properly, much less cook a dinner. Sarah (colored) was willing and pleasant, but insufferably untidy. Bridget was neatness itself, but she had no conception of the value of time. Her meals were always from thirty to sixty minutes late, and half-cooked at that. Vera sang—when she wasn't whistling—and as she was generally off the key, and always off the tune, her almost frantic mistress dismissed her before twenty-four hours had passed. Then came Mary Ellen.

Mary Ellen began well. She was neat, capable, and obliging; but it did not take her long to discover just how much—and how little—her mistress really knew of practical housekeeping. Matters and things were very different then. Mary Ellen became argumentative, impertinent, and domineering. She openly shirked her work, when it pleased her so to do, and demanded perquisites and privileges so insolently that even William asked Billy one day whether Mary Ellen or Billy herself were the mistress of the Strata: and Bertram, with mock humility, inquired how *soon* Mary Ellen would be wanting the house. Billy, in weary despair, submitted to this bullying for almost a week; then, in a sudden accession of outraged dignity that left Mary Ellen gasping with surprise, she told the girl to go.

And thus the days passed. The maids came and the maids went, and, to Billy, each one seemed a little worse than the one before. Nowhere was there comfort, rest, or peacefulness. The nights were a torture of apprehension, and the days an even greater torture of fulfilment. Noise, confusion, meals poorly cooked and worse served, dust, disorder, and uncertainty. And this was *home*, Billy told herself bitterly. No wonder that Bertram telephoned more and more frequently that he had met a friend, and was dining in town. No wonder that William pushed back his plate almost every meal with his food scarcely touched, and then wandered about the house with that hungry, homesick, homeless look that nearly broke her heart. No wonder, indeed!

And so it had come. It was true. Aunt Hannah and Kate and the "Talk to Young Wives" were right. She had not been fit to marry Bertram. She had not been fit to marry anybody. Her honeymoon was not only waning, but going into a total eclipse. Had not Bertram already declared that if she would tend to her husband and her home a little more—

Billy clenched her small hands and set her round chin squarely.

Very well, she would show them. She would tend to her husband and her home. She fancied she could *learn* to run that house, and run it well! And forthwith she descended to the kitchen and told the then reigning tormentor that her wages would be paid until the end of the week, but that her services would be immediately dispensed with.

Billy was well aware now that housekeeping was a matter of more than muffins and date puffs. She could gauge, in a measure, the magnitude of the task to which she had set herself. But she did not falter; and very systematically she set about making her plans.

With a good stout woman to come in twice a week for the heavier work, she believed she could manage by herself very well until Eliza could come back. At least she could serve more palatable meals than the most of those that had appeared lately; and at least she could try to make a home that would not drive Bertram to club dinners, and Uncle William to hungry wanderings from room to room. Meanwhile, all the time, she could be learning, and in due course she would reach that shining goal of Housekeeping Efficiency, short of which—according to Aunt Hannah and the "Talk to Young Wives"—no woman need hope for a waneless honeymoon.

So chaotic and erratic had been the household service, and so quietly did Billy slip into her new role, that it was not until the second meal after the maid's departure that the master of the house discovered what had happened. Then, as his wife rose to get some forgotten article, he questioned, with uplifted eyebrows:

"Too good to wait upon us, is my lady now, eh?"

"My lady is waiting on you," smiled Billy.

"Yes, I see *this* lady is," retorted Bertram, grimly; "but I mean our real lady in the kitchen. Great Scott, Billy, how long are you going to stand this?"

Billy tossed her head airily, though she shook in her shoes. Billy had been dreading this moment.

"I'm not standing it. She's gone," responded Billy, cheerfully, resuming her seat. "Uncle William, sha'n't I give you some more pudding?"

"Gone, so soon?" groaned Bertram, as William passed his plate, with a smiling nod. "Oh, well," went on Bertram, resignedly, "she stayed longer than the last one. When is the next one coming?"

"She's already here."

Bertram frowned.

"Here? But—you served the dessert, and—" At something in Billy's face, a quick suspicion came into his own. "Billy, you don't mean that you— you—"

"Yes," she nodded brightly, "that's just what I mean. I'm the next one."

"Nonsense!" exploded Bertram, wrathfully. "Oh, come, Billy, we've been all over this before. You know I can't have it."

"Yes, you can. You've got to have it," retorted Billy, still with that disarming, airy cheerfulness. "Besides, 'twon't be half so bad as you think. Wasn't that a good pudding to-night? Didn't you both come back for more? Well, I made it."

"Puddings!" ejaculated Bertram, with an impatient gesture. "Billy, as I've said before, it takes something besides puddings to run this house."

"Yes, I know it does," dimpled Billy, "and I've got Mrs. Durgin for that part. She's coming twice a week, and more, if I need her. Why, dearie, you don't know anything about how comfortable you're going to be! I'll leave it to Uncle William if—"

But Uncle William had gone. Silently he had slipped from his chair and disappeared. Uncle William, it might be mentioned in passing, had never quite forgotten Aunt Hannah's fateful call with its dire revelations concerning a certain unwanted, superfluous, third-party husband's brother. Remembering this, there were times when he thought absence was both safest and best. This was one of the times.

"But, Billy, dear," still argued Bertram, irritably, "how can you? You don't know how. You've had no experience."

Billy threw back her shoulders. An ominous light came to her eyes. She was no longer airily playful.

"That's exactly it, Bertram. I don't know how—but I'm going to learn. I haven't had experience—but I'm going to get it. I *can't* make a worse mess of it than we've had ever since Eliza went, anyway!"

"But if you'd get a maid—a good maid," persisted Bertram, feebly.

"I had *one*—Mary Ellen. She was a good maid—until she found out how little her mistress knew; then—well, you know what it was then. Do you think I'd let that thing happen to me again? No, sir! I'm going into training for—my next Mary Ellen!" And with a very majestic air Billy rose from the table and began to clear away the dishes.

CHAPTER XVII
THE EFFICIENCY STAR—AND BILLY

Billy was not a young woman that did things by halves. Long ago, in the days of her childhood, her Aunt Ella had once said of her: "If only Billy didn't go into things all over, so; but whether it's measles or mud pies, I always know that she'll be the measliest or the muddiest of any child in town!" It could not be expected, therefore, that Billy would begin to play her new rôle now with any lack of enthusiasm. But even had she needed any incentive, there was still ever ringing in her ears Bertram's accusing: "If you'd tend to your husband and your home a little more—" Billy still declared very emphatically that she had forgiven Bertram; but she knew, in her heart, that she had not forgotten.

Certainly, as the days passed, it could not be said that Billy was not tending to her husband and her home. From morning till night, now, she tended to nothing else. She seldom touched her piano—save to dust it—and she never touched her half-finished song-manuscript, long since banished to the oblivion of the music cabinet. She made no calls except occasional flying visits to the Annex, or to the pretty new home where Marie and Cyril were now delightfully settled. The opera and the Symphony were over for the season, but even had they not been, Billy could not have attended them. She had no time. Surely she was not doing any "gallivanting" now, she told herself sometimes, a little aggrievedly.

There was, indeed, no time. From morning until night Billy was busy, flying from one task to another. Her ambition to have everything just right was equalled only by her dogged determination to "just show them" that she could do this thing. At first, of course, hampered as she was by ignorance and inexperience, each task consumed about twice as much time as was necessary. Yet afterwards, when accustomedness had brought its reward of speed, there was still for Billy no time; for increased knowledge had only opened the way to other paths, untrodden and alluring. Study of cookbooks had led to the study of food values. Billy discovered suddenly that potatoes, beef, onions, oranges, and puddings were something besides vegetables, meat, fruit, and dessert. They possessed attributes known as proteids, fats, and carbohydrates. Faint memories of long forgotten school days hinted that these terms had been heard before; but never, Billy was sure, had she fully realized what they meant.

It was at this juncture that Billy ran across a book entitled "Correct Eating for Efficiency." She bought it at once, and carried it home in triumph. It proved to be a marvelous book. Billy had not read two chapters before she began to wonder how the family had managed to live thus far with any sort of success, in the face of their dense ignorance and her own criminal carelessness concerning their daily bill of fare.

At dinner that night Billy told Bertram and William of her discovery, and, with growing excitement, dilated on the wonderful good that it was to bring to them.

"Why, you don't know, you can't imagine what a treasure it is!" she exclaimed. "It gives a complete table for the exact balancing of food."

"For what?" demanded Bertram, glancing up.

"The exact balancing of food; and this book says that's the biggest problem that modern scientists have to solve."

"Humph!" shrugged Bertram. "Well, you just balance my food to my hunger, and I'll agree not to complain."

"Oh, but, Bertram, it's serious, really," urged Billy, looking genuinely distressed. "Why, it says that what you eat goes to make up what you are. It makes your vital energies. Your brain power and your body power come from what you eat. Don't you see? If you're going to paint a picture you need something different from what you would if you were going to—to saw wood; and what this book tells is—is what I ought to give you to make you do each one, I should think, from what I've read so far. Now don't you see how important it is? What if I should give you the saw-wood kind of a breakfast when you were just going up-stairs to paint all day? And what if I should give Uncle William a—a soldier's breakfast when all he is going to do is to go down on State Street and sit still all day?"

"But—but, my dear," began Uncle William, looking slightly worried, "there's my eggs that I *always* have, you know."

"For heaven's sake, Billy, what *have* you got hold of now?" demanded Bertram, with just a touch of irritation.

Billy laughed merrily.

"Well, I suppose I didn't sound very logical," she admitted. "But the book—you just wait. It's in the kitchen. I'm going to get it." And with laughing eagerness she ran from the room.

In a moment she had returned, book in hand.

"Now listen. *This* is the real thing—not my garbled inaccuracies. 'The food which we eat serves three purposes: it builds the body substance, bone, muscle, etc., it produces heat in the body, and it generates vital energy. Nitrogen in different chemical combinations contributes largely to the manufacture of body substances; the fats produce heat; and the starches and sugars go to make the vital energy. The nitrogenous food elements we call proteins; the fats and oils, fats; and the starches and sugars (because of the predominance of carbon), we call carbohydrates. Now in selecting the diet for the day you should take care to choose those foods which give the proteins, fats, and carbohydrates in just the right proportion.'"

"Oh, Billy!" groaned Bertram.

"But it's so, Bertram," maintained Billy, anxiously. "And it's every bit here. I don't have to guess at it at all. They even give the quantities of calories of energy required for different sized men. I'm going to measure you both to-morrow; and you must be weighed, too," she continued, ignoring the sniffs of remonstrance from her two listeners. "Then I'll know just how many calories to give each of you. They say a man of average size and weight, and sedentary occupation, should have at least 2,000 calories— and some authorities say 3,000—in this proportion: proteins, 300 calories, fats, 350 calories, carbohydrates, 1,350 calories. But you both are taller than five feet five inches, and I should think you weighed more than 145 pounds; so I can't tell just yet how many calories you will need."

"How many we will need, indeed!" ejaculated Bertram.

"But, my dear, you know I have to have my eggs," began Uncle William again, in a worried voice.

"Of course you do, dear; and you shall have them," soothed Billy, brightly. "It's only that I'll have to be careful and balance up the other things for the day accordingly. Don't you see? Now listen. We'll see what eggs are." She turned the leaves rapidly. "Here's the food table. It's lovely. It tells everything. I never saw anything so wonderful. A—b—c—d—e—here we are. 'Eggs, scrambled or boiled, fats and proteins, one egg, 100.' If it's poached it's only 50; but you like yours boiled, so we'll have to reckon on the 100. And you always have two, so that means 200 calories in fats and proteins. Now, don't you see? If you can't have but 300 proteins and 350 fats all day, and you've already eaten 200 in your two eggs, that'll leave just— er—450 for all the rest of the day,—of fats and proteins, you understand. And you've no idea how fast that'll count up. Why, just one serving of butter is 100 of fats, and eight almonds is another, while a serving of lentils is 100 of proteins. So you see how it'll go."

"Yes, I see," murmured Uncle William, casting a mournful glance about the generously laden table, much as if he were bidding farewell to a departing friend. "But if I should want more to eat—" He stopped helplessly, and Bertram's aggrieved voice filled the pause.

"Look here, Billy, if you think I'm going to be measured for an egg and weighed for an almond, you're much mistaken; because I'm not. I want to eat what I like, and as much as I like, whether it's six calories or six thousand!"

Billy chuckled, but she raised her hands in pretended shocked protest.

"Six thousand! Mercy! Bertram, I don't know what would happen if you ate that quantity; but I'm sure you couldn't paint. You'd just have to saw wood and dig ditches to use up all that vital energy."

"Humph!" scoffed Bertram.

"Besides, this is for *efficiency*," went on Billy, with an earnest air. "This man owns up that some may think a 2,000 calory ration is altogether too small, and he advises such to begin with 3,000 or even 3,500—graded, of course, according to a man's size, weight, and occupation. But he says one famous man does splendid work on only 1,800 calories, and another on even 1,600. But that is just a matter of chewing. Why, Bertram, you have no idea what perfectly wonderful things chewing does."

"Yes, I've heard of that," grunted Bertram; "ten chews to a cherry, and sixty to a spoonful of soup. There's an old metronome up-stairs that Cyril left. You might bring it down and set it going on the table—so many ticks to a mouthful, I suppose. I reckon, with an incentive like that to eat, just about two calories would do me. Eh, William?"

"Bertram! Now you're only making fun," chided Billy; "and when it's really serious, too. Now listen," she admonished, picking up the book again. "'If a man consumes a large amount of meat, and very few vegetables, his diet will be too rich in protein, and too lacking in carbohydrates. On the other hand, if he consumes great quantities of pastry, bread, butter, and tea, his meals will furnish too much energy, and not enough building material.' There, Bertram, don't you see?"

"Oh, yes, I see," teased Bertram. "William, better eat what you can to-night. I foresee it's the last meal of just *food* we'll get for some time. Hereafter we'll have proteins, fats, and carbohydrates made into calory croquettes, and—"

"Bertram!" scolded Billy.

But Bertram would not be silenced.

"Here, just let me take that book," he insisted, dragging the volume from Billy's reluctant fingers. "Now, William, listen. Here's your breakfast to-morrow morning: strawberries, 100 calories; whole-wheat bread, 75 calories; butter, 100 calories (no second helping, mind you, or you'd ruin the balance and something would topple); boiled eggs, 200 calories; cocoa, 100 calories—which all comes to 570 calories. Sounds like an English bill of fare with a new kind of foreign money, but 'tisn't, really, you know. Now for luncheon you can have tomato soup, 50 calories; potato salad—that's cheap, only 30 calories, and—" But Billy pulled the book away then, and in righteous indignation carried it to the kitchen.

"You don't deserve anything to eat," she declared with dignity, as she returned to the dining-room.

"No?" queried Bertram, his eyebrows uplifted. "Well, as near as I can make out we aren't going to get—much."

But Billy did not deign to answer this.

In spite of Bertram's tormenting gibes, Billy did, for some days, arrange her meals in accordance with the wonderful table of food given in "Correct Eating for Efficiency." To be sure, Bertram, whatever he found before him during those days, anxiously asked whether he were eating fats, proteins, or carbohydrates; and he worried openly as to the possibility of his meal's producing one calory too much or too little, thus endangering his "balance."

Billy alternately laughed and scolded, to the unvarying good nature of her husband. As it happened, however, even this was not for long, for Billy ran across a magazine article on food adulteration; and this so filled her with terror lest, in the food served, she were killing her family by slow poison, that she forgot all about the proteins, fats, and carbohydrates. Her talk these days was of formaldehyde, benzoate of soda, and salicylic acid.

Very soon, too, Billy discovered an exclusive Back Bay school for instruction in household economics and domestic hygiene. Billy investigated it at once, and was immediately aflame with enthusiasm. She told Bertram that it taught everything, *everything* she wanted to know; and forthwith she enrolled herself as one of its most devoted pupils, in spite of her husband's protests that she knew enough, more than enough, already. This school attendance, to her consternation, Billy discovered took added time; but in some way she contrived to find it to take.

And so the days passed. Eliza's mother, though better, was still too ill for her daughter to leave her. Billy, as the warm weather approached, began to look pale and thin. Billy, to tell the truth, was working altogether too hard; but she would not admit it, even to herself. At first the novelty of the work, and her determination to conquer at all costs, had given a fictitious strength to her endurance. Now that the novelty had become accustomedness, and the conquering a surety, Billy discovered that she had a back that could ache, and limbs that, at times, could almost refuse to move from weariness. There was still, however, one spur that never failed to urge her to fresh endeavor, and to make her, at least temporarily, forget both ache and weariness; and that was the comforting thought that now, certainly, even Bertram himself must admit that she was tending to her home and her husband.

As to Bertram—Bertram, it is true, had at first uttered frequent and vehement protests against his wife's absorption of both mind and body in "that plaguy housework," as he termed it. But as the days passed, and blessed order superseded chaos, peace followed discord, and delicious, well-served meals took the place of the horrors that had been called meals in the past, he gradually accepted the change with tranquil satisfaction, and forgot to question how it was brought about; though he did still, sometimes, rebel because Billy was always too tired, or too busy, to go out with him. Of late, however, he had not done even this so frequently, for a new "Face of a Girl" had possessed his soul; and all his thoughts and most of his time had gone to putting on canvas the vision of loveliness that his mind's eye saw.

By June fifteenth the picture was finished. Bertram awoke then to his surroundings. He found summer was upon him with no plans made for its enjoyment. He found William had started West for a two weeks' business trip. But what he did not find one day—at least at first—was his wife, when he came home unexpectedly at four o'clock. And Bertram especially wanted to find his wife that day, for he had met three people whose words had disquieted him not a little. First, Aunt Hannah. She had said:

"Bertram, where is Billy? She hasn't been out to the Annex for a week; and the last time she was there she looked sick. I was real worried about her."

Cyril had been next.

"Where's Billy?" he had asked abruptly. "Marie says she hasn't seen her for two weeks. Marie's afraid she's sick. She says Billy didn't look well a bit, when she did see her."

Calderwell had capped the climax. He had said:

"Great Scott, Henshaw, where have you been keeping yourself? And where's your wife? Not one of us has caught more than a glimpse of her for weeks. She hasn't sung with us, nor played for us, nor let us take her anywhere for a month of Sundays. Even Miss Greggory says *she* hasn't seen much of her, and that Billy always says she's too busy to go anywhere. But Miss Greggory says she looks pale and thin, and that *she* thinks she's worrying too much over running the house. I hope she isn't sick!"

"Why, no, Billy isn't sick. Billy's all right," Bertram had answered. He had spoken lightly, nonchalantly, with an elaborate air of carelessness; but after he had left Calderwell, he had turned his steps abruptly and a little hastily toward home.

And he had not found Billy—at least, not at once. He had gone first down into the kitchen and dining-room. He remembered then, uneasily, that he had always looked for Billy in the kitchen and dining-room, of late. To-day, however, she was not there.

On the kitchen table Bertram did see a book wide open, and, mechanically, he picked it up. It was a much-thumbed cookbook, and it was open where two once-blank pages bore his wife's handwriting. On the first page, under the printed heading "Things to Remember," he read these sentences:

"That rice swells till every dish in the house is full, and that spinach shrinks till you can't find it.

"That beets boil dry if you look out the window.

"That biscuits which look as if they'd been mixed up with a rusty stove poker haven't really been so, but have only got too much undissolved soda in them."

There were other sentences, but Bertram's eyes chanced to fall on the opposite page where the "Things to Remember" had been changed to "Things to Forget"; and here Billy had written just four words: "Burns," "cuts," and "yesterday's failures."

Bertram dropped the book then with a spasmodic clearing of his throat, and hurriedly resumed his search. When he did find his wife, at last, he gave a cry of dismay—she was on her own bed, huddled in a little heap, and shaking with sobs.

"Billy! Why, Billy!" he gasped, striding to the bedside.

Billy sat up at once, and hastily wiped her eyes.

"Oh, is it you, B-Bertram? I didn't hear you come in. You—you s-said you weren't coming till six o'clock!" she choked.

"Billy, what is the meaning of this?"

"N-nothing. I—I guess I'm just tired."

"What have you been doing?" Bertram spoke sternly, almost sharply. He was wondering why he had not noticed before the little hollows in his wife's cheeks. "Billy, what have you been doing?"

"Why, n-nothing extra, only some sweeping, and cleaning out the refrigerator."

"Sweeping! Cleaning! *You!* I thought Mrs. Durgin did that."

"She does. I mean she did. But she couldn't come. She broke her leg— fell off the stepladder where she was three days ago. So I *had* to do it. And to-day, someway, everything went wrong. I burned me, and I cut me, and I used two sodas with not any cream of tartar, and I should think I didn't know anything, not anything!" And down went Billy's head into the pillows again in another burst of sobs.

With gentle yet uncompromising determination, Bertram gathered his wife into his arms and carried her to the big chair. There, for a few minutes, he soothed and petted her as if she were a tired child—which, indeed, she was.

"Billy, this thing has got to stop," he said then. There was a very inexorable ring of decision in his voice.

"What thing?"

"This housework business."

Billy sat up with a jerk.

"But, Bertram, it isn't fair. You can't—you mustn't—just because of to-day! I *can* do it. I have done it. I've done it days and days, and it's gone beautifully—even if they did say I couldn't!"

"Couldn't what?"

"Be an e-efficient housekeeper."

"Who said you couldn't?"

"Aunt Hannah and K-Kate."

Bertram said a savage word under his breath.

"Holy smoke, Billy! I didn't marry you for a cook or a scrub-lady. If you *had* to do it, that would be another matter, of course; and if we did have to do it, we wouldn't have a big house like this for you to do it in. But I didn't marry for a cook, and I knew I wasn't getting one when I married you."

Billy bridled into instant wrath.

"Well, I like that, Bertram Henshaw! Can't I cook? Haven't I proved that I can cook?"

Bertram laughed, and kissed the indignant lips till they quivered into an unwilling smile.

"Bless your spunky little heart, of course you have! But that doesn't mean that I want you to do it. You see, it so happens that you can do other things, too; and I'd rather you did those. Billy, you haven't played to me for a week, nor sung to me for a month. You're too tired every night to talk, or read together, or go anywhere with me. I married for companionship—not cooking and sweeping!"

Billy shook her head stubbornly. Her mouth settled into determined lines.

"That's all very well to say. You aren't hungry now, Bertram. But it's different when you are, and they said 'twould be."

"Humph! 'They' are Aunt Hannah and Kate, I suppose."

"Yes—and the 'Talk to Young Wives.'"

"The w-what?"

Billy choked a little. She had forgotten that Bertram did not know about the "Talk to Young Wives." She wished that she had not mentioned the book, but now that she had, she would make the best of it. She drew herself up with dignity.

"It's a book; a very nice book. It says lots of things—that have come true."

"Where is that book? Let me see it, please."

With visible reluctance Billy got down from her perch on Bertram's knee, went to her desk and brought back the book.

Bertram regarded it frowningly, so frowningly that Billy hastened to its defense.

"And it's true—what it says in there, and what Aunt Hannah and Kate said. It *is* different when they're hungry! You said yourself if I'd tend to my husband and my home a little more, and—"

Bertram looked up with unfeigned amazement.

"I said what?" he demanded.

In a voice shaken with emotion, Billy repeated the fateful words.

"I never—when did I say that?"

"The night Uncle William and I came home from—Pete's."

For a moment Bertram stared dumbly; then a shamed red swept to his forehead.

"Billy, *did* I say that? I ought to be shot if I did. But, Billy, you said you'd forgiven me!"

"I did, dear—truly I did; but, don't you see?—it was true. I *hadn't* tended to things. So I've been doing it since."

A sudden comprehension illuminated Bertram's face.

"Heavens, Billy! And is that why you haven't been anywhere, or done anything? Is that why Calderwell said to-day that you hadn't been with them anywhere, and that—Great Scott, Billy! Did you think I was such a selfish brute as that?"

"Oh, but when I was going with them I *was* following the book—I thought," quavered Billy; and hurriedly she turned the leaves to a carefully marked passage. "It's there—about the outside interests. See? I *was* trying to brush up against them, so that I wouldn't interfere with your Art. Then, when you accused me of gallivanting off with—" But Bertram swept her back into his arms, and not for some minutes could Billy make a coherent speech again.

Then Bertram spoke.

"See here, Billy," he exploded, a little shakily, "if I could get you off somewhere on a desert island, where there weren't any Aunt Hannahs or Kates, or Talks to Young Wives, I think there'd be a chance to make you happy; but—"

"Oh, but there was truth in it," interrupted Billy, sitting erect again. "I *didn't* know how to run a house, and it was perfectly awful while we were having all those dreadful maids, one after the other; and no woman should be a wife who doesn't know—"

"All right, all right, dear," interrupted Bertram, in his turn. "We'll concede that point, if you like. But you *do* know now. You've got the efficient housewife racket down pat even to the last calory your husband should be fed; and I'll warrant there isn't a Mary Ellen in Christendom who can find a spot of ignorance on you as big as a pinhead! So we'll call that settled. What you need now is a good rest; and you're going to have it, too. I'm going to have six Mary Ellens here to-morrow morning. Six! Do you hear? And all you've got to do is to get your gladdest rags together for a trip to Europe with me next month. Because we're going. I shall get the tickets to-morrow, *after* I send the six Mary Ellens packing up here. Now come, put on your bonnet. We're going down town to dinner."

CHAPTER XVIII
BILLY TRIES HER HAND AT "MANAGING"

Bertram did not engage six Mary Ellens the next morning, nor even one, as it happened; for that evening, Eliza—who had not been unaware of conditions at the Strata—telephoned to say that her mother was so much better now she believed she could be spared to come to the Strata for several hours each day, if Mrs. Henshaw would like to have her begin in that way.

Billy agreed promptly, and declared herself as more than willing to put up with such an arrangement. Bertram, it is true, when he heard of the plan, rebelled, and asserted that what Billy needed was a rest, an entire rest from care and labor. In fact, what he wanted her to do, he said, was to gallivant—to gallivant all day long.

"Nonsense!" Billy had laughed, coloring to the tips of her ears. "Besides, as for the work, Bertram, with just you and me here, and with all my vast experience now, and Eliza here for several hours every day, it'll be nothing but play for this little time before we go away. You'll see!"

"All right, I'll *see*, then," Bertram had nodded meaningly. "But just make sure that it *is* play for you!"

"I will," laughed Billy; and there the matter had ended.

Eliza began work the next day, and Billy did indeed soon find herself "playing" under Bertram's watchful insistence. She resumed her music, and brought out of exile the unfinished song. With Bertram she took drives and walks; and every two or three days she went to see Aunt Hannah and Marie. She was pleasantly busy, too, with plans for her coming trip; and it was not long before even the remorseful Bertram had to admit that Billy was looking and appearing quite like her old self.

At the Annex Billy found Calderwell and Arkwright, one day. They greeted her as if she had just returned from a far country.

"Well, if you aren't the stranger lady," began Calderwell, looking frankly pleased to see her. "We'd thought of advertising in the daily press somewhat after this fashion: 'Lost, strayed, or stolen, one Billy; comrade, good friend, and kind cheerer-up of lonely hearts. Any information thankfully received by her bereft, sorrowing friends.'"

Billy joined in the laugh that greeted this sally, but Arkwright noticed that she tried to change the subject from her own affairs to a discussion of the new song on Alice Greggory's piano. Calderwell, however, was not to be silenced.

"The last I heard of this elusive Billy," he resumed, with teasing cheerfulness, "she was running down a certain lost calory that had slipped away from her husband's breakfast, and—"

Billy wheeled sharply.

"Where did you get hold of that?" she demanded.

"Oh, I didn't," returned the man, defensively. "I never got hold of it at all. I never even saw the calory—though, for that matter, I don't think I should know one if I did see it! What we feared was, that, in hunting the lost calory, you had lost yourself, and—" But Billy would hear no more. With her disdainful nose in the air she walked to the piano.

"Come, Mr. Arkwright," she said with dignity. "Let's try this song."

Arkwright rose at once and accompanied her to the piano.

They had sung the song through twice when Billy became uneasily aware that, on the other side of the room, Calderwell and Alice Greggory were softly chuckling over something they had found in a magazine. Billy frowned, and twitched the corners of a pile of music, with restless fingers.

"I wonder if Alice hasn't got some quartets here somewhere," she murmured, her disapproving eyes still bent on the absorbed couple across the room.

Arkwright was silent. Billy, throwing a hurried glance into his face, thought she detected a somber shadow in his eyes. She thought, too, she knew why it was there. So possessed had Billy been, during the early winter, of the idea that her special mission in life was to inaugurate and foster a love affair between disappointed Mr. Arkwright and lonely Alice Greggory, that now she forgot, for a moment, that Arkwright himself was quite unaware of her efforts. She thought only that the present shadow on his face must be caused by the same thing that brought worry to her own heart—the manifest devotion of Calderwell to Alice Greggory just now across the room. Instinctively, therefore, as to a coworker in a common cause, she turned a disturbed face to the man at her side.

"It is, indeed, high time that I looked after something besides lost calories," she said significantly. Then, at the evident uncomprehension in Arkwright's face, she added: "Has it been going on like this—very long?"

Arkwright still, apparently, did not understand.

"Has—what been going on?" he questioned.

"That—over there," answered Billy, impatiently, scarcely knowing whether to be more irritated at the threatened miscarriage of her cherished plans, or at Arkwright's (to her) wilfully blind insistence on her making her meaning more plain. "Has it been going on long—such utter devotion?"

As she asked the question Billy turned and looked squarely into Arkwright's face. She saw, therefore, the great change that came to it, as her meaning became clear to him. Her first feeling was one of shocked realization that Arkwright had, indeed, been really blind. Her second—she turned away her eyes hurriedly from what she thought she saw in the man's countenance.

With an assumedly gay little cry she sprang to her feet.

"Come, come, what are you two children chuckling over?" she demanded, crossing the room abruptly. "Didn't you hear me say I wanted you to come and sing a quartet?"

Billy blamed herself very much for what she called her stupidity in so baldly summoning Arkwright's attention to Calderwell's devotion to Alice Greggory. She declared that she ought to have known better, and she asked herself if this were the way she was "furthering matters" between Alice Greggory and Arkwright.

Billy was really seriously disturbed. She had never quite forgiven herself for being so blind to Arkwright's feeling for herself during those days when he had not known of her engagement to Bertram. She had never forgotten, either, the painful scene when he had hopefully told of his love, only to be met with her own shocked repudiation. For long weeks after that, his face had haunted her. She had wished, oh, so ardently, that she could do something in some way to bring him happiness. When, therefore, it had come to her knowledge afterward that he was frequently with his old friend, Alice Greggory, she had been so glad. It was very easy then to fan hope into conviction that here, in this old friend, he had found sweet balm for his wounded heart; and she determined at once to do all that she could do to help. So very glowing, indeed, was her eagerness in the matter, that it looked suspiciously as if she thought, could she but bring this thing about, that old scores against herself would be erased.

Billy told herself, virtuously, however, that not only for Arkwright did she desire this marriage to take place, but for Alice Greggory. In the very nature of things Alice would one day be left alone. She was poor, and not very strong. She sorely needed the shielding love and care of a good husband. What more natural than that her old-time friend and almost-sweetheart, M. J. Arkwright, should be that good husband?

That really it was more Arkwright and less Alice that was being considered, however, was proved when the devotion of Calderwell began to be first suspected, then known for a fact. Billy's distress at this turn of affairs indicated very plainly that it was not just a husband, but a certain one particular husband that she desired for Alice Greggory. All the more disturbed was she, therefore, when to-day, seeing her three friends together again for the first time for some weeks, she discovered increased evidence that her worst fears were to be realized. It was to be Alice and Calderwell, not Alice and Arkwright. Arkwright was again to be disappointed in his dearest hopes.

Telling herself indignantly that it could not be, it *should* not be, Billy determined to remain after the men had gone, and speak to Alice. Just what she would say she did not know. Even what she could say, she was not sure. But certainly there must be something, some little thing that she could say, which would open Alice's eyes to what she was doing, and what she ought to do.

It was in this frame of mind, therefore, that Billy, after Arkwright and Calderwell had gone, spoke to Alice. She began warily, with assumed nonchalance.

"I believe Mr. Arkwright sings better every time I hear him."

There was no answer. Alice was sorting music at the piano.

"Don't you think so?" Billy raised her voice a little.

Alice turned almost with a start.

"What's that? Oh, yes. Well, I don't know; maybe I do."

"You would—if you didn't hear him any oftener than I do," laughed Billy. "But then, of course you do hear him oftener."

"I? Oh, no, indeed. Not so very much oftener." Alice had turned back to her music. There was a slight embarrassment in her manner. "I wonder—where—that new song—is," she murmured.

Billy, who knew very well where the song lay, was not to be diverted.

"Nonsense! As if Mr. Arkwright wasn't always telling how Alice liked this song, and didn't like that one, and thought the other the best yet! I don't believe he sings a thing that he doesn't first sing to you. For that matter, I fancy he asks your opinion of everything, anyway."

"Why, Billy, he doesn't!" exclaimed Alice, a deep red flaming into her cheeks. "You know he doesn't."

Billy laughed gleefully. She had not been slow to note the color in her friend's face, or to ascribe to it the one meaning she wished to ascribe to it. So sure, indeed, was she now that her fears had been groundless, that she flung caution to the winds.

"Ho! My dear Alice, you can't expect us all to be blind," she teased. "Besides, we all think it's such a lovely arrangement that we're just glad to see it. He's such a fine fellow, and we like him so much! We couldn't ask for a better husband for you than Mr. Arkwright, and—" From sheer amazement at the sudden white horror in Alice Greggory's face, Billy stopped short. "Why, Alice!" she faltered then.

With a visible effort Alice forced her trembling lips to speak.

"My husband—*Mr. Arkwright!* Why, Billy, you couldn't have seen— you haven't seen—there's nothing you *could* see! He isn't—he wasn't—he can't be! We—we're nothing but friends, Billy, just good friends!"

Billy, though dismayed, was still not quite convinced.

"Friends! Nonsense! When—"

But Alice interrupted feverishly. Alice, in an agony of fear lest the true state of affairs should be suspected, was hiding behind a bulwark of pride.

"Now, Billy, please! Say no more. You're quite wrong, entirely. You'll never, never hear of my marrying Mr. Arkwright. As I said before, we're friends—the best of friends; that is all. We couldn't be anything else, possibly!"

Billy, plainly discomfited, fell back; but she threw a sharp glance into her friend's flushed countenance.

"You mean—because of—Hugh Calderwell?" she demanded. Then, for the second time that afternoon throwing discretion to the winds, she went on plaintively: "You won't listen, of course. Girls in love never do. Hugh is all right, and I like him; but there's more real solid worth in Mr. Arkwright's little finger than there is in Hugh's whole self. And—" But a merry peal of laughter from Alice Greggory interrupted.

"And, pray, do you think I'm in love with Hugh Calderwell?" she demanded. There was a curious note of something very like relief in her voice.

"Well, I didn't know," began Billy, uncertainly.

"Then I'll tell you now," smiled Alice. "I'm not. Furthermore, perhaps it's just as well that you should know right now that I don't intend to marry—ever."

"Oh, Alice!"

"No." There was determination, and there was still that curious note of relief in the girl's voice. It was as if, somewhere, a great danger had been avoided. "I have my music. That is enough. I'm not intending to marry."

"Oh, but Alice, while I will own up I'm glad it isn't Hugh Calderwell, there *is* Mr. Arkwright, and I did hope—" But Alice shook her head and turned resolutely away. At that moment, too, Aunt Hannah came in from the street, so Billy could say no more.

Aunt Hannah dropped herself a little wearily into a chair.

"I've just come from Marie's," she said.

"How is she?" asked Billy.

Aunt Hannah smiled, and raised her eyebrows.

"Well, just now she's quite exercised over another rattle—from her cousin out West, this time. There were four little silver bells on it, and she hasn't got any janitor's wife now to give it to."

Billy laughed softly, but Aunt Hannah had more to say.

"You know she isn't going to allow any toys but Teddy bears and woolly lambs, of which, I believe, she has already bought quite an assortment. She says they don't rattle or squeak. I declare, when I see the woolen pads and rubber hushers that that child has put everywhere all over the house, I don't know whether to laugh or cry. And she's so worried! It seems Cyril must needs take just this time to start composing a new opera or symphony, or something; and never before has she allowed him to be interrupted by anything on such an occasion. But what he'll do when the baby comes she says she doesn't know, for she says she can't—she just can't keep it from bothering him some, she's afraid. As if any opera or symphony that ever lived was of more consequence than a man's own child!" finished Aunt Hannah, with an indignant sniff, as she reached for her shawl.

CHAPTER XIX
A TOUGH NUT TO CRACK FOR CYRIL

It was early in the forenoon of the first day of July that Eliza told her mistress that Mrs. Stetson was asking for her at the telephone. Eliza's face was not a little troubled.

"I'm afraid, maybe, it isn't good news," she stammered, as her mistress hurriedly arose. "She's at Mr. Cyril Henshaw's—Mrs. Stetson is—and she seemed so terribly upset about something that there was no making real sense out of what she said. But she asked for you, and said to have you come quick."

Billy, her own face paling, was already at the telephone.

"Yes, Aunt Hannah. What is it?"

"Oh, my grief and conscience, Billy, if you *can*, come up here, please. You must come! *Can't* you come?"

"Why, yes, of course. But—but—*Marie!* The—the *baby!*"

A faint groan came across the wires.

"Oh, my grief and conscience, Billy! It isn't *the* baby. It's *babies!* It's twins—boys. Cyril has them now—the nurse hasn't got here yet."

"Twins! *Cyril* has them!" broke in Billy, hysterically.

"Yes, and they're crying something terrible. We've sent for a second nurse to come, too, of course, but she hasn't got here yet, either. And those babies—if you could hear them! That's what we want you for, to—"

But Billy was almost laughing now.

"All right, I'll come out—and hear them," she called a bit wildly, as she hung up the receiver.

Some little time later, a palpably nervous maid admitted Billy to the home of Mr. and Mrs. Cyril Henshaw. Even as the door was opened, Billy heard faintly, but unmistakably, the moaning wails of two infants.

"Mrs. Stetson says if you will please to help Mr. Henshaw with the babies," stammered the maid, after the preliminary questions and answers.

"I've been in when I could, and they're all right, only they're crying. They're in his den. We had to put them as far away as possible—their crying worried Mrs. Henshaw so."

"Yes, I see," murmured Billy. "I'll go to them at once. No, don't trouble to come. I know the way. Just tell Mrs. Stetson I'm here, please," she finished, as she tossed her hat and gloves on to the hall table, and turned to go upstairs.

Billy's feet made no sound on the soft rugs. The crying, however, grew louder and louder as she approached the den. Softly she turned the knob and pushed open the door. She stopped short, then, at what she saw.

Cyril had not heard her, nor seen her. His back was partly toward the door. His coat was off, and his hair stood fiercely on end as if a nervous hand had ruffled it. His usually pale face was very red, and his forehead showed great drops of perspiration. He was on his feet, hovering over the couch, at each end of which lay a rumpled roll of linen, lace, and flannel, from which emerged a prodigiously puckered little face, two uncertainly waving rose-leaf fists, and a wail of protesting rage that was not uncertain in the least.

In one hand Cyril held a Teddy bear, in the other his watch, dangling from its fob chain. Both of these he shook feebly, one after the other, above the tiny faces.

"Oh, come, come, pretty baby, good baby, hush, hush," he begged agitatedly.

In the doorway Billy clapped her hands to her lips and stifled a laugh. Billy knew, of course, that what she should do was to go forward at once, and help this poor, distracted man; but Billy, just then, was not doing what she knew she ought to do.

With a muttered ejaculation (which Billy, to her sorrow, could not catch) Cyril laid down the watch and flung the Teddy bear aside. Then, in very evident despair, he gingerly picked up one of the rumpled rolls of flannel, lace, and linen, and held it straight out before him. After a moment's indecision he began awkwardly to jounce it, teeter it, rock it back and forth, and to pat it jerkily.

"Oh, come, come, pretty baby, good baby, hush, hush," he begged again, frantically.

Perhaps it was the change of position; perhaps it was the novelty of the motion, perhaps it was only utter weariness, or lack of breath. Whatever the cause, the wailing sobs from the bundle in his arms dwindled suddenly to a gentle whisper, then ceased altogether.

With a ray of hope illuminating his drawn countenance, Cyril carefully laid the baby down and picked up the other. Almost confidently now he began the jouncing and teetering and rocking as before.

"There, there! Oh, come, come, pretty baby, good baby, hush, hush," he chanted again.

This time he was not so successful. Perhaps he had lost his skill. Perhaps it was merely the world-old difference in babies. At all events, this infant did not care for jerks and jounces, and showed it plainly by emitting loud and yet louder wails of rage—wails in which his brother on the couch speedily joined.

"Oh, come, come, pretty baby, good baby, hush, hush—*confound it*, HUSH, I say!" exploded the frightened, weary, baffled, distracted man, picking up the other baby, and trying to hold both his sons at once.

Billy hurried forward then, tearfully, remorsefully, her face all sympathy, her arms all tenderness.

"Here, Cyril, let me help you," she cried.

Cyril turned abruptly.

"Thank God, *some* one's come," he groaned, holding out both the babies, with an exuberance of generosity. "Billy, you've saved my life!"

Billy laughed tremulously.

"Yes, I've come, Cyril, and I'll help every bit I can; but I don't know a thing—not a single thing about them myself. Dear me, aren't they cunning? But, Cyril, do they always cry so?"

The father-of-an-hour drew himself stiffly erect.

"Cry? What do you mean? Why shouldn't they cry?" he demanded indignantly. "I want you to understand that Doctor Brown said those were A number I fine boys! Anyhow, I guess there's no doubt they've got lungs all right," he added, with a grim smile, as he pulled out his handkerchief and drew it across his perspiring brow.

Billy did not have an opportunity to show Cyril how much or how little she knew about babies, for in another minute the maid had appeared with the extra nurse; and that young woman, with trained celerity and easy confidence, assumed instant command, and speedily had peace and order restored.

Cyril, freed from responsibility, cast longing eyes, for a moment, upon his work; but the next minute, with a despairing glance about him, he turned and fled precipitately.

Billy, following the direction of his eyes, suppressed a smile. On the top of Cyril's manuscript music on the table lay a hot-water bottle. Draped over the back of his favorite chair was a pink-bordered baby blanket. On the piano-stool rested a beribboned and beruffled baby's toilet basket. From behind the sofa pillow leered ridiculously the Teddy bear, just as it had left Cyril's desperate hand.

No wonder, indeed, that Billy smiled. Billy was thinking of what Marie had said not a week before:

"I shall keep the baby, of course, in the nursery. I've been in homes where they've had baby things strewn from one end of the house to the other; but it won't be that way here. In the first place, I don't believe in it; but, even if I did, I'd have to be careful on account of Cyril. Imagine Cyril's trying to write his music with a baby in the room! No! I shall keep the baby in the nursery, if possible; but wherever it is, it won't be anywhere near Cyril's den, anyway."

Billy suppressed many a smile during the days that immediately followed the coming of the twins. Some of the smiles, however, refused to be suppressed. They became, indeed, shamelessly audible chuckles.

Billy was to sail the tenth, and, naturally, during those early July days, her time was pretty much occupied with her preparations for departure; but nothing could keep her from frequent, though short, visits to the home of her brother-in-law.

The twins were proving themselves to be fine, healthy boys. Two trained maids, and two trained nurses ruled the household with a rod of iron. As to Cyril—Billy declared that Cyril was learning something every day of his life now.

"Oh, yes, he's learning things," she said to Aunt Hannah, one morning; "lots of things. For instance: he has his breakfast now, not when he wants it, but when the maid wants to give it to him—which is precisely at eight o'clock every morning. So he's learning punctuality. And for the first time in his life he has discovered the astounding fact that there are several things more important in the world than is the special piece of music he happens to be composing—chiefly the twins' bath, the twins' nap, the twins' airing, and the twins' colic."

Aunt Hannah laughed, though she frowned, too.

"But, surely, Billy, with two nurses and the maids, Cyril doesn't have to—to—" She came to a helpless pause.

"Oh, no," laughed Billy; "Cyril doesn't have to really attend to any of those things—though I have seen each of the nurses, at different times, unhesitatingly thrust a twin into his arms and bid him hold the child till she comes back. But it's this way. You see, Marie must be kept quiet, and the nursery is very near her room. It worries her terribly when either of the children cries. Besides, the little rascals have apparently fixed up some sort of labor-union compact with each other, so that if one cries for something or nothing, the other promptly joins in and helps. So the nurses have got into the habit of picking up the first disturber of the peace, and hurrying him to quarters remote; and Cyril's den being the most remote of all, they usually fetch up there."

"You mean—they take those babies into Cyril's den—*now*?" Even Aunt Hannah was plainly aghast.

"Yes," twinkled Billy. "I fancy their Hygienic Immaculacies approved of Cyril's bare floors, undraped windows, and generally knick-knackless condition. Anyhow, they've made his den a sort of—of annex to the nursery."

"But—but Cyril! What does he say?" stammered the dumfounded Aunt Hannah. "Think of Cyril's standing a thing like that! Doesn't he do anything—or say anything?"

Billy smiled, and lifted her brows quizzically.

"My dear Aunt Hannah, did you ever know *many* people to have the courage to 'say things' to one of those becapped, beaproned, bespotless creatures of loftily superb superiority known as trained nurses? Besides, you wouldn't recognize Cyril now. Nobody would. He's as meek as Moses, and has been ever since his two young sons were laid in his reluctant, trembling arms. He breaks into a cold sweat at nothing, and moves about his own home as if he were a stranger and an interloper, endured merely on sufferance in this abode of strange women and strange babies."

"Nonsense!" scoffed Aunt Hannah.

"But it's so," maintained Billy, merrily. "Now, for instance. You know Cyril always has been in the habit of venting his moods on the piano (just as I do, only more so) by playing exactly as he feels. Well, as near as I can gather, he was at his usual trick the next day after the twins arrived; and you can imagine about what sort of music it would be, after what he had been through the preceding forty-eight hours.

"Of course I don't know exactly what happened, but Julia—Marie's second maid, you know—tells the story. She's been with them long enough to know something of the way the whole household always turns on the pivot of the master's whims; so she fully appreciated the situation. She says she heard him begin to play, and that she never heard such queer, creepy, shivery music in her life; but that he hadn't been playing five minutes before one of the nurses came into the living-room where Julia was dusting, and told her to tell whoever was playing to stop that dreadful noise, as they wanted to take the twins in there for their nap.

"'But I didn't do it, ma'am,' Julia says. 'I wa'n't lookin' for losin' my place, an' I let the young woman do the job herself. An' she done it, pert as you please. An' jest as I was seekin' a hidin'-place for the explosion, if Mr. Henshaw didn't come out lookin' a little wild, but as meek as a lamb; an' when he sees me he asked wouldn't I please get him a cup of coffee, good an' strong. An' I got it.'

"So you see," finished Billy, "Cyril is learning things—lots of things."

"Oh, my grief and conscience! I should say he was," half-shivered Aunt Hannah. "*Cyril* looking meek as a lamb, indeed!"

Billy laughed merrily.

"Well, it must be a new experience—for Cyril. For a man whose daily existence for years has been rubber-heeled and woolen-padded, and whose family from boyhood has stood at attention and saluted if he so much as looked at them, it must be quite a change, as things are now. However, it'll be different, of course, when Marie is on her feet again."

"Does she know at all how things are going?"

"Not very much, as yet, though I believe she has begun to worry some. She confided to me one day that she was glad, of course, that she had two darling babies, instead of one; but that she was afraid it might be hard, just at first, to teach them both at once to be quiet; for she was afraid that while she was teaching one, the other would be sure to cry, or do something noisy."

"Do something noisy, indeed!" ejaculated Aunt Hannah.

"As for the real state of affairs, Marie doesn't dream that Cyril's sacred den is given over to Teddy bears and baby blankets. All is, I hope she'll be measurably strong before she does find it out," laughed Billy, as she rose to go.

CHAPTER XX
ARKWRIGHT'S EYES ARE OPENED

William came back from his business trip the eighth of July, and on the ninth Billy and Bertram went to New York. Eliza's mother was so well now that Eliza had taken up her old quarters in the Strata, and the household affairs were once more running like clockwork. Later in the season William would go away for a month's fishing trip, and the house would be closed.

Mr. and Mrs. Bertram Henshaw were not expected to return until the first of October; but with Eliza to look after the comfort of William, the mistress of the house did no worrying. Ever since Pete's going, Eliza had said that she preferred to be the only maid, with a charwoman to come in for the heavier work; and to this arrangement her mistress had willingly consented, for the present.

Marie and the babies were doing finely, and Aunt Hannah's health, and affairs at the Annex, were all that could be desired. As Billy, indeed, saw it, there was only one flaw to mar her perfect content on this holiday trip with Bertram, and that was her disappointment over the very evident disaster that had come to her cherished matrimonial plans for Arkwright and Alice Greggory. She could not forget Arkwright's face that day at the Annex, when she had so foolishly called his attention to Calderwell's devotion; and she could not forget, either, Alice Greggory's very obvious perturbation a little later, and her suspiciously emphatic assertion that she had no intention of marrying any one, certainly not Arkwright. As Billy thought of all this now, she could not but admit that it did look dark for Arkwright—poor Arkwright, whom she, more than any one else in the world, perhaps, had a special reason for wishing to see happily married.

There was, then, this one cloud on Billy's horizon as the big boat that was to bear her across the water steamed down the harbor that beautiful July day.

As it chanced, naturally, perhaps, not only was Billy thinking of Arkwright that morning, but Arkwright was thinking of Billy.

Arkwright had thought frequently of Billy during the last few days, particularly since that afternoon meeting at the Annex when the four had renewed their old good times together. Up to that day Arkwright had been trying not to think of Billy. He had been "fighting his tiger skin." Sternly he had been forcing himself to meet her, to see her, to talk with her, to sing with her, or to pass her by—all with the indifference properly expected to be shown in association with Mrs. Bertram Henshaw, another man's wife. He had known, of course, that deep down in his heart he loved her, always had loved her, and always would love her. Hopelessly and drearily he accepted this as a fact even while with all his might fighting that tiger skin. So sure was he, indeed, of this, so implicitly had he accepted it as an unalterable certainty, that in time even his efforts to fight it became almost mechanical and unconscious in their stern round of forced indifference.

Then came that day at the Annex—and the discovery: the discovery which he had made when Billy called his attention to Calderwell and Alice Greggory across the room in the corner; the discovery which had come with so blinding a force, and which even now he was tempted to question as to its reality; the discovery that not Billy Neilson, nor Mrs. Bertram Henshaw, nor even the tender ghost of a lost love held the center of his heart—but Alice Greggory.

The first intimation of all this had come with his curious feeling of unreasoning hatred and blind indignation toward Calderwell as, through Billy's eyes, he had seen the two together. Then had come the overwhelming longing to pick up Alice Greggory and run off with her—somewhere, anywhere, so that Calderwell could not follow.

At once, however, he had pulled himself up short with the mental cry of "Absurd!" What was it to him if Calderwell did care for Alice Greggory? Surely he himself was not in love with the girl. He was in love with Billy; that is—

It was all confusion then, in his mind, and he was glad indeed when he could leave the house. He wanted to be alone. He wanted to think. He must, in some way, thrash out this astounding thing that had come to him.

Arkwright did not visit the Annex again for some days. Until he was more nearly sure of himself and of his feelings, he did not wish to see Alice Greggory. It was then that he began to think of Billy, deliberately, purposefully, for it must be, of course, that he had made a mistake, he told himself. It must be that he did, really, still care for Billy—though of course he ought not to.

Arkwright made another discovery then. He learned that, however deliberately he started in to think of Billy, he ended every time in thinking of Alice. He thought of how good she had been to him, and of how faithful she had been in helping him to fight his love for Billy. Just here he decided, for a moment, that probably, after all, his feeling of anger against Calderwell was merely the fear of losing this helpful comradeship that he so needed. Even with himself, however, Arkwright could not keep up this farce long, and very soon he admitted miserably that it was not the comradeship of Alice Greggory that he wanted or needed, but the love.

He knew it now. No longer was there any use in beating about the bush. He did love Alice Greggory; but so curiously and unbelievably stupid had he been that he had not found it out until now. And now it was too late. Had not even Billy called his attention to the fact of Calderwell's devotion? Besides, had not he himself, at the very first, told Calderwell that he might have a clear field?

Fool that he had been to let another thus lightly step in and win from under his very nose what might have been his if he had but known his own mind before it was too late!

But was it, after all, quite too late? He and Alice were old friends. Away back in their young days in their native town they had been, indeed, almost sweethearts, in a boy-and-girl fashion. It would not have taken much in those days, he believed, to have made the relationship more interesting. But changes had come. Alice had left town, and for years they had drifted apart. Then had come Billy, and Billy had found Alice, thus bringing about the odd circumstance of their renewing of acquaintanceship. Perhaps, at that time, if he had not already thought he cared for Billy, there would have been something more than acquaintanceship.

But he *had* thought he cared for Billy all these years; and now, at this late day, to wake up and find that he cared for Alice! A pretty mess he had made of things! Was he so inconstant then, so fickle? Did he not know his own mind five minutes at a time? What would Alice Greggory think, even if he found the courage to tell her? What could she think? What could anybody think?

Arkwright fairly ground his teeth in impotent wrath—and he did not know whether he were the most angry that he did not love Billy, or that he had loved Billy, or that he loved somebody else now.

It was while he was in this unenviable frame of mind that he went to see Alice. Not that he had planned definitely to speak to her of his discovery, nor yet that he had planned not to. He had, indeed, planned nothing. For a man usually so decided as to purpose and energetic as to action, he was in a most unhappy state of uncertainty and changeableness. One thing only was unmistakably clear to him, and that was that he must see Alice.

For months, now, he had taken to Alice all his hopes and griefs, perplexities and problems; and never had he failed to find comfort in the shape of sympathetic understanding and wise counsel. To Alice, therefore, now he turned as a matter of course, telling himself vaguely that, perhaps, after he had seen Alice, he would feel better.

Just how intimately this particular problem of his concerned Alice herself, he did not stop to realize. He did not, indeed, think of it at all from Alice's standpoint—until he came face to face with the girl in the living-room at the Annex. Then, suddenly, he did. His manner became at once, consequently, full of embarrassment and quite devoid of its usual frank friendliness.

As it happened, this was perhaps the most unfortunate thing that could have occurred, so far as it concerned the attitude of Alice Greggory, for thereby innumerable tiny sparks of suspicion that had been tormenting the girl for days were instantly fanned into consuming flames of conviction.

Alice had not been slow to note Arkwright's prolonged absence from the Annex. Coming as it did so soon after her most disconcerting talk with Billy in regard to her own relations with him, it had filled her with frightened questionings.

If Billy had seen things to make her think of linking their names together, perhaps Arkwright himself had heard some such idea put forth somewhere, and that was why he was staying away—to show the world that there was no foundation for such rumors. Perhaps he was even doing it to show *her* that—

Even in her thoughts Alice could scarcely bring herself to finish the sentence. That Arkwright should ever suspect for a moment that she cared for him was intolerable. Painfully conscious as she was that she did care for him, it was easy to fear that others must be conscious of it, too. Had she not already proof that Billy suspected it? Why, then, might not it be quite possible, even probable, that Arkwright suspected it, also; and, because he did suspect it, had decided that it would be just as well, perhaps, if he did not call so often.

In spite of Alice's angry insistence to herself that, after all, this could not be the case—that the man *knew* she understood he still loved Billy—she could not help fearing, in the face of Arkwright's unusual absence, that it might yet be true. When, therefore, he finally did appear, only to become at once obviously embarrassed in her presence, her fears instantly became convictions. It was true, then. The man did believe she cared for him, and he had been trying to teach her—to save her.

To teach her! To save her, indeed! Very well, he should see! And forthwith, from that moment, Alice Greggory's chief reason for living became to prove to Mr. M. J. Arkwright that he needed not to teach her, to save her, nor yet to sympathize with her.

"How do you do?" she greeted him, with a particularly bright smile. "I'm sure I *hope* you are well, such a beautiful day as this."

"Oh, yes, I'm well, I suppose. Still, I have felt better in my life," smiled Arkwright, with some constraint.

"Oh, I'm sorry," murmured the girl, striving so hard to speak with impersonal unconcern that she did not notice the inaptness of her reply.

"Eh? Sorry I've felt better, are you?" retorted Arkwright, with nervous humor. Then, because he was embarrassed, he said the one thing he had meant not to say: "Don't you think I'm quite a stranger? It's been some time since I've been here."

Alice, smarting under the sting of what she judged to be the only possible cause for his embarrassment, leaped to this new opportunity to show her lack of interest.

"Oh, has it?" she murmured carelessly. "Well, I don't know but it has, now that I come to think of it."

Arkwright frowned gloomily. A week ago he would have tossed back a laughingly aggrieved remark as to her unflattering indifference to his presence. Now he was in no mood for such joking. It was too serious a matter with him.

"You've been busy, no doubt, with—other matters," he presumed forlornly, thinking of Calderwell.

"Yes, I have been busy," assented the girl. "One is always happier, I think, to be busy. Not that I meant that I needed the work to *be* happy," she added hastily, in a panic lest he think she had a consuming sorrow to kill.

"No, of course not," he murmured abstractedly, rising to his feet and crossing the room to the piano. Then, with an elaborate air of trying to appear very natural, he asked jovially: "Anything new to play to me?"

Alice arose at once.

"Yes. I have a little nocturne that I was playing to Mr. Calderwell last night."

"Oh, to Calderwell!" Arkwright had stiffened perceptibly.

"Yes. *He* didn't like it. I'll play it to you and see what you say," she smiled, seating herself at the piano.

"Well, if he had liked it, it's safe to say I shouldn't," shrugged Arkwright.

"Nonsense!" laughed the girl, beginning to appear more like her natural self. "I should think you were Mr. Cyril Henshaw! Mr. Calderwell *is* partial to ragtime, I'll admit. But there are some good things he likes."

"There are, indeed, *some* good things he likes," returned Arkwright, with grim emphasis, his somber eyes fixed on what he believed to be the one especial object of Calderwell's affections at the moment.

Alice, unaware both of the melancholy gaze bent upon herself and of the cause thereof, laughed again merrily.

"Poor Mr. Calderwell," she cried, as she let her fingers slide into soft, introductory chords. "He isn't to blame for not liking what he calls our lost spirits that wail. It's just the way he's made."

Arkwright vouchsafed no reply. With an abrupt gesture he turned and began to pace the room moodily. At the piano Alice slipped from the chords into the nocturne. She played it straight through, then, with a charm and skill that brought Arkwright's feet to a pause before it was half finished.

"By George, that's great!" he breathed, when the last tone had quivered into silence.

"Yes, isn't it—beautiful?" she murmured.

The room was very quiet, and in semi-darkness. The last rays of a late June sunset had been filling the room with golden light, but it was gone now. Even at the piano by the window, Alice had barely been able to see clearly enough to read the notes of her nocturne.

To Arkwright the air still trembled with the exquisite melody that had but just left her fingers. A quick fire came to his eyes. He forgot everything but that it was Alice there in the half-light by the window—Alice, whom he loved. With a low cry he took a swift step toward her.

"Alice!"

Instantly the girl was on her feet. But it was not toward him that she turned. It was away—resolutely, and with a haste that was strangely like terror.

Alice, too, had forgotten, for just a moment. She had let herself drift into a dream world where there was nothing but the music she was playing and the man she loved. Then the music had stopped, and the man had spoken her name.

Alice remembered then. She remembered Billy, whom this man loved. She remembered the long days just passed when this man had stayed away, presumably to teach *her*—to save *her*. And now, at the sound of his voice speaking her name, she had almost bared her heart to him.

No wonder that Alice, with a haste that looked like terror, crossed the floor and flooded the room with light.

"Dear me!" she shivered, carefully avoiding Arkwright's eyes. "If Mr. Calderwell were here now he'd have some excuse to talk about our lost spirits that wail. That *is* a creepy piece of music when you play it in the dark!" And, for fear that he should suspect how her heart was aching, she gave a particularly brilliant and joyous smile.

Once again at the mention of Calderwell's name Arkwright stiffened perceptibly. The fire left his eyes. For a moment he did not speak; then, gravely, he said:

"Calderwell? Yes, perhaps he would; and—you ought to be a judge, I should think. You see him quite frequently, don't you?"

"Why, yes, of course. He often comes out here, you know."

"Yes; I had heard that he did—since *you* came."

His meaning was unmistakable. Alice looked up quickly. A prompt denial of his implication was on her lips when the thought came to her that perhaps just here lay a sure way to prove to this man before her that there was, indeed, no need for him to teach her, to save her, or yet to sympathize with her. She could not affirm, of course; but she need not deny—yet.

"Nonsense!" she laughed lightly, pleased that she could feel what she hoped would pass for a telltale color burning her cheeks. "Come, let us try some duets," she proposed, leading the way to the piano. And Arkwright, interpreting the apparently embarrassed change of subject exactly as she had hoped that he would interpret it, followed her, sick at heart.

"'O wert thou in the cauld blast,'" sang Arkwright's lips a few moments later.

"I can't tell her now—when I *know* she cares for Calderwell," gloomily ran his thoughts, the while. "It would do no possible good, and would only make her unhappy to grieve me."

"'O wert thou in the cauld blast,'" chimed in Alice's alto, low and sweet.

"I reckon now he won't be staying away from here any more just to *save* me!" ran Alice's thoughts, palpitatingly triumphant.

CHAPTER XXI
BILLY TAKES HER TURN AT QUESTIONING

Arkwright did not call to see Alice Greggory for some days. He did not want to see Alice now. He told himself wearily that she could not help him fight this tiger skin that lay across his path, The very fact of her presence by his side would, indeed, incapacitate himself for fighting. So he deliberately stayed away from the Annex until the day before he sailed for Germany. Then he went out to say good-by.

Chagrined as he was at what he termed his imbecile stupidity in not knowing his own heart all these past months, and convinced, as he also was, that Alice and Calderwell cared for each other, he could see no way for him but to play the part of a man of kindliness and honor, leaving a clear field for his preferred rival, and bringing no shadow of regret to mar the happiness of the girl he loved.

As for being his old easy, frank self on this last call, however, that was impossible; so Alice found plenty of fuel for her still burning fires of suspicion—fires which had, indeed, blazed up anew at this second long period of absence on the part of Arkwright. Naturally, therefore, the call was anything but a joy and comfort to either one. Arkwright was nervous, gloomy, and abnormally gay by turns. Alice was nervous and abnormally gay all the time. Then they said good-by and Arkwright went away. He sailed the next day, and Alice settled down to the summer of study and hard work she had laid out for herself.

On the tenth of September Billy came home. She was brown, plump-cheeked, and smiling. She declared that she had had a perfectly beautiful time, and that there couldn't be anything in the world nicer than the trip she and Bertram had taken—just they two together. In answer to Aunt Hannah's solicitous inquiries, she asserted that she was all well and rested now. But there was a vaguely troubled questioning in her eyes that Aunt Hannah did not quite like. Aunt Hannah, however, said nothing even to Billy herself about this.

One of the first friends Billy saw after her return was Hugh Calderwell. As it happened Bertram was out when he came, so Billy had the first half-hour of the call to herself. She was not sorry for this, as it gave her a chance to question Calderwell a little concerning Alice Greggory—something she had long ago determined to do at the first opportunity.

"Now tell me everything—everything about everybody," she began diplomatically, settling herself comfortably for a good visit.

"Thank you, I'm well, and have had a passably agreeable summer, barring the heat, sundry persistent mosquitoes, several grievous disappointments, and a felon on my thumb," he began, with shameless imperturbability. "I have been to Revere once, to the circus once, to Nantasket three times, and to Keith's and the 'movies' ten times, perhaps—to be accurate. I have also— But perhaps there was some one else you desired to inquire for," he broke off, turning upon his hostess a bland but unsmiling countenance.

"Oh, no, how could there be?" twinkled Billy. "Really, Hugh, I always knew you had a pretty good opinion of yourself, but I didn't credit you with thinking you were *everybody*. Go on. I'm so interested!"

Hugh chuckled softly; but there was a plaintive tone in his voice as he answered.

"Thanks, no. I've rather lost my interest now. Lack of appreciation always did discourage me. We'll talk of something else, please. You enjoyed your trip?"

"Very much. It just couldn't have been nicer!"

"You were lucky. The heat here has been something fierce!"

"What made you stay?"

"Reasons too numerous, and one too heart-breaking, to mention. Besides, you forget," with dignity. "There is my profession. I have joined the workers of the world now, you know."

"Oh, fudge, Hugh!" laughed Billy. "You know very well you're as likely as not to start for the ends of the earth to-morrow morning!"

Hugh drew himself up.

"I don't seem to succeed in making people understand that I'm serious," he began aggrievedly. "I—" With an expressive flourish of his hands he relaxed suddenly, and fell back in his chair. A slow smile came to his lips. "Well, Billy, I'll give up. You've hit it," he confessed. "I *have* thought seriously of starting to-morrow morning for *half-way* to the ends of the earth—Panama."

"Hugh!"

"Well, I have. Even this call was to be a good-by—if I went."

"Oh, Hugh! But I really thought—in spite of my teasing—that you had settled down, this time."

"Yes, so did I," sighed the man, a little soberly. "But I guess it's no use, Billy. Oh, I'm coming back, of course, and link arms again with their worthy Highnesses, John Doe and Richard Roe; but just now I've got a restless fit on me. I want to see the wheels go 'round. Of course, if I had my bread and butter and cigars to earn, 'twould be different. But I haven't, and I know I haven't; and I suspect that's where the trouble lies. If it wasn't for those natal silver spoons of mine that Bertram is always talking about, things might be different. But the spoons are there, and always have been; and I know they're all ready to dish out mountains to climb and lakes to paddle in, any time I've a mind to say the word. So—I just say the word. That's all."

"And you've said it now?"

"Yes, I think so; for a while."

"And—those reasons that *have* kept you here all summer," ventured Billy, "they aren't in—er—commission any longer?"

"No."

Billy hesitated, regarding her companion meditatively. Then, with the feeling that she had followed a blind alley to its termination, she retreated and made a fresh start.

"Well, you haven't yet told me everything about everybody, you know," she hinted smilingly. "You might begin that—I mean the less important everybodies, of course, now that I've heard about you."

"Meaning—"

"Oh, Aunt Hannah, and the Greggorys, and Cyril and Marie, and the twins, and Mr. Arkwright, and all the rest."

"But you've had letters, surely."

"Yes, I've had letters from some of them, and I've seen most of them since I came back. It's just that I wanted to know *your* viewpoint of what's happened through the summer."

"Very well. Aunt Hannah is as dear as ever, wears just as many shawls, and still keeps her clock striking twelve when it's half-past eleven. Mrs. Greggory is just as sweet as ever—and a little more frail, I fear,—bless her heart! Mr. Arkwright is still abroad, as I presume you know. I hear he is doing great stunts over there, and will sing in Berlin and Paris this winter. I'm thinking of going across from Panama later. If I do I shall look him up. Mr. and Mrs. Cyril are as well as could be expected when you realize that they haven't yet settled on a pair of names for the twins."

"I know it—and the poor little things three months old, too! I think it's a shame. You've heard the reason, I suppose. Cyril declares that naming babies is one of the most serious and delicate operations in the world, and that, for his part, he thinks people ought to select their own names when they've arrived at years of discretion. He wants to wait till the twins are eighteen, and then make each of them a birthday present of the name of their own choosing."

"Well, if that isn't the limit!" laughed Calderwell. "I'd heard some such thing before, but I hadn't supposed it was really so."

"Well, it is. He says he knows more tomboys and enormous fat women named 'Grace' and 'Lily,' and sweet little mouse-like ladies staggering along under a sonorous 'Jerusha Theodosia' or 'Zenobia Jane'; and that if he should name the boys 'Franz' and 'Felix' after Schubert and Mendelssohn as Marie wants to, they'd as likely as not turn out to be men who hated the sound of music and doted on stocks and dry goods."

"Humph!" grunted Calderwell. "I saw Cyril last week, and he said he hadn't named the twins yet, but he didn't tell me why. I offered him two perfectly good names myself, but he didn't seem interested."

"What were they?"

"Eldad and Bildad."

"Hugh!" protested Billy.

"Well, why not?" bridled the man. "I'm sure those are new and unique, and really musical, too—'way ahead of your Franz and Felix."

"But those aren't really names!"

"Indeed they are."

"Where did you get them?"

"Off our family tree, though they're Bible names, Belle says. Perhaps you didn't know, but Sister Belle has been making the dirt fly quite lively of late around that family tree of ours, and she wrote me some of her discoveries. It seems two of the roots, or branches—say, are ancestors roots, or branches?—were called Eldad and Bildad. Now I thought those names were good enough to pass along, but, as I said before, Cyril wasn't interested."

"I should say not," laughed Billy. "But, honestly, Hugh, it's really serious. Marie wants them named *something*, but she doesn't say much to Cyril. Marie wouldn't really breathe, you know, if she thought Cyril disapproved of breathing. And in this case Cyril does not hesitate to declare that the boys shall name themselves."

"What a situation!" laughed Calderwell.

"Isn't it? But, do you know, I can sympathize with it, in a way, for I've always mourned so over *my* name. 'Billy' was always such a trial to me! Poor Uncle William wasn't the only one that prepared guns and fishing rods to entertain the expected boy. I don't know, though, I'm afraid if I'd been allowed to select my name I should have been a 'Helen Clarabella' all my days, for that was the name I gave all my dolls, with 'first,' 'second,' 'third,' and so on, added to them for distinction. Evidently I thought that 'Helen Clarabella' was the most feminine appellation possible, and the most foreign to the despised 'Billy.' So you see I can sympathize with Cyril to a certain extent."

"But they must call the little chaps *something*, now," argued Hugh.

Billy gave a sudden merry laugh.

"They do," she gurgled, "and that's the funniest part of it. Oh, Cyril doesn't. He always calls them impersonally 'they' or 'it.' He doesn't see much of them anyway, now, I understand. Marie was horrified when she realized how the nurses had been using his den as a nursery annex and she changed all that instanter, when she took charge of things again. The twins stay in the nursery now, I'm told. But about the names—the nurses, it seems, have got into the way of calling them 'Dot' and 'Dimple.' One has a dimple in his cheek, and the other is a little smaller of the two. Marie is no end distressed, particularly as she finds that she herself calls them that; and she says the idea of boys being 'Dot' and 'Dimple'!"

"I should say so," laughed Calderwell. "Not I regard that as worse than my 'Eldad' and 'Bildad.'"

"I know it, and Alice says—By the way, you haven't mentioned Alice, but I suppose you see her occasionally."

Billy paused in evident expectation of a reply. Billy was, in fact, quite pluming herself on the adroit casualness with which she had introduced the subject nearest her heart.

Calderwell raised his eyebrows.

"Oh, yes, I see her."

"But you hadn't mentioned her."

There was the briefest of pauses; then with a half-quizzical dejection, there came the remark:

"You seem to forget. I told you that I stayed here this summer for reasons too numerous, and one too heart-breaking, to mention. She was the *one*."

"You mean—"

"Yes. The usual thing. She turned me down. Oh, I haven't asked her yet as many times as I did you, but—"

"*Hugh!*"

Hugh tossed her a grim smile and went on imperturbably.

"I'm older now, of course, and know more, perhaps. Besides, the finality of her remarks was not to be mistaken."

Billy, in spite of her sympathy for Calderwell, was conscious of a throb of relief that at least one stumbling-block was removed from Arkwright's possible pathway to Alice's heart.

"Did she give any special reason?" hazarded Billy, a shade too anxiously.

"Oh, yes. She said she wasn't going to marry anybody—only her music."

"Nonsense!" ejaculated Billy, falling back in her chair a little.

"Yes, I said that, too," gloomed the man; "but it didn't do any good. You see, I had known another girl who'd said the same thing once." (He did not look up, but a vivid red flamed suddenly into Billy's cheeks.) "And she—when the right one came—forgot all about the music, and married the man. So I naturally suspected that Alice would do the same thing. In fact, I said so to her. I was bold enough to even call the man by name—I hadn't been jealous of Arkwright for nothing, you see—but she denied it, and flew into such an indignant allegation that there wasn't a word of truth in it, that I had to sue for pardon before I got anything like peace."

"Oh-h!" said Billy, in a disappointed voice, falling quite back in her chair this time.

"And so that's why I'm wanting especially just now to see the wheels go 'round," smiled Calderwell, a little wistfully. "Oh, I shall get over it, I suppose. It isn't the first time, I'll own—but some day I take it there will be a last time. Enough of this, however! You haven't told me a thing about yourself. How about it? When I come back, are you going to give me a dinner cooked by your own fair hands? Going to still play Bridget?"

Billy laughed and shook her head.

"No; far from it. Eliza has come back, and her cousin from Vermont is coming as second girl to help her. But I *could* cook a dinner for you if I had to now, sir, and it wouldn't be potato-mush and cold lamb," she bragged shamelessly, as there sounded Bertram's peculiar ring, and the click of his key in the lock.

It was the next afternoon that Billy called on Marie. From Marie's, Billy went to the Annex, which was very near Cyril's new house; and there, in Aunt Hannah's room, she had what she told Bertram afterwards was a perfectly lovely visit.

Aunt Hannah, too, enjoyed the visit very much, though yet there was one thing that disturbed her—the vaguely troubled look in Billy's eyes, which to-day was more apparent than ever. Not until just before Billy went home did something occur to give Aunt Hannah a possible clue as to what was the meaning of it. That something was a question from Billy.

"Aunt Hannah, why don't I feel like Marie did? why don't I feel like everybody does in books and stories? Marie went around with such a detached, heavenly, absorbed look in her eyes, before the twins came to her home. But I don't. I don't find anything like that in my face, when I look in the glass. And I don't feel detached and absorbed and heavenly. I'm happy, of course; but I can't help thinking of the dear, dear times Bertram and I have together, just we two, and I can't seem to imagine it at all with a third person around."

"Billy! *Third person*, indeed!"

"There! I knew 'twould shock you," mourned Billy. "It shocks me. I *want* to feel detached and heavenly and absorbed."

"But Billy, dear, think of it—calling your own baby a third person!"

Billy sighed despairingly.

"Yes, I know. And I suppose I might as well own up to the rest of it too. I—I'm actually afraid of babies, Aunt Hannah! Well, I am," she reiterated, in answer to Aunt Hannah's gasp of disapproval. "I'm not used to them at all. I never had any little brothers and sisters, and I don't know how to treat babies. I—I'm always afraid they'll break, or something. I'm just as afraid of the twins as I can be. How Marie can handle them, and toss them about as she does, I don't see."

"Toss them about, indeed!"

"Well, it looks that way to me," sighed Billy. "Anyhow, I know I can never get to handle them like that—and that's no way to feel! And I'm ashamed of myself because I *can't* be detached and heavenly and absorbed," she added, rising to go. "Everybody always is, it seems, but just me."

"Fiddlededee, my dear!" scoffed Aunt Hannah, patting Billy's downcast face. "Wait till a year from now, and we'll see about that third-person bugaboo you're worrying about. *I'm* not worrying now; so you'd better not!"

CHAPTER XXII
A DOT AND A DIMPLE

On the day Cyril Henshaw's twins were six months old, a momentous occurrence marked the date with a flaming red letter of remembrance; and it all began with a baby's smile.

Cyril, in quest of his wife at about ten o'clock that morning, and not finding her, pursued his search even to the nursery—a room he very seldom entered. Cyril did not like to go into the nursery. He felt ill at ease, and as if he were away from home—and Cyril was known to abhor being away from home since he was married. Now that Marie had taken over the reins of government again, he had been obliged to see very little of those strange women and babies. Not but that he liked the babies, of course. They were his sons, and he was proud of them. They should have every advantage that college, special training, and travel could give them. He quite anticipated what they would be to him—when they really knew anything. But, of course, *now*, when they could do nothing but cry and wave their absurd little fists, and wobble their heads in so fearsome a manner, as if they simply did not know the meaning of the word backbone—and, for that matter, of course they didn't—why, he could not be expected to be anything but relieved when he had his den to himself again, with a reasonable chance of finding his manuscript as he had left it, and not cut up into a ridiculous string of paper dolls holding hands, as he had once found it, after a visit from a woman with a small girl.

Since Marie had been at the helm, however, he had not been troubled in such a way. He had, indeed, known almost his old customary peace and freedom from interruption, with only an occasional flitting across his path of the strange women and babies—though he had realized, of course, that they were in the house, especially in the nursery. For that reason, therefore, he always avoided the nursery when possible. But to-day he wanted his wife, and his wife was not to be found anywhere else in the house. So, reluctantly, he turned his steps toward the nursery, and, with a frown, knocked and pushed open the door.

"Is Mrs. Henshaw here?" he demanded, not over gently.

Absolute silence greeted his question. The man saw then that there was no one in the room save a baby sitting on a mat in the middle of the floor, barricaded on all sides with pillows.

With a deeper frown the man turned to go, when a gleeful "Ah—goo!" halted his steps midway. He wheeled sharply.

"Er—eh?" he queried, uncertainly eyeing his small son on the floor.

"Ah—goo!" observed the infant (who had been very lonesome), with greater emphasis; and this time he sent into his father's eyes the most bewitching of smiles.

"Well, by George!" murmured the man, weakly, a dawning amazement driving the frown from his face.

"Spgggh—oo—wah!" gurgled the boy, holding out two tiny fists.

A slow smile came to the man's face.

"Well, I'll—be—darned," he muttered half-shamefacedly, wholly delightedly. "If the rascal doesn't act as if he—knew me!"

"Ah—goo—spggghh!" grinned the infant, toothlessly, but entrancingly.

With almost a stealthy touch Cyril closed the door back of him, and advanced a little dubiously toward his son. His countenance carried a mixture of guilt, curiosity, and dogged determination so ludicrous that it was a pity none but baby eyes could see it. As if to meet more nearly on a level this baffling new acquaintance, Cyril got to his knees—somewhat stiffly, it must be confessed—and faced his son.

"Goo—eee—ooo—yah!" crowed the baby now, thrashing legs and arms about in a transport of joy at the acquisition of this new playmate.

"Well, well, young man, you—you don't say so!" stammered the growingly-proud father, thrusting a plainly timid and unaccustomed finger toward his offspring. "So you do know me, eh? Well, who am I?"

"Da—da!" gurgled the boy, triumphantly clutching the outstretched finger, and holding on with a tenacity that brought a gleeful chuckle to the lips of the man.

"Jove! but aren't you the strong little beggar, though! Needn't tell me you don't know a good thing when you see it! So I'm 'da-da,' am I?" he went on, unhesitatingly accepting as the pure gold of knowledge the shameless imitation vocabulary his son was foisting upon him. "Well, I expect I am, and—"

"Oh, Cyril!" The door had opened, and Marie was in the room. If she gave a start of surprise at her husband's unaccustomed attitude, she quickly controlled herself. "Julia said you wanted me. I must have been going down the back stairs when you came up the front, and—"

"Please, Mrs. Henshaw, is it Dot you have in here, or Dimple?" asked a new voice, as the second nurse entered by another door.

Before Mrs. Henshaw could answer, Cyril, who had got to his feet, turned sharply.

"Is it—*who*?" he demanded.

"Oh! Oh, Mr. Henshaw," stammered the girl. "I beg your pardon. I didn't know you were here. It was only that I wanted to know which baby it was. We thought we had Dot with us, until—"

"Dot! Dimple!" exploded the man. "Do you mean to say you have given my *sons* the ridiculous names of '*Dot*' and '*Dimple*'?"

"Why, no—yes—well, that is—we had to call them something," faltered the nurse, as with a despairing glance at her mistress, she plunged through the doorway.

Cyril turned to his wife.

"Marie, what is the meaning of this?" he demanded.

"Why, Cyril, dear, don't—don't get so wrought up," she begged. "It's only as Mary said, we *had* to call them something, and—"

"Wrought up, indeed!" interrupted Cyril, savagely. "Who wouldn't be? 'Dot' and 'Dimple'! Great Scott! One would think those boys were a couple of kittens or puppies; that they didn't know anything—didn't have any brains! But they have—if the other is anything like this one, at least," he declared, pointing to his son on the floor, who, at this opportune moment joined in the conversation to the extent of an appropriate "Ah—goo—da—da!"

"There, hear that, will you?" triumphed the father. "What did I tell you? That's the way he's been going on ever since I came into the room; The little rascal knows me—so soon!"

Marie clapped her fingers to her lips and turned her back suddenly, with a spasmodic little cough; but her husband, if he noticed the interruption, paid no heed.

"Dot and Dimple, indeed!" he went on wrathfully. "That settles it. We'll name those boys to-day, Marie, *to-day!* Not once again will I let the sun go down on a Dot and a Dimple under my roof."

Marie turned with a quick little cry of happiness.

"Oh, Cyril, I'm so glad! I've so wanted to have them named, you know! And shall we call them Franz and Felix, as we'd talked?"

"Franz, Felix, John, James, Paul, Charles—anything, so it's sane and sensible! I'd even adopt Calderwell's absurd Bildad and—er—Tomdad, or whatever it was, rather than have those poor little chaps insulted a day longer with a 'Dot' and a 'Dimple.' Great Scott!" And, entirely forgetting what he had come to the nursery for, Cyril strode from the room.

"Ah—goo—spggggh!" commented baby from the middle of the floor.

It was on a very windy March day that Bertram Henshaw's son, Bertram, Jr., arrived at the Strata. Billy went so far into the Valley of the Shadow of Death for her baby that it was some days before she realized in all its importance the presence of the new member of her family. Even when the days had become weeks, and Bertram, Jr., was a month and a half old, the extreme lassitude and weariness of his young mother was a source of ever-growing anxiety to her family and friends. Billy was so unlike herself, they all said.

"If something could only rouse her," suggested the Henshaw's old family physician one day. "A certain sort of mental shock—if not too severe—would do the deed, I think, and with no injury—only benefit. Her physical condition is in just the state that needs a stimulus to stir it into new life and vigor."

As it happened, this was said on a certain Monday. Two days later Bertram's sister Kate, on her way with her husband to Mr. Hartwell's old home in Vermont, stopped over in Boston for a two days' visit. She made her headquarters at Cyril's home, but very naturally she went, without much delay, to pay her respects to Bertram, Jr.

"Mr. Hartwell's brother isn't well," she explained to Billy, after the greetings were over. "You know he's the only one left there, since Mother and Father Hartwell came West. We shall go right on up to Vermont in a couple of days, but we just had to stay over long enough to see the baby; and we hadn't ever seen the twins, either, you know. By the way, how perfectly ridiculous Cyril is over those boys!"

"Is he?" smiled Billy, faintly.

"Yes. One would think there were never any babies born before, to hear him talk. He thinks they're the most wonderful things in the world—and they are cunning little fellows, I'll admit. But Cyril thinks they *know* so much," went on Kate, laughingly. "He's always bragging of something one or the other of them has done. Think of it—*Cyril!* Marie says it all started from the time last January when he discovered the nurses had been calling them Dot and Dimple."

"Yes, I know," smiled Billy again, faintly, lifting a thin, white, very un-Billy-like hand to her head.

Kate frowned, and regarded her sister-in-law thoughtfully.

"Mercy! how you look, Billy!" she exclaimed, with cheerful tactlessness. "They said you did, but, I declare, you look worse than I thought."

Billy's pale face reddened perceptibly.

"Nonsense! It's just that I'm so—so tired," she insisted. "I shall be all right soon. How did you leave the children?"

"Well, and happy—'specially little Kate, because mother was going away. Kate is mistress, you know, when I'm gone, and she takes herself very seriously."

"Mistress! A little thing like her! Why, she can't be more than ten or eleven," murmured Billy.

"She isn't. She was ten last month. But you'd think she was forty, the airs she gives herself, sometimes. Oh, of course there's Nora, and the cook, and Miss Winton, the governess, there to really manage things, and Mother Hartwell is just around the corner; but little Kate *thinks* she's managing, so she's happy."

Billy suppressed a smile. Billy was thinking that little Kate came naturally by at least one of her traits.

"Really, that child is impossible, sometimes," resumed Mrs. Hartwell, with a sigh. "You know the absurd things she was always saying two or three years ago, when we came on to Cyril's wedding."

"Yes, I remember."

"Well, I thought she would get over it. But she doesn't. She's worse, if anything; and sometimes her insight, or intuition, or whatever you may call it, is positively uncanny. I never know what she's going to remark next, when I take her anywhere; but it's safe to say, whatever it is, it'll be unexpected and *usually* embarrassing to somebody. And—is that the baby?" broke off Mrs. Hartwell, as a cooing laugh and a woman's voice came from the next room.

"Yes. The nurse has just brought him in, I think," said Billy.

"Then I'll go right now and see him," rejoined Kate, rising to her feet and hurrying into the next room.

Left alone, Billy lay back wearily in her reclining-chair. She wondered why Kate always tired her so. She wished she had had on her blue kimono, then perhaps Kate would not have thought she looked so badly. Blue was always more becoming to her than—

Billy turned her head suddenly. From the next room had come Kate's clear-cut, decisive voice.

"Oh, no, I don't think he looks a bit like his father. That little snubby nose was never the Henshaw nose."

Billy drew in her breath sharply, and pulled herself half erect in her chair. From the next room came Kate's voice again, after a low murmur from the nurse.

"Oh, but he isn't, I tell you. He isn't one bit of a Henshaw baby! The Henshaw babies are always *pretty* ones. They have more hair, and they look—well, different."

Billy gave a low cry, and struggled to her feet.

"Oh, no," spoke up Kate, in answer to another indistinct something from the nurse. "I don't think he's near as pretty as the twins. Of course the twins are a good deal older, but they have such a *bright* look,—and they did have, from the very first. I saw it in their tiniest baby pictures. But this baby—"

"*This* baby is *mine*, please," cut in a tremulous, but resolute voice; and Mrs. Hartwell turned to confront Bertram, Jr.'s mother, manifestly weak and trembling, but no less manifestly blazing-eyed and determined.

"Why, Billy!" expostulated Mrs. Hartwell, as Billy stumbled forward and snatched the child into her arms.

"Perhaps he doesn't look like the Henshaw babies. Perhaps he isn't as pretty as the twins. Perhaps he hasn't much hair, and does have a snub nose. He's my baby just the same, and I shall not stay calmly by and see him abused! Besides, *I* think he's prettier than the twins ever thought of being; and he's got all the hair I want him to have, and his nose is just exactly what a baby's nose ought to be!" And, with a superb gesture, Billy turned and bore the baby away.

CHAPTER XXIII
BILLY AND THE ENORMOUS RESPONSIBILITY

When the doctor heard from the nurse of Mrs. Hartwell's visit and what had come of it, he only gave a discreet smile, as befitted himself and the occasion; but to his wife privately, that night, the doctor said, when he had finished telling the story:

"And I couldn't have prescribed a better pill if I'd tried!"

"*Pill*—Mrs. Hartwell! Oh, Harold," reproved the doctor's wife, mildly.

But the doctor only chuckled the more, and said:

"You wait and see."

If Billy's friends were worried before because of her lassitude and lack of ambition, they were almost as worried now over her amazing alertness and insistent activity. Day by day, almost hour by hour, she seemed to gain in strength; and every bit she acquired she promptly tested almost to the breaking point, so plainly eager was she to be well and strong. And always, from morning until night, and again from night until morning, the pivot of her existence, around which swung all thoughts, words, actions, and plans, was the sturdy little plump-cheeked, firm-fleshed atom of humanity known as Bertram, Jr. Even Aunt Hannah remonstrated with her at last.

"But, Billy, dear," she exclaimed, "one would almost get the idea that you thought there wasn't a thing in the world but that baby!"

Billy laughed.

"Well, do you know, sometimes I 'most think there isn't," she retorted unblushingly.

"Billy!" protested Aunt Hannah; then, a little severely, she demanded: "And who was it that just last September was calling this same only-object-in-the-world a third person in your home?"

"Third person, indeed! Aunt Hannah, did I? Did I really say such a dreadful thing as that? But I didn't know, then, of course. I couldn't know how perfectly wonderful a baby is, especially such a baby as Bertram, Jr., is. Why, Aunt Hannah, that little thing knows a whole lot already. He's known me for weeks; I know he has. And ages and ages ago he began to give me little smiles when he saw me. They were smiles—real smiles! Oh, yes, I know nurse said they weren't smiles at the first," admitted Billy, in answer to Aunt Hannah's doubting expression. "I know nurse said it was only wind on his stomach. Think of it—wind on his stomach! Just as if I didn't know the difference between my own baby's smile and wind on his stomach! And you don't know how soon he began to follow my moving finger with his eyes!"

"Yes, I tried that one day, I remember," observed Aunt Hannah demurely. "I moved my finger. He looked at the ceiling—*fixedly*."

"Well, probably he *wanted* to look at the ceiling, then," defended the young mother, promptly. "I'm sure I wouldn't give a snap for a baby if he didn't sometimes have a mind of his own, and exercise it!"

"Oh, Billy, Billy," laughed Aunt Hannah, with a shake of her head as Billy turned away, chin uptilted.

By the time Bertram, Jr., was three months old, Billy was unmistakably her old happy, merry self, strong and well. Affairs at the Strata once more were moving as by clockwork—only this time it was a baby's hand that set the clock, and that wound it, too.

Billy told her husband very earnestly that now they had entered upon a period of Enormous Responsibility. The Life, Character, and Destiny of a Human Soul was intrusted to their care, and they must be Wise, Faithful, and Efficient. They must be at once Proud and Humble at this their Great Opportunity. They must Observe, Learn, and Practice. First and foremost in their eyes must always be this wonderful Important Trust.

Bertram laughed at first very heartily at Billy's instructions, which, he declared, were so bristling with capitals that he could fairly see them drop from her lips. Then, when he found how really very much in earnest she was, and how hurt she was at his levity, he managed to pull his face into something like sobriety while she talked to him, though he did persist in dropping kisses on her cheeks, her chin, her finger-tips, her hair, and the little pink lobes of her ears—"just by way of punctuation" to her sentences, he said. And he told her that he wasn't really slighting her lips, only that they moved so fast he could not catch them. Whereat Billy pouted, and told him severely that he was a bad, naughty boy, and that he did not deserve to be the father of the dearest, most wonderful baby in the world.

"No, I know I don't," beamed Bertram, with cheerful unrepentance; "but I am, just the same," he finished triumphantly. And this time he contrived to find his wife's lips.

"Oh, Bertram," sighed Billy, despairingly.

"You're an old dear, of course, and one just can't be cross with you; but you don't, you just *don't* realize your Immense Responsibility."

"Oh, yes, I do," maintained Bertram so seriously that even Billy herself almost believed him.

In spite of his assertions, however, it must be confessed that Bertram was much more inclined to regard the new member of his family as just his son rather than as an Important Trust; and there is little doubt that he liked to toss him in the air and hear his gleeful crows of delight, without any bother of Observing him at all. As to the Life and Character and Destiny intrusted to his care, it is to be feared that Bertram just plain gloried in his son, poked him in the ribs, and chuckled him under the chin whenever he pleased, and gave never so much as a thought to Character and Destiny. It is to be feared, too, that he was Proud without being Humble, and that the only Opportunity he really appreciated was the chance to show off his wife and baby to some less fortunate fellow-man.

But not so Billy. Billy joined a Mothers' Club and entered a class in Child Training with an elaborate system of Charts, Rules, and Tests. She subscribed to each new "Mothers' Helper," and the like, that she came across, devouring each and every one with an eagerness that was tempered only by a vague uneasiness at finding so many differences of opinion among Those Who Knew.

Undeniably Billy, if not Bertram, was indeed realizing the Enormous Responsibility, and was keeping ever before her the Important Trust.

In June Bertram took a cottage at the South Shore, and by the time the really hot weather arrived the family were well settled. It was only an hour away from Boston, and easy of access, but William said he guessed he would not go; he would stay in Boston, sleeping at the house, and getting his meals at the club, until the middle of July, when he was going down in Maine for his usual fishing trip, which he had planned to take a little earlier than usual this year.

"But you'll be so lonesome, Uncle William," Billy demurred, "in this great house all alone!"

"Oh, no, I sha'n't," rejoined Uncle William. "I shall only be sleeping here, you know," he finished, with a slightly peculiar smile.

It was well, perhaps, that Billy did not exactly realize the significance of that smile, nor the unconscious emphasis on the word "sleeping," for it would have troubled her not a little.

William, to tell the truth, was quite anticipating that sleeping. William's nights had not been exactly restful since the baby came. His evenings, too, had not been the peaceful things they were wont to be.

Some of Billy's Rules and Tests were strenuously objected to on the part of her small son, and the young man did not hesitate to show it. Billy said that it was good for the baby to cry, that it developed his lungs; but William was very sure that it was not good for *him*. Certainly, when the baby did cry, William never could help hovering near the center of disturbance, and he always *had* to remind Billy that it might be a pin, you know, or some cruel thing that was hurting. As if he, William, a great strong man, could sit calmly by and smoke a pipe, or lie in his comfortable bed and sleep, while that blessed little baby was crying his heart out like that! Of course, if one did not *know* he was crying—Hence William's anticipation of those quiet, restful nights when he could not know it.

Very soon after Billy's arrival at the cottage, Aunt Hannah and Alice Greggory came down for a day's visit. Aunt Hannah had been away from Boston for several weeks, so it was some time since she had seen the baby.

"My, but hasn't he grown!" she exclaimed, picking the baby up and stooping to give him a snuggling kiss. The next instant she almost dropped the little fellow, so startling had been Billy's cry.

"No, no, wait, Aunt Hannah, please," Billy was entreating, hurrying to the little corner cupboard. In a moment she was back with a small bottle and a bit of antiseptic cotton. "We always sterilize our lips now before we kiss him—it's so much safer, you know."

Aunt Hannah sat down limply, the baby still in her arms.

"Fiddlededee, Billy! What an absurd idea! What have you got in that bottle?"

"Why, Aunt Hannah, it's just a little simple listerine," bridled Billy, "and it isn't absurd at all. It's very sensible. My 'Hygienic Guide for Mothers' says—"

"Well, I suppose I may kiss his hand," interposed Aunt Hannah, just a little curtly, "without subjecting myself to a City Hospital treatment!"

Billy laughed shamefacedly, but she still held her ground.

"No, you can't—nor even his foot. He might get them in his mouth. Aunt Hannah, why does a baby think that everything, from his own toes to his father's watch fob and the plush balls on a caller's wrist-bag, is made to eat? As if I could sterilize everything, and keep him from getting hold of germs somewhere!"

"You'll have to have a germ-proof room for him," laughed Alice Greggory, playfully snapping her fingers at the baby in Aunt Hannah's lap.

Billy turned eagerly.

"Oh, did you read about that, too?" she cried. "I thought it was *so* interesting, and I wondered if I could do it."

Alice stared frankly.

"You don't mean to say they actually *have* such things," she challenged.

"Well, I read about them in a magazine," asserted Billy, "—how you could have a germ-proof room. They said it was very simple, too. Just pasteurize the air, you know, by heating it to one hundred and ten and one-half degrees Fahrenheit for seventeen and one-half minutes. I remember just the figures."

"Simple, indeed! It sounds so," scoffed Aunt Hannah, with uplifted eyebrows.

"Oh, well, I couldn't do it, of course," admitted Billy, regretfully. "Bertram never'd stand for that in the world. He's always rushing in to show the baby off to every Tom, Dick and Harry and his wife that comes; and of course if you opened the nursery door, that would let in those germ things, and you *couldn't* very well pasteurize your callers by heating them to one hundred and ten and one-half degrees for seventeen and one-half minutes! I don't see how you could manage such a room, anyway, unless you had a system of—of rooms like locks, same as they do for water in canals."

"Oh, my grief and conscience—locks, indeed!" almost groaned Aunt Hannah. "Here, Alice, will you please take this child—that is, if you have a germ-proof certificate about you to show to his mother. I want to take off my bonnet and gloves."

"Take him? Of course I'll take him," laughed Alice; "and right under his mother's nose, too," she added, with a playful grimace at Billy. "And we'll make pat-a-cakes, and send the little pigs to market, and have such a beautiful time that we'll forget there ever was such a thing in the world as an old germ. Eh, babykins?"

"Babykins" cooed his unqualified approval of this plan; but his mother looked troubled.

"That's all right, Alice. You may play with him," she frowned doubtfully; "but you mustn't do it long, you know—not over five minutes."

"Five minutes! Well, I like that, when I've come all the way from Boston purposely to see him," pouted Alice. "What's the matter now? Time for his nap?"

"Oh, no, not for—thirteen minutes," replied Billy, consulting the watch at her belt. "But we never play with Baby more than five minutes at a time. My 'Scientific Care of Infants' says it isn't wise; that with some babies it's positively dangerous, until after they're six months old. It makes them nervous, and forces their mind, you know," she explained anxiously. "So of course we'd want to be careful. Bertram, Jr., isn't quite four, yet."

"Why, yes, of course," murmured Alice, politely, stopping a pat-a-cake before it was half baked.

The infant, as if suspecting that he was being deprived of his lawful baby rights, began to fret and whimper.

"Poor itty sing," crooned Aunt Hannah, who, having divested herself of bonnet and gloves, came hurriedly forward with outstretched hands. "Do they just 'buse 'em? Come here to your old auntie, sweetems, and we'll go walkee. I saw a bow-wow—such a tunnin' ickey wickey bow-wow on the steps when I came in. Come, we go see ickey wickey bow-wow?"

"Aunt Hannah, *please!*" protested Billy, both hands upraised in horror. "*Won't* you say 'dog,' and leave out that dreadful 'ickey wickey'? Of course he can't understand things now, really, but we never know when he'll begin to, and we aren't ever going to let him hear baby-talk at all, if we can help it. And truly, when you come to think of it, it is absurd to expect a child to talk sensibly and rationally on the mental diet of 'moo-moos' and 'choo-choos' served out to them. Our Professor of Metaphysics and Ideology in our Child Study Course says that nothing is so receptive and plastic as the Mind of a Little Child, and that it is perfectly appalling how we fill it with trivial absurdities that haven't even the virtue of being accurate. So that's why we're trying to be so careful with Baby. You didn't mind my speaking, I know, Aunt Hannah."

"Oh, no, of course not, Billy," retorted Aunt Hannah, a little tartly, and with a touch of sarcasm most unlike her gentle self. "I'm sure I shouldn't wish to fill this infant's plastic mind with anything so appalling as trivial inaccuracies. May I be pardoned for suggesting, however," she went on as the baby's whimper threatened to become a lusty wail, "that this young gentleman cries as if he were sleepy and hungry?"

"Yes, he is," admitted Billy.

"Well, doesn't your system of scientific training allow him to be given such trivial absurdities as food and naps?" inquired the lady, mildly.

"Of course it does, Aunt Hannah," retorted Billy, laughing in spite of herself. "And it's almost time now. There are only a few more minutes to wait."

"Few more minutes to wait, indeed!" scorned Aunt Hannah. "I suppose the poor little fellow might cry and cry, and you wouldn't set that clock ahead by a teeny weeny minute!"

"Certainly not," said the young mother, decisively. "My 'Daily Guide for Mothers' says that a time for everything and everything in its time, is the very A B C and whole alphabet of Right Training. He does everything by the clock, and to the minute," declared Billy, proudly.

Aunt Hannah sniffed, obviously skeptical and rebellious. Alice Greggory laughed.

"Aunt Hannah looks as if she'd like to bring down her clock that strikes half an hour ahead," she said mischievously; but Aunt Hannah did not deign to answer this.

"How long do you rock him?" she demanded of Billy. "I suppose I may do that, mayn't I?"

"Mercy, I don't rock him at all, Aunt Hannah," exclaimed Billy.

"Nor sing to him?"

"Certainly not."

"But you did—before I went away. I remember that you did."

"Yes, I know I did," admitted Billy, "and I had an awful time, too. Some evenings, every single one of us, even to Uncle William, had to try before we could get him off to sleep. But that was before I got my 'Efficiency of Mother and Child,' or my 'Scientific Training,' and, oh, lots of others. You see, I didn't know a thing then, and I loved to rock him, so I did it—though the nurse said it wasn't good for him; but I didn't believe *her*. I've had an awful time changing; but I've done it. I just put him in his little crib, or his carriage, and after a while he goes to sleep. Sometimes, now, he doesn't cry hardly any. I'm afraid, to-day, though, he will," she worried.

"Yes, I'm afraid he will," almost screamed Aunt Hannah, in order to make herself heard above Bertram, Jr., who, by this time, was voicing his opinion of matters and things in no uncertain manner.

It was not, after all, so very long before peace and order reigned; and, in due course, Bertram, Jr., in his carriage, lay fast asleep. Then, while Aunt Hannah went to Billy's room for a short rest, Billy and Alice went out on to the wide veranda which faced the wonderful expanse of sky and sea.

"Now tell me of yourself," commanded Billy, almost at once. "It's been ages since I've heard or seen a thing of you."

"There's nothing to tell."

"Nonsense! But there must be," insisted Billy. "You know it's months since I've seen anything of you, hardly."

"I know. We feel quite neglected at the Annex," said Alice.

"But I don't go anywhere," defended Billy. "I can't. There isn't time."

"Even to bring us the extra happiness?" smiled Alice.

A quick change came to Billy's face. Her eyes glowed deeply.

"No; though I've had so much that ought to have gone—such loads and loads of extra happiness, which I couldn't possibly use myself! Sometimes I'm so happy, Alice, that—that I'm just frightened. It doesn't seem as if anybody ought to be so happy."

"Oh, Billy, dear," demurred Alice, her eyes filling suddenly with tears.

"Well, I've got the Annex. I'm glad I've got that for the overflow, anyway," resumed Billy, trying to steady her voice. "I've sent a whole lot of happiness up there mentally, if I haven't actually carried it; so I'm sure you must have got it. Now tell me of yourself."

"There's nothing to tell," insisted Alice, as before.

"You're working as hard as ever?"

"Yes—harder."

"New pupils?"

"Yes, and some concert engagements—good ones, for next season. Accompaniments, you know."

Billy nodded.

"Yes; I've heard of you already twice, lately, in that line, and very flatteringly, too."

"Have you? Well, that's good."

"Hm-m." There was a moment's silence, then, abruptly, Billy changed the subject. "I had a letter from Belle Calderwell, yesterday." She paused expectantly, but there was no comment.

"You don't seem interested," she frowned, after a minute.

Alice laughed.

"Pardon me, but—I don't know the Lady, you see. Was it a good letter?"

"You know her brother."

"Very true." Alice's cheeks showed a deeper color. "Did she say anything of him?"

"Yes. She said he was coming back to Boston next winter."

"Indeed!"

"Yes. She says that this time he declares he really *is* going to settle down to work," murmured Billy, demurely, with a sidelong glance at her companion. "She says he's engaged to be married—one of her friends over there."

There was no reply. Alice appeared to be absorbed in watching a tiny white sail far out at sea.

Again Billy was silent. Then, with studied carelessness, she said:

"Yes, and you know Mr. Arkwright, too. She told of him."

"Yes? Well, what of him?" Alice's voice was studiedly indifferent.

"Oh, there was quite a lot of him. Belle had just been to hear him sing, and then her brother had introduced him to her. She thinks he's perfectly wonderful, in every way, I should judge. In fact, she simply raved over him. It seems that while we've been hearing nothing from him all winter, he's been winning no end of laurels for himself in Paris and Berlin. He's been studying, too, of course, as well as singing; and now he's got a chance to sing somewhere—create a rôle, or something—Belle said she wasn't quite clear on the matter herself, but it was a perfectly splendid chance, and one that was a fine feather in his cap."

"Then he won't be coming home—that is, to Boston—at all this winter, probably," said Alice, with a cheerfulness that sounded just a little forced.

"Not until February. But he is coming then. He's been engaged for six performances with the Boston Opera Company—as a star tenor, mind you! Isn't that splendid?"

"Indeed it is," murmured Alice.

"Belle writes that Hugh says he's improved wonderfully, and that even he can see that his singing is marvelous. He says Paris is wild over him; but—for my part, I wish he'd come home and stay here where he belongs," finished Billy, a bit petulantly.

"Why, why, Billy!" murmured her friend, a curiously startled look coming into her eyes.

"Well, I do," maintained Billy; then, recklessly, she added: "I had such beautiful plans for him, once, Alice. Oh, if you only could have cared for him, you'd have made such a splendid couple!"

A vivid scarlet flew to Alice's face.

"Nonsense!" she cried, getting quickly to her feet and bending over one of the flower boxes along the veranda railing. "Mr. Arkwright never thought of marrying me—and I'm not going to marry anybody but my music."

Billy sighed despairingly.

"I know that's what you say now; but if—" She stopped abruptly. Around the turn of the veranda had appeared Aunt Hannah, wheeling Bertram, Jr., still asleep in his carriage.

"I came out the other door," she explained softly. "And it was so lovely I just had to go in and get the baby. I thought it would be so nice for him to finish his nap out here."

Billy arose with a troubled frown.

"But, Aunt Hannah, he mustn't—he can't stay out here. I'm sorry, but we'll have to take him back."

Aunt Hannah's eyes grew mutinous.

"But I thought the outdoor air was just the thing for him. I'm sure your scientific hygienic nonsense says *that!*"

"They do—they did—that is, some of them do," acknowledged Billy, worriedly; "but they differ, so! And the one I'm going by now says that Baby should always sleep in an *even* temperature—seventy degrees, if possible; and that's exactly what the room in there was, when I left him. It's not the same out here, I'm sure. In fact I looked at the thermometer to see, just before I came out myself. So, Aunt Hannah, I'm afraid I'll have to take him back."

"But you used to have him sleep out of doors all the time, on that little balcony out of your room," argued Aunt Hannah, still plainly unconvinced.

"Yes, I know I did. I was following the other man's rules, then. As I said, if only they wouldn't differ so! Of course I want the best; but it's so hard to always know the best, and—"

At this very inopportune moment Master Bertram took occasion to wake up, which brought even a deeper wrinkle of worry to his fond mother's forehead; for she said that, according to the clock, he should have been sleeping exactly ten and one-half more minutes, and that of course he couldn't commence the next thing until those ten and one-half minutes were up, or else his entire schedule for the day would be shattered. So what she should do with him for those should-have-been-sleeping ten minutes and a half, she did not know. All of which drew from Aunt Hannah the astounding exclamation of:

"Oh, my grief and conscience, Billy, if you aren't the—the limit!" Which, indeed, she must have been, to have brought circumspect Aunt Hannah to the point of actually using slang.

CHAPTER XXIV
A NIGHT OFF

The Henshaw family did not return to the Strata until late in September. Billy said that the sea air seemed to agree so well with the baby it would be a pity to change until the weather became really too cool at the shore to be comfortable.

William came back from his fishing trip in August, and resumed his old habit of sleeping at the house and taking his meals at the club. To be sure, for a week he went back and forth between the city and the beach house; but it happened to be a time when Bertram, Jr., was cutting a tooth, and this so wore upon William's sympathy—William still could not help insisting it *might* be a pin—that he concluded peace lay only in flight. So he went back to the Strata.

Bertram had stayed at the cottage all summer, painting industriously. Heretofore he had taken more of a vacation through the summer months, but this year there seemed to be nothing for him to do but to paint. He did not like to go away on a trip and leave Billy, and she declared she could not take the baby nor leave him, and that she did not need any trip, anyway.

"All right, then, we'll just stay at the beach, and have a fine vacation together," he had answered her.

As Bertram saw it, however, he could detect very little "vacation" to it. Billy had no time for anything but the baby. When she was not actually engaged in caring for it, she was studying how to care for it. Never had she been sweeter or dearer, and never had Bertram loved her half so well. He was proud, too, of her devotion, and of her triumphant success as a mother; but he did wish that sometimes, just once in a while, she would remember she was a wife, and pay a little attention to him, her husband.

Bertram was ashamed to own it, even to himself, but he was feeling just a little abused that summer; and he knew that, in his heart, he was actually getting jealous of his own son, in spite of his adoration of the little fellow. He told himself defensively that it was not to be expected that he should not want the love of his wife, the attentions of his wife, and the companionship of his wife—a part of the time. It was nothing more than natural that occasionally he should like to see her show some interest in subjects not mentioned in Mothers' Guides and Scientific Trainings of Infants; and he did not believe he could be blamed for wanting his residence to be a home for himself as well as a nursery for his offspring.

Even while he thus discontentedly argued with himself, however, Bertram called himself a selfish brute just to think such things when he had so dear and loving a wife as Billy, and so fine and splendid a baby as Bertram, Jr. He told himself, too, that very likely when they were back in their own house again, and when motherhood was not so new to her, Billy would not be so absorbed in the baby. She would return to her old interest in her husband, her music, her friends, and her own personal appearance. Meanwhile there was always, of course, for him, his painting. So he would paint, accepting gladly what crumbs of attention fell from the baby's table, and trust to the future to make Billy none the less a mother, perhaps, but a little more the wife.

Just how confidently he was counting on this coming change, Bertram hardly realized himself; but certainly the family was scarcely settled at the Strata before the husband gayly proposed one evening that he and Billy should go to the theater to see "Romeo and Juliet."

Billy was clearly both surprised and shocked.

"Why, Bertram, I can't—you know I can't!" she exclaimed reprovingly.

Bertram's heart sank; but he kept a brave front.

"Why not?"

"What a question! As if I'd leave Baby!"

"But, Billy, dear, you'd be gone less than three hours, and you say Delia's the most careful of nurses."

Billy's forehead puckered into an anxious frown.

"I can't help it. Something might happen to him, Bertram. I couldn't be happy a minute."

"But, dearest, aren't you *ever* going to leave him?" demanded the young husband, forlornly.

"Why, yes, of course, when it's reasonable and necessary. I went out to the Annex yesterday afternoon. I was gone almost two whole hours."

"Well, did anything happen?"

"N-no; but then I telephoned, you see, several times, so I *knew* everything was all right."

"Oh, well, if that's all you want, I could telephone, you know, between every act," suggested Bertram, with a sarcasm that was quite lost on the earnest young mother.

"Y-yes, you could do that, couldn't you?" conceded Billy; "and, of course, I *haven't* been anywhere much, lately."

"Indeed I could," agreed Bertram, with a promptness that carefully hid his surprise at her literal acceptance of what he had proposed as a huge joke. "Come, is it a go? Shall I telephone to see if I can get seats?"

"You think Baby'll surely be all right?"

"I certainly do."

"And you'll telephone home between every act?"

"I will." Bertram's voice sounded almost as if he were repeating the marriage service.

"And we'll come straight home afterwards as fast as John and Peggy can bring us?"

"Certainly."

"Then I think—I'll—go," breathed Billy, tremulously, plainly showing what a momentous concession she thought she was making. "I do love 'Romeo and Juliet,' and I haven't seen it for ages!"

"Good! Then I'll find out about the tickets," cried Bertram, so elated at the prospect of having an old-time evening out with his wife that even the half-hourly telephones did not seem too great a price to pay.

When the time came, they were a little late in starting. Baby was fretful, and though Billy usually laid him in his crib and unhesitatingly left the room, insisting that he should go to sleep by himself in accordance with the most approved rules in her Scientific Training; yet to-night she could not bring herself to the point of leaving the house until he was quiet. Hurried as they were when they did start, Billy was conscious of Bertram's frowning disapproval of her frock.

"You don't like it, of course, dear, and I don't blame you," she smiled remorsefully.

"Oh, I like it—that is, I did, when it was new," rejoined her husband, with apologetic frankness. "But, dear, didn't you have anything else? This looks almost—well, mussy, you know."

"No—well, yes, maybe there were others," admitted Billy; "but this was the quickest and easiest to get into, and it all came just as I was getting Baby ready for bed, you know. I am a fright, though, I'll acknowledge, so far as clothes go. I haven't had time to get a thing since Baby came. I must get something right away, I suppose."

"Yes, indeed," declared Bertram, with emphasis, hurrying his wife into the waiting automobile.

Billy had to apologize again at the theater, for the curtain had already risen on the ancient quarrel between the houses of Capulet and Montague, and Billy knew her husband's special abhorrence of tardy arrivals. Later, though, when well established in their seats, Billy's mind was plainly not with the players on the stage.

"Do you suppose Baby *is* all right?" she whispered, after a time.

"Sh-h! Of course he is, dear!"

There was a brief silence, during which Billy peered at her program in the semi-darkness. Then she nudged her husband's arm ecstatically.

"Bertram, I couldn't have chosen a better play if I'd tried. There are *five* acts! I'd forgotten there were so many. That means you can telephone four times!"

"Yes, dear." Bertram's voice was sternly cheerful.

"You must be sure they tell you exactly how Baby is."

"All right, dear. Sh-h! Here's Romeo."

Billy subsided. She even clapped a little in spasmodic enthusiasm. Presently she peered at her program again.

"There wouldn't be time, I suppose, to telephone between the scenes," she hazarded wistfully. "There are sixteen of those!"

"Well, hardly! Billy, you aren't paying one bit of attention to the play!"

"Why, of course I am," whispered Billy, indignantly. "I think it's perfectly lovely, and I'm perfectly contented, too—since I found out about those five acts, and as long as I *can't* have the sixteen scenes," she added, settling back in her seat.

As if to prove that she was interested in the play, her next whisper, some time later, had to do with one of the characters on the stage.

"Who's that—the nurse? Mercy! We wouldn't want her for Baby, would we?"

In spite of himself Bertram chuckled this time. Billy, too, laughed at herself. Then, resolutely, she settled into her seat again.

The curtain was not fairly down on the first act before Billy had laid an urgent hand on her husband's arm.

"Now, remember; ask if he's waked up, or anything," she directed. "And be sure to say I'll come right home if they need me. Now hurry."

"Yes, dear." Bertram rose with alacrity. "I'll be back right away."

"Oh, but I don't want you to hurry *too* much," she called after him, softly. "I want you to take plenty of time to ask questions."

"All right," nodded Bertram, with a quizzical smile, as he turned away.

Obediently Bertram asked all the question she could think of, then came back to his wife. There was nothing in his report that even Billy could disapprove of, or worry about; and with almost a contented look on her face she turned toward the stage as the curtain went up on the second act.

"I love this balcony scene," she sighed happily.

Romeo, however, had not half finished his impassioned love-making when Billy clutched her husband's arm almost fiercely.

"Bertram," she fairly hissed in a tragic whisper, "I've just happened to think! Won't it be awful when Baby falls in love? I know I shall just hate that girl for taking him away from me!"

"Sh-h! *Billy!*" expostulated her husband, choking with half-stifled laughter. "That woman in front heard you, I know she did!"

"Well, I shall," sighed Billy, mournfully, turning back to the stage.

"'Good night, good night! parting is such sweet sorrow,
That I shall say good night, till it be morrow,'"

sighed Juliet passionately to her Romeo.

"Mercy! I hope not," whispered Billy flippantly in Bertram's ear. "I'm sure I don't want to stay here till to-morrow! I want to go home and see Baby."

"*Billy!*" pleaded Bertram so despairingly, that Billy, really conscience-smitten, sat back in her seat and remained, for the rest of the act, very quiet indeed.

Deceived by her apparent tranquillity, Bertram turned as the curtain went down.

"Now, Billy, surely you don't think it'll be necessary to telephone so soon as this again," he ventured.

Miss Billy—Married | 173

Billy's countenance fell.

"But, Bertram, you *said* you would! Of course if you aren't willing to—but I've been counting on hearing all through this horrid long act, and—"

"Goodness me, Billy, I'll telephone every minute for you, of course, if you want me to," cried Bertram, springing to his feet, and trying not to show his impatience.

He was back more promptly this time.

"Everything O. K.," he smiled reassuringly into Billy's anxious eyes. "Delia said she'd just been up, and the little chap was sound asleep."

To the man's unbounded surprise, his wife grew actually white.

"Up! Up!" she exclaimed. "Do you mean that Delia went down-stairs to *stay*, and left my baby up there alone?"

"But, Billy, she said he was all right," murmured Bertram, softly, casting uneasy sidelong glances at his too interested neighbors.

"'All right'! Perhaps he was, *then*—but he may not be, later. Delia should stay in the next room all the time, where she could hear the least thing."

"Yes, dear, she will, I'm sure, if you tell her to," soothed Bertram, quickly. "It'll be all right next time."

Billy shook her head. She was obviously near to crying.

"But, Bertram, I can't stand it to sit here enjoying myself all safe and comfortable, and know that Baby is *alone* up there in that great big room! Please, *please* won't you go and telephone Delia to go up *now* and stay there?"

Bertram, weary, sorely tried, and increasingly aware of those annoyingly interested neighbors, was on the point of saying a very decided no; but a glance into Billy's pleading eyes settled it. Without a word he went back to the telephone.

The curtain was up when he slipped into his seat, very red of face. In answer to Billy's hurried whisper he shook his head; but in the short pause between the first and second scenes he said, in a low voice:

"I'm sorry, Billy, but I couldn't get the house at all."

"Couldn't get them! But you'd just been talking with them!"

"That's exactly it, probably. I had just telephoned, so they weren't watching for the bell. Anyhow, I couldn't get them."

"Then you didn't get Delia at all!"

"Of course not."

"And Baby is still—all alone!"

"But he's all right, dear. Delia's keeping watch of him."

For a moment there was silence; then, with clear decisiveness came Billy's voice.

"Bertram, I am going home."

"Billy!"

"I am."

"Billy, for heaven's sake don't be a silly goose! The play's half over already. We'll soon be going, anyway."

Billy's lips came together in a thin little determined line.

"Bertram, I am going home now, please," she said. "You needn't come with me; I can go alone."

Bertram said two words under his breath which it was just as well, perhaps, that Billy—and the neighbors—did not hear; then he gathered up their wraps and, with Billy, stalked out of the theater.

At home everything was found to be absolutely as it should be. Bertram, Jr., was peacefully sleeping, and Delia, who had come up from downstairs, was sewing in the next room.

"There, you see," observed Bertram, a little sourly.

Billy drew a long, contented sigh.

"Yes, I see; everything is all right. But that's exactly what I wanted to do, Bertram, you know—to *see for myself*," she finished happily.

And Bertram, looking at her rapt face as she hovered over the baby's crib, called himself a brute and a beast to mind *anything* that could make Billy look like that.

CHAPTER XXV
"SHOULD AULD ACQUAINTANCE BE FORGOT"

Bertram did not ask Billy very soon again to go to the theater. For some days, indeed, he did not ask her to do anything. Then, one evening, he did beg for some music.

"Billy, you haven't played to me or sung to me since I could remember," he complained. "I want some music."

Billy gave a merry laugh and wriggled her fingers experimentally.

"Mercy, Bertram! I don't believe I could play a note. You know I'm all out of practice."

"But why *don't* you practice?"

"Why, Bertram, I can't. In the first place I don't seem to have any time except when Baby's asleep; and I can't play then-I'd wake him up."

Bertram sighed irritably, rose to his feet, and began to walk up and down the room. He came to a pause at last, his eyes bent a trifle disapprovingly on his wife.

"Billy, dear, *don't* you wear anything but those wrapper things nowadays?" he asked plaintively.

Again Billy laughed. But this time a troubled frown followed the laugh.

"I know, Bertram, I suppose they do look dowdy, sometimes," she confessed; "but, you see, I hate to wear a really good dress—Baby rumples them up so; and I'm usually in a hurry to get to him mornings, and these are so easy to slip into, and so much more comfortable for me to handle him in!"

"Yes, of course, of course; I see," mumbled Bertram, listlessly taking up his walk again.

Billy, after a moment's silence, began to talk animatedly. Baby had done a wonderfully cunning thing that morning, and Billy had not had a chance yet to tell Bertram. Baby was growing more and more cunning anyway, these days, and there were several things she believed she had not told him; so she told them now.

Bertram listened politely, interestedly. He told himself that he *was* interested, too. Of course he was interested in the doings of his own child! But he still walked up and down the room a little restlessly, coming to a halt at last by the window, across which the shade had not been drawn.

"Billy," he cried suddenly, with his old boyish eagerness, "there's a glorious moon. Come on! Let's take a little walk—a real fellow-and-his-best-girl walk! Will you?"

"Mercy! dear, I couldn't," cried Billy springing to her feet. "I'd love to, though, if I could," she added hastily, as she saw disappointment cloud her husband's face. "But I told Delia she might go out. It isn't her regular evening, of course, but I told her I didn't mind staying with Baby a bit. So I'll have to go right up now. She'll be going soon. But, dear, you go and take your walk. It'll do you good. Then you can come back and tell me all about it—only you must come in quietly, so not to wake the baby," she finished, giving her husband an affectionate kiss, as she left the room.

After a disconsolate five minutes of solitude, Bertram got his hat and coat and went out for his walk—but he told himself he did not expect to enjoy it.

Bertram Henshaw knew that the old rebellious jealousy of the summer had him fast in its grip. He was heartily ashamed of himself, but he could not help it. He wanted Billy, and he wanted her then. He wanted to talk to her. He wanted to tell her about a new portrait commission he had just obtained; and he wanted to ask her what she thought of the idea of a brand-new "Face of a Girl" for the Bohemian Ten Exhibition next March. He wanted—but then, what would be the use? She would listen, of course, but he would know by the very looks of her face that she would not be really thinking of what he was saying; and he would be willing to wager his best canvas that in the very first pause she would tell about the baby's newest tooth or latest toy. Not but that he liked to hear about the little fellow, of course; and not but that he was proud as Punch of him, too; but that he would like sometimes to hear Billy talk of something else. The sweetest melody in the world, if dinned into one's ears day and night, became something to be fled from.

And Billy ought to talk of something else, too! Bertram, Jr., wonderful as he was, really was not the only thing in the world, or even the only baby; and other people—outsiders, their friends—had a right to expect that sometimes other matters might be considered—their own, for instance. But Billy seemed to have forgotten this. No matter whether the subject of conversation had to do with the latest novel or a trip to Europe, under Billy's guidance it invariably led straight to Baby's Jack-and-Jill book, or to a perambulator journey in the Public Garden. If it had not been so serious, it would have been really funny the way all roads led straight to one goal. He himself, when alone with Billy, had started the most unusual and foreign subjects, sometimes, just to see if there were not somewhere a little bypath that did not bring up in his own nursery. He never, however, found one.

But it was not funny; it was serious. Was this glorious gift on parenthood to which he had looked forward as the crowning joy of his existence, to be nothing but a tragedy that would finally wreck his domestic happiness? It could not be. It must not be. He must be patient, and wait. Billy loved him. He was sure she did. By and by this obsession of motherhood, which had her so fast in its grasp, would relax. She would remember that her husband had rights as well as her child. Once again she would give him the companionship, love, and sympathetic interest so dear to him. Meanwhile there was his work. He must bury himself in that. And fortunate, indeed, he was, he told himself, that he had something so absorbing.

It was at this point in his meditations that Bertram rounded a corner and came face to face with a man who stopped him short with a jovial:

"Isn't it—by George, it is Bertie Henshaw! Well, what do you think of that for luck?—and me only two days home from 'Gay Paree'!"

"Oh, Seaver! How are you? You *are* a stranger!" Bertram's voice and handshake were a bit more cordial than they would have been had he not at the moment been feeling so abused and forlorn. In the old days he had liked this Bob Seaver well. Seaver was an artist like himself, and was good company always. But Seaver and his crowd were a little too Bohemian for William's taste; and after Billy came, she, too, had objected to what she called "that horrid Seaver man." In his heart, Bertram knew that there was good foundation for their objections, so he had avoided Seaver for a time; and for some years, now, the man had been abroad, somewhat to Bertram's relief. To-night, however, Seaver's genial smile and hearty friendliness were like a sudden burst of sunshine on a rainy day—and Bertram detested rainy days. He was feeling now, too, as if he had just had a whole week of them.

"Yes, I am something of a stranger here," nodded Seaver. "But I tell you what, little old Boston looks mighty good to me, all the same. Come on! You're just the fellow we want. I'm on my way now to the old stamping ground. Come—right about face, old chap, and come with me!"

Bertram shook his head.

"Sorry—but I guess I can't, to-night," he sighed. Both gesture and words were unhesitating, but the voice carried the discontent of a small boy, who, while the sun is still shining, has been told to come into the house.

"Oh, rats! Yes, you can, too. Come on! Lots of the old crowd will be there—Griggs, Beebe, Jack Jenkins, and Tully. We need you to complete the show."

"Jack Jenkins? Is he here?" A new eagerness had come into Bertram's voice.

"Sure! He came on from New York last night. Great boy, Jenkins! Just back from Paris fairly covered with medals, you know."

"Yes, so I hear. I haven't seen him for four years."

"Better come to-night then."

"No-o," began Bertram, with obvious reluctance. "It's already nine o'clock, and—"

"Nine o'clock!" cut in Seaver, with a broad grin. "Since when has your limit been nine o'clock? I've seen the time when you didn't mind nine o'clock in the morning, Bertie! What's got—Oh, I remember. I met another friend of yours in Berlin; chap named Arkwright—and say, he's some singer, you bet! You're going to hear of him one of these days. Well, he told me all about how you'd settled down now—son and heir, fireside bliss, pretty wife, and all the fixings. But, I say, Bertie, doesn't she let you out—*any*?"

"Nonsense, Seaver!" flared Bertram in annoyed wrath.

"Well, then, why don't you come to-night? If you want to see Jenkins you'll have to; he's going back to New York to-morrow."

For only a brief minute longer did Bertram hesitate; then he turned squarely about with an air of finality.

"Is he? Well, then, perhaps I will," he said. "I'd hate to miss Jenkins entirely."

"Good!" exclaimed his companion, as they fell into step. "Have a cigar?"

"Thanks. Don't mind if I do."

If Bertram's chin was a little higher and his step a little more decided than usual, it was all merely by way of accompaniment to his thoughts.

Certainly it was right that he should go, and it was sensible. Indeed, it was really almost imperative—due to Billy, as it were—after that disagreeable taunt of Seaver's. As if she did not want him to go when and where he pleased! As if she would consent for a moment to figure in the eyes of his friends as a tyrannical wife who objected to her husband's passing a social evening with his friends! To be sure, in this particular case, she might not favor Seaver's presence, but even she would not mind this once— and, anyhow, it was Jenkins that was the attraction, not Seaver. Besides, he himself was no undeveloped boy now. He was a man, presumedly able to take care of himself. Besides, again, had not Billy herself told him to go out and enjoy the evening without her, as she had to stay with the baby? He would telephone her, of course, that he had met some old friends, and that he might be late; then she would not worry.

And forthwith, having settled the matter in his mind, and to his complete satisfaction, Bertram gave his undivided attention to Seaver, who had already plunged into an account of a recent Art Exhibition he had attended in Paris.

CHAPTER XXVI
GHOSTS THAT WALKED FOR BERTRAM

October proved to be unusually mild, and about the middle of the month, Bertram, after much unselfish urging on the part of Billy, went to a friend's camp in the Adirondacks for a week's stay. He came back with an angry, lugubrious face—and a broken arm.

"Oh, Bertram! And your right one, too—the same one you broke before!" mourned Billy, tearfully.

"Of course," retorted Bertram, trying in vain to give an air of jauntiness to his reply. "Didn't want to be too changeable, you know!"

"But how did you do it, dear?"

"Fell into a silly little hole covered with underbrush. But—oh, Billy, what's the use? I did it, and I can't undo it—more's the pity!"

"Of course you can't, you poor boy," sympathized Billy; "and you sha'n't be tormented with questions. We'll just be thankful 'twas no worse. You can't paint for a while, of course; but we won't mind that. It'll just give Baby and me a chance to have you all to ourselves for a time, and we'll love that!'

"Yes, of course," sighed Bertram, so abstractedly that Billy bridled with pretty resentment.

"Well, I like your enthusiasm, sir," she frowned. "I'm afraid you don't appreciate the blessings you do have, young man! Did you realize what I said? I remarked that you could be with *Baby* and *me*," she emphasized.

Bertram laughed, and gave his wife an affectionate kiss.

"Indeed I do appreciate my blessings, dear—when those blessings are such treasures as you and Baby, but—" Only his doleful eyes fixed on his injured arm finished his sentence.

"I know, dear, of course, and I understand," murmured Billy, all tenderness at once.

They were not easy for Bertram—those following days. Once again he was obliged to accept the little intimate personal services that he so disliked. Once again he could do nothing but read, or wander disconsolately into his studio and gaze at his half-finished "Face of a Girl." Occasionally, it is true, driven nearly to desperation by the haunting vision in his mind's eye, he picked up a brush and attempted to make his left hand serve his will; but a bare half-dozen irritating, ineffectual strokes were usually enough to make him throw down his brush in disgust. He never could do anything with his left hand, he told himself dejectedly.

Many of his hours, of course, he spent with Billy and his son, and they were happy hours, too; but they always came to be restless ones before the day was half over. Billy was always devotion itself to him—when she was not attending to the baby; he had no fault to find with Billy. And the baby was delightful—he could find no fault with the baby. But the baby *was* fretful—he was teething, Billy said—and he needed a great deal of attention; so, naturally, Bertram drifted out of the nursery, after a time, and went down into his studio, where were his dear, empty palette, his orderly brushes, and his tantalizing "Face of a Girl." From the studio, generally, Bertram went out on to the street.

Sometimes he dropped into a fellow-artist's studio. Sometimes he strolled into a club or café where he knew he would be likely to find some friend who would help him while away a tiresome hour. Bertram's friends quite vied with each other in rendering this sort of aid, so much so, indeed, that—naturally, perhaps—Bertram came to call on their services more and more frequently.

Particularly was this the case when, after the splints were removed, Bertram found, as the days passed, that his arm was not improving as it should improve. This not only disappointed and annoyed him, but worried him. He remembered sundry disquieting warnings given by the physician at the time of the former break—warnings concerning the probable seriousness of a repetition of the injury. To Billy, of course, Bertram said nothing of all this; but just before Christmas he went to see a noted specialist.

An hour later, almost in front of the learned surgeon's door, Bertram met Bob Seaver.

"Great Scott, Bertie, what's up?" ejaculated Seaver. "You look as if you'd seen a ghost."

"I have," answered Bertram, with grim bitterness. "I've seen the ghost of—of every 'Face of a Girl' I ever painted."

"Gorry! So bad as that? No wonder you look as if you'd been disporting in graveyards," chuckled Seaver, laughing at his own joke "What's the matter—arm on a rampage to day?"

He paused for reply, but as Bertram did not answer at once, he resumed, with gay insistence: "Come on! You need cheering up. Suppose we go down to Trentini's and see who's there."

"All right," agreed Bertram, dully. "Suit yourself."

Bertram was not thinking of Seaver, Trentini's, or whom he might find there. Bertram was thinking of certain words he had heard less than half an hour ago. He was wondering, too, if ever again he could think of anything but those words.

"The truth?" the great surgeon had said. "Well, the truth is—I'm sorry to tell you the truth, Mr. Henshaw, but if you will have it—you've painted the last picture you'll ever paint with your right hand, I fear. It's a bad case. This break, coming as it did on top of the serious injury of two or three years ago, was bad enough; but, to make matters worse, the bone was imperfectly set and wrongly treated, which could not be helped, of course, as you were miles away from skilled surgeons at the time of the injury. We'll do the best we can, of course; but—well, you asked for the truth, you remember; so I had to give it to you."

CHAPTER XXVII
THE MOTHER—THE WIFE

Bertram made up his mind at once that, for the present, at least, he would tell no one what the surgeon had said to him. He had placed himself under the man's care, and there was nothing to do but to take the prescribed treatment and await results as patiently as he could. Meanwhile there was no need to worry Billy, or William, or anybody else with the matter.

Billy was so busy with her holiday plans that she was only vaguely aware of what seemed to be an increase of restlessness on the part of her husband during those days just before Christmas.

"Poor dear, is the arm feeling horrid to-day?" she asked one morning, when the gloom on her husband's face was deeper than usual.

Bertram frowned and did not answer directly.

"Lots of good I am these days!" he exclaimed, his moody eyes on the armful of many-shaped, many-sized packages she carried. "What are those for—the tree?"

"Yes; and it's going to be so pretty, Bertram," exulted Billy. "And, do you know, Baby positively acts as if he suspected things—little as he is," she went on eagerly. "He's as nervous as a witch. I can't keep him still a minute!"

"How about his mother?" hinted Bertram, with a faint smile.

Billy laughed.

"Well, I'm afraid she isn't exactly calm herself," she confessed, as she hurried out of the room with her parcels.

Bertram looked after her longingly, despondently.

"I wonder what she'd say if she—knew," he muttered. "But she sha'n't know—till she just has to," he vowed suddenly, under his breath, striding into the hall for his hat and coat.

Never had the Strata known such a Christmas as this was planned to be. Cyril, Marie, and the twins were to be there, also Kate, her husband and three children, Paul, Egbert, and little Kate, from the West. On Christmas Day there was to be a big family dinner, with Aunt Hannah down from the Annex. Then, in concession to the extreme youth of the young host and his twin cousins, there was to be an afternoon tree. The shades were to be drawn and the candles lighted, however, so that there might be no loss of effect. In the evening the tree was to be once more loaded with fascinating packages and candy-bags, and this time the Greggorys, Tommy Dunn, and all the rest from the Annex were to have the fun all over again.

From garret to basement the Strata was aflame with holly, and aglitter with tinsel. Nowhere did there seem to be a spot that did not have its bit of tissue paper or its trail of red ribbon. And everything—holly, ribbon, tissue, and tinsel—led to the mysteriously closed doors of the great front drawing-room, past which none but Billy and her accredited messengers might venture. No wonder, indeed, that even Baby scented excitement, and that Baby's mother was not exactly calm. No wonder, too, that Bertram, with his helpless right arm, and his heavy heart, felt peculiarly forlorn and "out of it." No wonder, also, that he took himself literally out of it with growing frequency.

Mr. and Mrs. Hartwell and little Kate were to stay at the Strata. The boys, Paul and Egbert, were to go to Cyril's. Promptly at the appointed time, two days before Christmas, they arrived. And from that hour until two days after Christmas, when the last bit of holly, ribbon, tissue, and tinsel disappeared from the floor, Billy moved in a whirl of anxious responsibility that was yet filled with fun, frolic, and laughter.

It was a great success, the whole affair. Everybody seemed pleased and happy—that is, everybody but Bertram; and he very plainly tried to seem pleased and happy. Even Cyril unbent to the extent of not appearing to mind the noise one bit; and Sister Kate (Bertram said) found only the extraordinarily small number of four details to change in the arrangements. Baby obligingly let his teeth-getting go, for the occasion, and he and the twins, Franz and Felix, were the admiration and delight of all. Little Kate, to be sure, was a trifle disconcerting once or twice, but everybody was too absorbed to pay much attention to her. Billy did, however, remember her opening remarks.

"Well, little Kate, do you remember me?" Billy had greeted her pleasantly.

"Oh, yes," little Kate had answered, with a winning smile. "You're my Aunt Billy what married my Uncle Bertram instead of Uncle William as you said you would first."

Everybody laughed, and Billy colored, of course; but little Kate went on eagerly:

"And I've been wanting just awfully to see you," she announced.

"Have you? I'm glad, I'm sure. I feel highly flattered," smiled Billy.

"Well, I have. You see, I wanted to ask you something. Have you ever wished that you *had* married Uncle William instead of Uncle Bertram, or that you'd tried for Uncle Cyril before Aunty Marie got him?"

"Kate!" gasped her horrified mother. "I told you—You see," she broke off, turning to Billy despairingly. "She's been pestering me with questions like that ever since she knew she was coming. She never has forgotten the way you changed from one uncle to the other. You may remember; it made a great impression on her at the time."

"Yes, I—I remember," stammered Billy, trying to laugh off her embarrassment.

"But you haven't told me yet whether you did wish you'd married Uncle William, or Uncle Cyril," interposed little Kate, persistently.

"No, no, of course not!" exclaimed Billy, with a vivid blush, casting her eyes about for a door of escape, and rejoicing greatly when she spied Delia with the baby coming toward them. "There, look, my dear, here's your new cousin, little Bertram!" she exclaimed. "Don't you want to see him?"

Little Kate turned dutifully.

"Yes'm, Aunt Billy, but I'd rather see the twins. Mother says *they're* real pretty and cunning."

"Er—y-yes, they are," murmured Billy, on whom the emphasis of the "they're" had not been lost.

Naturally, as may be supposed, therefore, Billy had not forgotten little Kate's opening remarks.

Immediately after Christmas Mr. Hartwell and the boys went back to their Western home, leaving Mrs. Hartwell and her daughter to make a round of visits to friends in the East. For almost a week after Christmas they remained at the Strata; and it was on the last day of their stay that little Kate asked the question that proved so momentous in results.

Billy, almost unconsciously, had avoided tête-á-têtes with her small guest. But to-day they were alone together.

"Aunt Billy," began the little girl, after a meditative gaze into the other's face, "you *are* married to Uncle Bertram, aren't you?"

"I certainly am, my dear," smiled Billy, trying to speak unconcernedly.

"Well, then, what makes you forget it?"

"What makes me forget—Why, child, what a question! What do you mean? I don't forget it!" exclaimed Billy, indignantly.

"Then what *did* mother mean? I heard her tell Uncle William myself—she didn't know I heard, though—that she did wish you'd remember you were Uncle Bertram's wife as well as Cousin Bertram's mother."

Billy flushed scarlet, then grew very white. At that moment Mrs. Hartwell came into the room. Little Kate turned triumphantly.

"There, she hasn't forgotten, and I knew she hadn't, mother! I asked her just now, and she said she hadn't."

"Hadn't what?" questioned Mrs. Hartwell, looking a little apprehensively at her sister-in-law's white face and angry eyes.

"Hadn't forgotten that she was Uncle Bertram's wife."

"Kate," interposed Billy, steadily meeting her sister-in-law's gaze, "will you be good enough to tell me what this child is talking about?"

Mrs. Hartwell sighed, and gave an impatient gesture.

"Kate, I've a mind to take you home on the next train," she said to her daughter. "Run away, now, down-stairs. Your Aunt Billy and I want to talk. Come, come, hurry! I mean what I say," she added warningly, as she saw unmistakable signs of rebellion on the small young face.

"I wish," pouted little Kate, rising reluctantly, and moving toward the door, "that you didn't always send me away just when I wanted most to stay!"

"Well, Kate?" prompted Billy, as the door closed behind the little girl.

"Yes, I suppose I'll have to say it now, as long as that child has put her finger in the pie. But I hadn't intended to speak, no matter what I saw. I promised myself I wouldn't, before I came. I know, of course, how Bertram and Cyril, and William, too, say that I'm always interfering in affairs that don't concern me—though, for that matter, if my own brother's affairs don't concern me, I don't know whose should!

"But, as I said, I wasn't going to speak this time, no matter what I saw. And I haven't—except to William, and Cyril, and Aunt Hannah; but I suppose somewhere little Kate got hold of it. It's simply this, Billy. It seems to me it's high time you began to realize that you're Bertram's wife as well as the baby's mother."

"That, I am—I don't think I quite understand," said Billy, unsteadily.

"No, I suppose you don't," sighed Kate, "though where your eyes are, I don't see—or, rather, I do see: they're on the baby, *always*. It's all very well and lovely, Billy, to be a devoted mother, and you certainly are that. I'll say that much for you, and I'll admit I never thought you would be. But *can't* you see what you're doing to Bertram?"

"*Doing to Bertram!*—by being a devoted mother to his son!"

"Yes, doing to Bertram. Can't you see what a change there is in the boy? He doesn't act like himself at all. He's restless and gloomy and entirely out of sorts."

"Yes, I know; but that's his arm," pleaded Billy. "Poor boy—he's so tired of it!"

Kate shook her head decisively.

"It's more than his arm, Billy. You'd see it yourself if you weren't blinded by your absorption in that baby. Where is Bertram every evening? Where is he daytimes? Do you realize that he's been at home scarcely one evening since I came? And as for the days—he's almost never here."

"But, Kate, he can't paint now, you know, so of course he doesn't need to stay so closely at home," defended Billy. "He goes out to find distraction from himself."

"Yes, 'distraction,' indeed," sniffed Kate. "And where do you suppose he finds it? Do you *know* where he finds it? I tell you, Billy, Bertram Henshaw is not the sort of man that should find too much 'distraction' outside his home. His tastes and his temperament are altogether too Bohemian, and—"

Billy interrupted with a peremptorily upraised hand.

"Please remember, Kate, you are speaking of my husband to his wife; and his wife has perfect confidence in him, and is just a little particular as to what you say."

"Yes; well, I'm speaking of my brother, too, whom I know very well," shrugged Kate. "All is, you may remember sometime that I warned you—that's all. This trusting business is all very pretty; but I think 'twould be a lot prettier, and a vast deal more sensible, if you'd give him a little attention as well as trust, and see if you can't keep him at home a bit more. At least you'll know whom he's with, then. Cyril says he saw him last week with Bob Seaver."

"With—Bob—Seaver?" faltered Billy, changing color.

"Yes. I see you remember him," smiled Kate, not quite agreeably. "Perhaps now you'll take some stock in what I've said, and remember it."

"I'll remember it, certainly," returned Billy, a little proudly. "You've said a good many things to me, in the past, Mrs. Hartwell, and I've remembered them all—every one."

It was Kate's turn to flush, and she did it.

"Yes, I know. And I presume very likely sometimes there *hasn't* been much foundation for what I've said. I think this time, however, you'll find there is," she finished, with an air of hurt dignity.

Billy made no reply, perhaps because Delia, at that moment, brought in the baby.

Mrs. Hartwell and little Kate left the Strata the next morning. Until then Billy contrived to keep, before them, a countenance serene, and a manner free from unrest. Even when, after dinner that evening, Bertram put on his hat and coat and went out, Billy refused to meet her sister-in-law's meaning gaze. But in the morning, after they had left the house, Billy did not attempt to deceive herself. Determinedly, then, she set herself to going over in her mind the past months since the baby came; and she was appalled at what she found. Ever in her ears, too, was that feared name, "Bob Seaver"; and ever before her eyes was that night years ago when, as an eighteen-year-old girl, she had followed Bertram and Bob Seaver into a glittering café at eleven o'clock at night, because Bertram had been drinking and was not himself. She remembered Bertram's face when he had seen her, and what he had said when she begged him to come home. She remembered, too, what the family had said afterward. But she remembered, also, that years later Bertram had told her what that escapade of hers had really done for him, and that he believed he had actually loved her from that moment. After that night, at all events, he had had little to do with Bob Seaver.

And now Seaver was back again, it seemed—and with Bertram. They had been seen together. But if they had, what could she do? Surely she could hardly now follow them into a public café and demand that Seaver let her husband come home! But she could keep him at home, perhaps. (Billy quite brightened at this thought.) Kate had said that she was so absorbed in Baby that her husband received no attention at all. Billy did not believe this was true; but if it were true, she could at least rectify that mistake. If it were attention that he wanted—he should want no more. Poor Bertram! No wonder that he had sought distraction outside! When one had a horrid broken arm that would not let one do anything, what else could one do?

Just here Billy suddenly remembered the book, "A Talk to Young Wives." If she recollected rightly, there was a chapter that covered the very claim Kate had been making. Billy had not thought of the book for months, but she went at once to get it now. There might be, after all, something in it that would help her.

"The Coming of the First Baby." Billy found the chapter without difficulty and settled herself to read, her countenance alight with interest. In a surprisingly short time, however, a new expression came to her face; and at last a little gasp of dismay fell from her lips. She looked up then, with a startled gaze.

Had her walls possessed eyes and ears all these past months, only to give instructions to an unseen hand that it might write what the eyes and ears had learned? For it was such sentences as these that the conscience-smitten Billy read:

"Maternity is apt to work a miracle in a woman's life, but sometimes it spells disaster so far as domestic bliss is concerned. The young mother, wrapped up in the delights and duties of motherhood, utterly forgets that she has a husband. She lives and moves and has her being in the nursery. She thinks baby, talks baby, knows only baby. She refuses to dress up, because it is easier to take care of baby in a frowzy wrapper. She will not go out with her husband for fear something might happen to the baby. She gives up her music because baby won't let her practice. In vain her husband tries to interest her in his own affairs. She has neither eyes nor ears for him, only for baby.

"Now no man enjoys having his nose put out of joint, even by his own child. He loves his child devotedly, and is proud of him, of course; but that does not keep him from wanting the society of his wife occasionally, nor from longing for her old-time love and sympathetic interest. It is an admirable thing, certainly, for a woman to be a devoted mother; but maternal affection can be carried too far. Husbands have some rights as well as offspring; and the wife who neglects her husband for her babies does so at her peril. Home, with the wife eternally in the nursery, is apt to be a dull and lonely thing to the average husband, so he starts out to find amusement for himself—and he finds it. Then is the time when the new little life that is so precious, and that should have bound the two more closely together, becomes the wedge that drives them apart."

Billy did not read any more. With a little sobbing cry she flung the book back into her desk, and began to pull off her wrapper. Her fingers shook. Already she saw herself a Monster, a Wicked Destroyer of Domestic Bliss with her thoughtless absorption in Baby, until he had become that Awful Thing—a *Wedge*. And Bertram—poor Bertram, with his broken arm! She had not played to him, nor sung to him, nor gone out with him. And when had they had one of their good long talks about Bertram's work and plans?

But it should all be changed now. She would play, and sing, and go out with him. She would dress up, too. He should see no more wrappers. She would ask about his work, and seem interested. She *was* interested. She remembered now, that just before he was hurt, he had told her of a new portrait, and of a new "Face of a Girl" that he had planned to do. Lately he had said nothing about these. He had seemed discouraged—and no wonder, with his broken arm! But she would change all that. He should see! And forthwith Billy hurried to her closet to pick out her prettiest house frock.

Long before dinner Billy was ready, waiting in the drawing-room. She had on a pretty little blue silk gown that she knew Bertram liked, and she watched very anxiously for Bertram to come up the steps. She remembered now, with a pang, that he had long since given up his peculiar ring; but she meant to meet him at the door just the same.

Bertram, however, did not come. At a quarter before six he telephoned that he had met some friends, and would dine at the club.

"My, my, how pretty we are!" exclaimed Uncle William, when they went down to dinner together. "New frock?"

"Why, no, Uncle William," laughed Billy, a little tremulously. "You've seen it dozens of times!"

"Have I?" murmured the man. "I don't seem to remember it. Too bad Bertram isn't here to see you. Somehow, you look unusually pretty to-night."

And Billy's heart ached anew.

Billy spent the evening practicing—softly, to be sure, so as not to wake Baby—but *practicing*.

As the days passed Billy discovered that it was much easier to say she would "change things" than it was really to change them. She changed herself, it is true—her clothes, her habits, her words, and her thoughts; but it was more difficult to change Bertram. In the first place, he was there so little. She was dismayed when she saw how very little, indeed, he was at home—and she did not like to ask him outright to stay. That was not in accordance with her plans. Besides, the "Talk to Young Wives" said that indirect influence was much to be preferred, always, to direct persuasion— which last, indeed, usually failed to produce results.

So Billy "dressed up," and practiced, and talked (of anything but the baby), and even hinted shamelessly once or twice that she would like to go to the theater; but all to little avail. True, Bertram brightened up, for a minute, when he came home and found her in a new or a favorite dress, and he told her how pretty she looked. He appeared to like to have her play to him, too, even declaring once or twice that it was quite like old times, yes, it was. But he never noticed her hints about the theater, and he did not seem to like to talk about his work, even a little bit.

Billy laid this last fact to his injured arm. She decided that he had become blue and discouraged, and that he needed cheering up, especially about his work; so she determinedly and systematically set herself to doing it.

She talked of the fine work he had done, and of the still finer work he would yet do, when his arm was well. She told him how proud she was of him, and she let him see how dear his Art was to her, and how badly she would feel if she thought he had really lost all his interest in his work and would never paint again. She questioned him about the new portrait he was to begin as soon as his arm would let him; and she tried to arouse his enthusiasm in the picture he had planned to show in the March Exhibition of the Bohemian Ten, telling him that she was sure his arm would allow him to complete at least one canvas to hang.

In none of this, however, did Bertram appear in the least interested. The one thing, indeed, which he seemed not to want to talk about, was his work; and he responded to her overtures on the subject with only moody silence, or else with almost irritable monosyllables; all of which not only grieved but surprised Billy very much. For, according to the "Talk to Young Wives," she was doing exactly what the ideal, sympathetic, interested-in-her-husband's-work wife should do.

When February came, bringing with it no change for the better, Billy was thoroughly frightened. Bertram's arm plainly was not improving. He was more gloomy and restless than ever. He seemed not to want to stay at home at all; and Billy knew now for a certainty that he was spending more and more time with Bob Seaver and "the boys."

Poor Billy! Nowhere could she look these days and see happiness. Even the adored baby seemed, at times, almost to give an added pang. Had he not become, according to the "Talk to Young Wives" that awful thing, a *Wedge*? The Annex, too, carried its sting; for where was the need of an overflow house for happiness now, when there was no happiness to overflow? Even the little jade idol on Billy's mantel Billy could not bear to see these days, for its once bland smile had become a hideous grin, demanding, "Where, now, is your heap plenty velly good luckee?"

But, before Bertram, Billy still carried a bravely smiling face, and to him still she talked earnestly and enthusiastically of his work—which last, as it happened, was the worst course she could have pursued; for the one thing poor Bertram wished to forget, just now, was—his work.

CHAPTER XXVIII
CONSPIRATORS

Early in February came Arkwright's appearance at the Boston Opera House—the first since he had sung there as a student a few years before. He was an immediate and an unquestioned success. His portrait adorned the front page of almost every Boston newspaper the next morning, and captious critics vied with each other to do him honor. His full history, from boyhood up, was featured, with special emphasis on his recent triumphs in New York and foreign capitals. He was interviewed as to his opinion on everything from vegetarianism to woman's suffrage; and his preferences as to pies and pastimes were given headline prominence. There was no doubt of it. Mr. M. J. Arkwright was a star.

All Arkwright's old friends, including Billy, Bertram, Cyril, Marie, Calderwell, Alice Greggory, Aunt Hannah, and Tommy Dunn, went to hear him sing; and after the performance he held a miniature reception, with enough adulation to turn his head completely around, he declared deprecatingly. Not until the next evening, however, did he have an opportunity for what he called a real talk with any of his friends; then, in Calderwell's room, he settled back in his chair with a sigh of content.

For a time his own and Calderwell's affairs occupied their attention; then, after a short pause, the tenor asked abruptly:

"Is there anything—wrong with the Henshaws, Calderwell?"

Calderwell came suddenly erect in his chair.

"Thank you! I hoped you'd introduce that subject; though, for that matter, if you hadn't, I should. Yes, there is—and I'm looking to you, old man, to get them out of it."

"I?" Arkwright sat erect now.

"Yes."

"What do you mean?"

"In a way, the expected has happened—though I know now that I didn't really expect it to happen, in spite of my prophecies. You may remember I was always skeptical on the subject of Bertram's settling down to a domestic hearthstone. I insisted 'twould be the turn of a girl's head and the curve of her cheek that he wanted to paint."

Arkwright looked up with a quick frown.

"You don't mean that Henshaw has been cad enough to find another—"

Calderwell threw up his hand.

"No, no, not that! We haven't that to deal with—yet, thank goodness! There's no woman in it. And, really, when you come right down to it, if ever a fellow had an excuse to seek diversion, Bertram Henshaw has—poor chap! It's just this. Bertram broke his arm again last October."

"Yes, so I hear, and I thought he was looking badly."

"He is. It's a bad business. 'Twas improperly set in the first place, and it's not doing well now. In fact, I'm told on pretty good authority that the doctor says he probably will never use it again."

"Oh, by George! Calderwell!"

"Yes. Tough, isn't it? 'Specially when you think of his work, and know—as I happen to—that he's particularly dependent on his right hand for everything. He doesn't tell this generally, and I understand Billy and the family know nothing of it—how hopeless the case is, I mean. Well, naturally, the poor fellow has been pretty thoroughly discouraged, and to get away from himself he's gone back to his old Bohemian habits, spending much of his time with some of his old cronies that are none too good for him—Seaver, for instance."

"Bob Seaver? Yes, I know him." Arkwright's lips snapped together crisply.

"Yes. He said he knew you. That's why I'm counting on your help."

"What do you mean?"

"I mean I want you to get Henshaw away from him, and keep him away."

Arkwright's face darkened with an angry flush.

"Great Scott, Calderwell! What are you talking about? Henshaw is no kid to be toted home, and I'm no nursery governess to do the toting!"

Calderwell laughed quietly.

"No; I don't think any one would take you for a nursery governess, Arkwright, in spite of the fact that you are still known to some of your friends as 'Mary Jane.' But you can sing a song, man, which will promptly give you a through ticket to their innermost sacred circle. In fact, to my certain knowledge, Seaver is already planning a jamboree with you at the right hand of the toastmaster. There's your chance. Once in, stay in—long enough to get Henshaw out."

"But, good heavens, Calderwell, it's impossible! What can I do?" demanded Arkwright, savagely. "I can't walk up to the man, take him by the ear, and say: 'Here, you, sir—march home!' Neither can I come the 'I-am-holier-than-thou' act, and hold up to him the mirror of his transgressions."

"No, but you can get him out of it *some* way. You can find a way—for Billy's sake."

There was no answer, and, after a moment, Calderwell went on more quietly.

"I haven't seen Billy but two or three times since I came back to Boston—but I don't need to, to know that she's breaking her heart over something. And of course that something is—Bertram."

There was still no answer. Arkwright got up suddenly, and walked to the window.

"You see, I'm helpless," resumed Calderwell. "I don't paint pictures, nor sing songs, nor write stories, nor dance jigs for a living—and you have to do one or another to be in with that set. And it's got to be a Johnny-on-the-spot with Bertram. All is, something will have to be done to get him out of the state of mind and body he's in now, or—"

Arkwright wheeled sharply.

"When did you say this jamboree was going to be?" he demanded.

"Next week, some time. The date is not settled. They were going to consult you."

"Hm-m," commented Arkwright. And, though his next remark was a complete change of subject, Calderwell gave a contented sigh.

If, when the proposition was first made to him, Arkwright was doubtful of his ability to be a successful "Johnny-on-the-spot," he was even more doubtful of it as the days passed, and he was attempting to carry out the suggestion.

He had known that he was undertaking a most difficult and delicate task, and he soon began to fear that it was an impossible one, as well. With a dogged persistence, however, he adhered to his purpose, ever on the alert to be more watchful, more tactful, more efficient in emergencies.

Disagreeable as was the task, in a way, in another way it was a great pleasure to him. He was glad of the opportunity to do anything for Billy; and then, too, he was glad of something absorbing enough to take his mind off his own affairs. He told himself, sometimes, that this helping another man to fight his tiger skin was assisting himself to fight his own.

Arkwright was trying very hard not to think of Alice Greggory these days. He had come back hoping that he was in a measure "cured" of his "folly," as he termed it; but the first look into Alice Greggory's blue-gray eyes had taught him the fallacy of that idea. In that very first meeting with Alice, he feared that he had revealed his secret, for she was plainly so nervously distant and ill at ease with him that he could but construe her embarrassment and chilly dignity as pity for him and a desire to show him that she had nothing but friendship for him. Since then he had seen but little of her, partly because he did not wish to see her, and partly because his time was so fully occupied. Then, too, in a round-about way he had heard a rumor that Calderwell was engaged to be married; and, though no feminine name had been mentioned in connection with the story, Arkwright had not hesitated to supply in his own mind that of Alice Greggory.

Beginning with the "jamboree," which came off quite in accordance with Calderwell's prophecies, Arkwright spent the most of such time as was not given to his professional duties in deliberately cultivating the society of Bertram and his friends. To this extent he met with no difficulty, for he found that M. J. Arkwright, the new star in the operatic firmament, was obviously a welcome comrade. Beyond this it was not so easy. Arkwright wondered, indeed, sometimes, if he were making any progress at all. But still he persevered.

He walked with Bertram, he talked with Bertram, unobtrusively he contrived to be near Bertram almost always, when they were together with "the boys." Gradually he won from him the story of what the surgeon had said to him, and of how black the future looked in consequence. This established a new bond between them, so potent that Arkwright ventured to test it one day by telling Bertram the story of the tiger skin—the first tiger skin in his uncle's library years ago, and of how, since then, any difficulty he had encountered he had tried to treat as a tiger skin. In telling the story he was careful to draw no moral for his listener, and to preach no sermon. He told the tale, too, with all possible whimsical lightness of touch, and immediately at its conclusion he changed the subject. But that he had not failed utterly in his design was evidenced a few days later when Bertram grimly declared that he guessed *his* tiger skin was a lively beast, all right.

The first time Arkwright went home with Bertram, his presence was almost a necessity. Bertram was not quite himself that night. Billy admitted them. She had plainly been watching and waiting. Arkwright never forgot the look on her face as her eyes met his. There was a curious mixture of terror, hurt pride, relief, and shame, overtopped by a fierce loyalty which almost seemed to say aloud the words: "Don't you dare to blame him!"

Arkwright's heart ached with sympathy and admiration at the proudly courageous way in which Billy carried off the next few painful minutes. Even when he bade her good night a little later, only her eyes said "thank you." Her lips were dumb.

Arkwright often went home with Bertram after that. Not that it was always necessary—far from it. Some time, indeed, elapsed before he had quite the same excuse again for his presence. But he had found that occasionally he could get Bertram home earlier by adroit suggestions of one kind or another; and more and more frequently he was succeeding in getting him home for a game of chess.

Bertram liked chess, and was a fine player. Since breaking his arm he had turned to games with the feverish eagerness of one who looks for something absorbing to fill an unrestful mind. It was Seaver's skill in chess that had at first attracted Bertram to the man long ago; but Bertram could beat him easily—too easily for much pleasure in it now. So they did not play chess often these days. Bertram had found that, in spite of his injury, he could still take part in other games, and some of them, if not so intricate as chess, were at least more apt to take his mind off himself, especially if there were a bit of money up to add zest and interest.

As it happened, however, Bertram learned one day that Arkwright could play chess—and play well, too, as he discovered after their first game together. This fact contributed not a little to such success as Arkwright was having in his efforts to wean Bertram from his undesirable companions; for Bertram soon found out that Arkwright was more than a match for himself, and the occasional games he did succeed in winning only whetted his appetite for more. Many an evening now, therefore, was spent by the two men in Bertram's den, with Billy anxiously hovering near, her eyes longingly watching either her husband's absorbed face or the pretty little red and white ivory figures, which seemed to possess so wonderful a power to hold his attention. In spite of her joy at the chessmen's efficacy in keeping Bertram at home, however, she was almost jealous of them.

"Mr. Arkwright, couldn't you show *me* how to play, sometime?" she said wistfully, one evening, when the momentary absence of Bertram had left the two alone together. "I used to watch Bertram and Marie play years ago; but I never knew how to play myself. Not that I can see where the fun is in just sitting staring at a chessboard for half an hour at a time, though! But Bertram likes it, and so I—I want to learn to stare with him. Will you teach me?"

"I should be glad to," smiled Arkwright.

"Then will you come, maybe, sometimes when Bertram is at the doctor's? He goes every Tuesday and Friday at three o'clock for treatment. I'd rather you came then for two reasons: first, because I don't want Bertram to know I'm learning, till I can play *some*; and, secondly, because—because I don't want to take you away—from him."

The last words were spoken very low, and were accompanied by a painful blush. It was the first time Billy had ever hinted to Arkwright, in words, that she understood what he was trying to do.

"I'll come next Tuesday," promised Arkwright, with a cheerfully unobservant air. Then Bertram came in, bringing the book of Chess Problems, for which he had gone up-stairs.

CHAPTER XXIX
CHESS

Promptly at three o'clock Tuesday afternoon Arkwright appeared at the Strata, and for the next hour Billy did her best to learn the names and the moves of the pretty little ivory men. But at the end of the hour she was almost ready to give up in despair.

"If there weren't so many kinds, and if they didn't all insist on doing something different, it wouldn't be so bad," she sighed. "But how can you be expected to remember which goes diagonal, and which crisscross, and which can't go but one square, and which can skip 'way across the board, 'specially when that little pawn-thing can go straight ahead *two* squares sometimes, and the next minute only one (except when it takes things, and then it goes crooked one square) and when that tiresome little horse tries to go all ways at once, and can jump 'round and hurdle over *anybody's* head, even the king's—how can you expect folks to remember? But, then, Bertram remembers," she added, resolutely, "so I guess I can."

Whenever possible, after that, Arkwright came on Tuesdays and Fridays, and, in spite of her doubts, Billy did very soon begin to "remember." Spurred by her great desire to play with Bertram and surprise him, Billy spared no pains to learn well her lessons. Even among the baby's books and playthings these days might be found a "Manual of Chess," for Billy pursued her study at all hours; and some nights even her dreams were of ruined, castles where kings and queens and bishops disported themselves, with pawns for servants, and where a weird knight on horseback used the castle's highest tower for a hurdle, landing always a hundred yards to one side of where he would be expected to come down.

It was not long, of course, before Billy could play a game of chess, after a fashion, but she knew just enough to realize that she actually knew nothing; and she knew, too, that until she could play a really good game, her moves would not hold Bertram's attention for one minute. Not at present, therefore, was she willing Bertram should know what she was attempting to do.

Billy had not yet learned what the great surgeon had said to Bertram. She knew only that his arm was no better, and that he never voluntarily spoke of his painting. Over her now seemed to be hanging a vague horror. Something was the matter. She knew that. But what it was she could not fathom. She realized that Arkwright was trying to help, and her gratitude, though silent, knew no bounds. Not even to Aunt Hannah or Uncle William could she speak of this thing that was troubling her. That they, too, understood, in a measure, she realized. But still she said no word. Billy was wearing a proud little air of aloofness these days that was heart-breaking to those who saw it and read it aright for what it was: loyalty to Bertram, no matter what happened. And so Billy pored over her chessboard feverishly, tirelessly, having ever before her longing eyes the dear time when Bertram, across the table from her, should sit happily staring for half an hour at a move she had made.

Whatever Billy's chess-playing was to signify, however, in her own life, it was destined to play a part in the lives of two friends of hers that was most unexpected.

During Billy's very first lesson, as it chanced, Alice Greggory called and found Billy and Arkwright so absorbed in their game that they did not at first hear Eliza speak her name.

The quick color that flew to Arkwright's face at sight of herself was construed at once by Alice as embarrassment on his part at being found tête-á-tête with Bertram Henshaw's wife. And she did not like it. She was not pleased that he was there. She was less pleased that he blushed for being there.

It so happened that Alice found him there again several times. Alice gave a piano lesson at two o'clock every Tuesday and Friday afternoon to a little Beacon Street neighbor of Billy's, and she had fallen into the habit of stepping in to see Billy for a few minutes afterward, which brought her there at a little past three, just after the chess lesson was well started.

If, the first time that Alice Greggory found Arkwright opposite Billy at the chess-table, she was surprised and displeased, the second and third times she was much more so. When it finally came to her one day with sickening illumination, that always the tête-á-têtes were during Bertram's hour at the doctor's, she was appalled.

What could it mean? Had Arkwright given up his fight? Was he playing false to himself and to Bertram by trying thus, on the sly, to win the love of his friend's wife? Was this man, whom she had so admired for his brave stand, and to whom all unasked she had given her heart's best love (more the pity of it!)—was this idol of hers to show feet of clay, after all? She could not believe it. And yet—

Sick at heart, but imbued with the determination of a righteous cause, Alice Greggory resolved, for Billy's sake, to watch and wait. If necessary she should speak to some one—though to whom she did not know. Billy's happiness should not be put in jeopardy if she could help it. Indeed, no!

As the weeks passed, Alice came to be more and more uneasy, distressed, and grieved. Of Billy she could believe no evil; but of Arkwright she was beginning to think she could believe everything that was dishonorable and despicable. And to believe that of the man she still loved—no wonder that Alice did not look nor act like herself these days.

Incensed at herself because she did love him, angry at him because he seemed to be proving himself so unworthy of that love, and genuinely frightened at what she thought was the fast-approaching wreck of all happiness for her dear friend, Billy, Alice did not know which way to turn. At the first she had told herself confidently that she would "speak to somebody." But, as time passed, she saw the impracticability of that idea. Speak to somebody, indeed! To whom? When? Where? What should she say? Where was her right to say anything? She was not dealing with a parcel of naughty children who had pilfered the cake jar! She was dealing with grown men and women, who, presumedly, knew their own affairs, and who, certainly, would resent any interference from her. On the other hand, could she stand calmly by and see Bertram lose his wife, Arkwright his honor, Billy her happiness, and herself her faith in human nature, all because to do otherwise would be to meddle in other people's business? Apparently she could, and should. At least that seemed to be the rôle which she was expected to play.

It was when Alice had reached this unhappy frame of mind that Arkwright himself unexpectedly opened the door for her.

The two were alone together in Bertram Henshaw's den. It was Tuesday afternoon. Alice had called to find Billy and Arkwright deep in their usual game of chess. Then a matter of domestic affairs had taken Billy from the room.

"I'm afraid I'll have to be gone ten minutes, or more," she had said, as she rose from the table reluctantly. "But you might be showing Alice the moves, Mr. Arkwright," she had added, with a laugh, as she disappeared.

"Shall I teach you the moves?" he had smiled, when they were alone together.

Alice's reply had been so indignantly short and sharp that Arkwright, after a moment's pause, had said, with a whimsical smile that yet carried a touch of sadness:

"I am forced to surmise from your answer that you think it is *you* who should be teaching *me* moves. At all events, I seem to have been making some moves lately that have not suited you, judging by your actions. Have I offended you in any way, Alice?"

The girl turned with a quick lifting of her head. Alice knew that if ever she were to speak, it must be now. Never again could she hope for such an opportunity as this. Suddenly throwing circumspect caution quite aside, she determined that she would speak. Springing to her feet she crossed the room and seated herself in Billy's chair at the chess-table.

"Me! Offend me!" she exclaimed, in a low voice. "As if I were the one you were offending!"

"Why, *Alice!*" murmured the man, in obvious stupefaction.

Alice raised her hand, palm outward.

"Now don't, *please* don't pretend you don't know," she begged, almost piteously. "Please don't add that to all the rest. Oh, I understand, of course, it's none of my affairs, and I wasn't going to speak," she choked; "but, to-day, when you gave me this chance, I had to. At first I couldn't believe it," she plunged on, plainly hurrying against Billy's return. "After all you'd told me of how you meant to fight it—your tiger skin. And I thought it merely *happened* that you were here alone with her those days I came. Then, when I found out they were *always* the days Mr. Henshaw was away at the doctor's, I had to believe."

She stopped for breath. Arkwright, who, up to this moment had shown that he was completely mystified as to what she was talking about, suddenly flushed a painful red. He was obviously about to speak, but she prevented him with a quick gesture.

"There's a little more I've got to say, please. As if it weren't bad enough to do what you're doing *at all*, but you must needs take it at such a time as this when—when her husband *isn't* doing just what he ought to do, and we all know it—it's so unfair to take her now, and try to—to win—And you aren't even fair with him," she protested tremulously. "You pretend to be his friend. You go with him everywhere. It's just as if you were *helping* to—to pull him down. You're one with the whole bunch." (The blood suddenly receded from Arkwright's face, leaving it very white; but if Alice saw it, she paid no heed.) "Everybody says you are. Then to come here like this, on the sly, when you know he can't be here, I—Oh, can't you see what you're doing?"

There was a moment's pause, then Arkwright spoke. A deep pain looked from his eyes. He was still very pale, and his mouth had settled into sad lines.

"I think, perhaps, it may be just as well if I tell you what I *am* doing—or, rather, trying to do," he said quietly.

Then he told her.

"And so you see," he added, when he had finished the tale, "I haven't really accomplished much, after all, and it seems the little I have accomplished has only led to my being misjudged by you, my best friend."

Alice gave a sobbing cry. Her face was scarlet. Horror, shame, and relief struggled for mastery in her countenance.

"Oh, but I didn't know, I didn't know," she moaned, twisting her hands nervously. "And now, when you've been so brave, so true—for me to accuse you of—Oh, can you *ever* forgive me? But you see, knowing that you *did* care for her, it did look—" She choked into silence, and turned away her head.

He glanced at her tenderly, mournfully.

"Yes," he said, after a minute, in a low voice. "I can see how it did look; and so I'm going to tell you now something I had meant never to tell you. There really couldn't have been anything in that, you see, for I found out long ago that it was gone—whatever love there had been for—Billy."

"But your—tiger skin!"

"Oh, yes, I thought it was alive," smiled Arkwright, sadly, "when I asked you to help me fight it. But one day, very suddenly, I discovered that it was nothing but a dead skin of dreams and memories. But I made another discovery, too. I found that just beyond lay another one, and that was very much alive."

"Another one?" Alice turned to him in wonder. "But you never asked me to help you fight—that one!"

He shook his head.

"No; I couldn't, you see. You couldn't have helped me. You'd only have hindered me."

"Hindered you?"

"Yes. You see, it was my love for—you, that I was fighting—then."

Alice gave a low cry and flushed vividly; but Arkwright hurried on, his eyes turned away.

"Oh, I understand. I know. I'm not asking for—anything. I heard some time ago of your engagement to Calderwell. I've tried many times to say the proper, expected pretty speeches, but—I couldn't. I will now, though. I do. You have all my tenderest best wishes for your happiness—dear. If long ago I hadn't been such a blind fool as not to know my own heart—"

"But—but there's some mistake," interposed Alice, palpitatingly, with hanging head. "I—I'm not engaged to Mr. Calderwell."

Arkwright turned and sent a keen glance into her face.

"You're—not?"

"No."

"But I heard that Calderwell—" He stopped helplessly.

"You heard that Mr. Calderwell was engaged, very likely. But—it so happens he isn't engaged—to me," murmured Alice, faintly.

"But, long ago you said—" Arkwright paused, his eyes still keenly searching her face.

"Never mind what I said—long ago," laughed Alice, trying unsuccessfully to meet his gaze. "One says lots of things, at times, you know."

Into Arkwright's eyes came a new light, a light that plainly needed but a breath to fan it into quick fire.

"Alice," he said softly, "do you mean that maybe now—I needn't try to fight—that other tiger skin?"

There was no answer.

Arkwright reached out a pleading hand.

"Alice, dear, I've loved you so long," he begged unsteadily. "Don't you think that sometime, if I was very, very patient, you could just *begin*—to care a little for me?"

Still there was no answer. Then, slowly, Alice shook her head. Her face was turned quite away—which was a pity, for if Arkwright could have seen the sudden tender mischief in her eyes, his own would not have become so somber.

"Not even a little bit?"

"I couldn't ever—begin," answered a half-smothered voice.

"Alice!" cried the man, heart-brokenly.

Alice turned now, and for a fleeting instant let him see her eyes, glowing with the love so long kept in relentless exile.

"I couldn't, because, you see-I began—long ago," she whispered.

"Alice!" It was the same single word, but spoken with a world of difference, for into it now was crowded all the glory and the wonder of a great love. "Alice!" breathed the man again; and this time the word was, oh, so tenderly whispered into the little pink and white ear of the girl in his arms.

"I got delayed," began Billy, in the doorway.

"Oh-h!" she broke off, beating a hushed, but precipitate, retreat.

Fully thirty minutes later, Billy came to the door again. This time her approach was heralded by a snatch of song.

"I hope you'll excuse my being gone so long," she smiled, as she entered the room where her two guests sat decorously face to face at the chess-table.

"Well, you know you said you'd be gone ten minutes," Arkwright reminded her, politely.

"Yes, I know I did." And Billy, to her credit, did not even smile at the man who did not know ten minutes from fifty.

CHAPTER XXX
BY A BABY'S HAND

After all, it was the baby's hand that did it, as was proper, and perhaps to be expected; for surely, was it not Bertram, Jr.'s place to show his parents that he was, indeed, no Wedge, but a dear and precious Tie binding two loving, loyal hearts more and more closely together? It would seem, indeed, that Bertram, Jr., thought so, perhaps, and very bravely he set about it; though, to carry out his purpose, he had to turn his steps into an unfamiliar way—a way of pain, and weariness, and danger.

It was Arkwright who told Bertram that the baby was very sick, and that Billy wanted him. Bertram went home at once to find a distracted, white-faced Billy, and a twisted, pain-racked little creature, who it was almost impossible to believe was the happy, laughing baby boy he had left that morning.

For the next two weeks nothing was thought of in the silent old Beacon Street house but the tiny little life hovering so near Death's door that twice it appeared to have slipped quite across the threshold. All through those terrible weeks it seemed as if Billy neither ate nor slept; and always at her side, comforting, cheering, and helping wherever possible was Bertram, tender, loving, and marvelously thoughtful.

Then came the turning point when the universe itself appeared to hang upon a baby's breath. Gradually, almost imperceptibly, came the fluttering back of the tiny spirit into the longing arms stretched so far, far out to meet and hold it. And the father and the mother, looking into each other's sleepless, dark-ringed eyes, knew that their son was once more theirs to love and cherish.

When two have gone together with a dear one down into the Valley of the Shadow of Death, and have come back, either mourning or rejoicing, they find a different world from the one they had left. Things that were great before seem small, and some things that were small seem great. At least Bertram and Billy found their world thus changed when together they came back bringing their son with them.

In the long weeks of convalescence, when the healthy rosiness stole bit by bit into the baby's waxen face, and the light of recognition and understanding crept day by day into the baby's eyes, there was many a quiet hour for heart-to-heart talks between the two who so anxiously and joyously hailed every rosy tint and fleeting sparkle. And there was so much to tell, so much to hear, so much to talk about! And always, running through everything, was that golden thread of joy, beside which all else paled—that they had Baby and each other. As if anything else mattered!

To be sure, there was Bertram's arm. Very early in their talks Billy found out about that. But Billy, with Baby getting well, was not to be daunted, even by this.

"Nonsense, darling—not paint again, indeed! Why, Bertram, of course you will," she cried confidently.

"But, Billy, the doctor said," began Bertram; but Billy would not even listen.

"Very well, what if he did, dear?" she interrupted. "What if he did say you couldn't use your right arm much again?" Billy's voice broke a little, then quickly steadied into something very much like triumph. "You've got your left one!"

Bertram shook his head.

"I can't paint with that."

"Yes, you can," insisted Billy, firmly. "Why, Bertram, what do you suppose you were given two arms for if not to fight with both of them? And I'm going to be ever so much prouder of what you paint now, because I'll know how splendidly you worked to do it. Besides, there's Baby. As if you weren't ever going to paint for Baby! Why, Bertram, I'm going to have you paint Baby, one of these days. Think how pleased he'll be to see it when he grows up! He's nicer, anyhow, than any old 'Face of a Girl' you ever did. Paint? Why, Bertram, darling, of course you're going to paint, and better than you ever did before!"

Bertram shook his head again; but this time he smiled, and patted Billy's cheek with the tip of his forefinger.

"As if I could!" he disclaimed. But that afternoon he went into his long-deserted studio and hunted up his last unfinished picture. For some time he stood motionless before it; then, with a quick gesture of determination, he got out his palette, paints, and brushes. This time not until he had painted ten, a dozen, a score of strokes, did he drop his brush with a sigh and carefully erase the fresh paint on the canvas. The next day he worked longer, and this time he allowed a little, a very little, of what he had done to remain.

The third day Billy herself found him at his easel.

"I wonder—do you suppose I could?" he asked fearfully.

"Why, dearest, of course you can! Haven't you noticed? Can't you see how much more you can do with your left hand now? You've *had* to use it, you see. *I've* seen you do a lot of things with it, lately, that you never used to do at all. And, of course, the more you do with it, the more you can!"

"I know; but that doesn't mean that I can paint with it," sighed Bertram, ruefully eyeing the tiny bit of fresh color his canvas showed for his long afternoon's work.

"You wait and see," nodded Billy, with so overwhelming a cheery confidence that Bertram, looking into her glowing face, was conscious of a curious throb of exultation, almost as if already the victory were his.

But it was not always of Bertram's broken arm, nor even of his work that they talked. Bertram, hanging over the baby's crib to assure himself that the rosiness and the sparkle were really growing more apparent every day, used to wonder sometimes how ever in the world he could have been jealous of his son. He said as much one day to Billy.

To Billy it was a most astounding idea.

"You mean you were actually jealous of your own baby?" she gasped. "Why, Bertram, how could—And was that why you—you sought distraction and—Oh, but, Bertram, that was all my f-fault," she quavered remorsefully. "I wouldn't play, nor sing, nor go to walk, nor anything; and I wore horrid frowzy wrappers all the time, and—"

"Oh, come, come, Billy," expostulated the man. "I'm not going to have you talk like that about *my wife!*"

"But I did—the book said I did," wailed Billy.

"The book? Good heavens! Are there any books in this, too?" demanded Bertram.

"Yes, the same one; the—the 'Talks to Young Wives,'" nodded Billy. And then, because some things had grown small to them, and some others great, they both laughed happily.

But even this was not quite all; for one evening, very shyly, Billy brought out the chessboard.

"Of course I can't play well," she faltered; "and maybe you don't want to play with me at all."

But Bertram, when he found out why she had learned, was very sure he did want very much to play with her.

Billy did not beat, of course. But she did several times experience—for a few blissful minutes—the pleasure of seeing Bertram sit motionless, studying the board, because of a move she had made. And though, in the end, her king was ignominiously trapped with not an unguarded square upon which to set his poor distracted foot, the memory of those blissful minutes when she had made Bertram "stare" more than paid for the final checkmate.

By the middle of June the baby was well enough to be taken to the beach, and Bertram was so fortunate as to secure the same house they had occupied before. Once again William went down in Maine for his fishing trip, and the Strata was closed. In the beach house Bertram was painting industriously—with his left hand. Almost he was beginning to feel Billy's enthusiasm. Almost he was believing that he *was* doing good work. It was not the "Face of a Girl," now. It was the face of a baby: smiling, laughing, even crying, sometimes; at other times just gazing straight into your eyes with adorable soberness. Bertram still went into Boston twice a week for treatment, though the treatment itself had changed. The great surgeon had sent him to still another specialist.

"There's a chance—though perhaps a small one," he had said. "I'd like you to try it, anyway."

As the summer advanced, Bertram thought sometimes that he could see a slight improvement in his injured arm; but he tried not to think too much about this. He had thought the same thing before, only to be disappointed in the end. Besides, he was undeniably interested just now in seeing if he *could* paint with his left hand. Billy was so sure, and she had said that she would be prouder than ever of him, if he could—and he would like to make Billy proud! Then, too, there was the baby—he had no idea a baby could be so interesting to paint. He was not sure but that he was going to like to paint babies even better than he had liked to paint his "Face of a Girl" that had brought him his first fame.

In September the family returned to the Strata. The move was made a little earlier this year on account of Alice Greggory's wedding.

Alice was to be married in the pretty living-room at the Annex, just where Billy herself had been married a few short years before; and Billy had great plans for the wedding—not all of which she was able to carry out, for Alice, like Marie before her, had very strong objections to being placed under too great obligations.

"And you see, really, anyway," she told Billy, "I owe the whole thing to you, to begin with—even my husband."

"Nonsense! Of course you don't," disputed Billy.

"But I do. If it hadn't been for you I should never have found him again, and of course I shouldn't have had this dear little home to be married in. And I never could have left mother if she hadn't had Aunt Hannah and the Annex which means you. And if I hadn't found Mr. Arkwright, I might never have known how—how I could go back to my old home (as I am going on my honeymoon trip), and just know that every one of my old friends who shakes hands with me isn't pitying me now, because I'm my father's daughter. And that means you; for you see I never would have known that my father's name was cleared if it hadn't been for you. And—"

"Oh, Alice, please, please," begged Billy, laughingly raising two protesting hands. "Why don't you say that it's to me you owe just breathing, and be done with it?"

"Well, I will, then," avowed Alice, doggedly. "And it's true, too, for, honestly, my dear, I don't believe I would have been breathing to-day, nor mother, either, if you hadn't found us that morning, and taken us out of those awful rooms."

"I? Never! You wouldn't let me take you out," laughed Billy. "You proud little thing! Maybe you've forgotten how you turned poor Uncle William and me out into the cold, cold world that morning, just because we dared to aspire to your Lowestoft teapot; but I haven't!"

"Oh, Billy, please, don't," begged Alice, the painful color staining her face. "If you knew how I've hated myself since for the way I acted that day—and, really, you did take us away from there, you know."

"No, I didn't. I merely found two good tenants for Mr. and Mrs. Delano," corrected Billy, with a sober face.

"Oh, yes, I know all about that," smiled Alice, affectionately; "and you got mother and me here to keep Aunt Hannah company and teach Tommy Dunn; and you got Aunt Hannah here to keep us company and take care of Tommy Dunn; and you got Tommy Dunn here so Aunt Hannah and we could have somebody to teach and take care of; and, as for the others,—" But Billy put her hands to her ears and fled.

The wedding was to be on the fifteenth. From the West Kate wrote that of course it was none of her affairs, particularly as neither of the interested parties was a relation, but still she should think that for a man in Mr. Arkwright's position, nothing but a church wedding would do at all, as, of course, he did, in a way, belong to the public. Alice, however, declared that perhaps he did belong to the public, when he was Don Somebody-or-other in doublet and hose; but when he was just plain Michael Jeremiah Arkwright in a frock coat he was hers, and she did not propose to make a Grand Opera show of her wedding. And as Arkwright, too, very much disapproved of the church-wedding idea, the two were married in the Annex living-room at noon on the fifteenth as originally planned, in spite of Mrs. Kate Hartwell's letter.

It was soon after the wedding that Bertram told Billy he wished she would sit for him with Bertram, Jr.

"I want to try my hand at you both together," he coaxed.

"Why, of course, if you like, dear," agreed Billy, promptly, "though I think Baby is just as nice, and even nicer, alone."

Once again all over Bertram's studio began to appear sketches of Billy, this time a glorified, tender Billy, with the wonderful mother-love in her eyes. Then, after several sketches of trial poses, Bertram began his picture of Billy and the baby together.

Even now Bertram was not sure of his work. He knew that he could not yet paint with his old freedom and ease; he knew that his stroke was not so sure, so untrammeled. But he knew, too, that he had gained wonderfully, during the summer, and that he was gaining now, every day. To Billy he said nothing of all this. Even to himself he scarcely put his hope into words; but in his heart he knew that what he was really painting his "Mother and Child" picture for was the Bohemian Ten Club Exhibition in March—if he could but put upon canvas the vision that was spurring him on.

And so Bertram worked all through those short winter days, not always upon the one picture, of course, but upon some picture or sketch that would help to give his still uncertain left hand the skill that had belonged to its mate. And always, cheering, encouraging, insisting on victory, was Billy, so that even had Bertram been tempted, sometimes, to give up, he could not have done so—and faced Billy's grieved, disappointed eyes. And when at last his work was completed, and the pictured mother and child in all their marvelous life and beauty seemed ready to step from the canvas, Billy drew a long ecstatic breath.

"Oh, Bertram, it *is*, it is the best work you have ever done." Billy was looking at the baby. Always she had ignored herself as part of the picture. "And won't it be fine for the Exhibition!"

Bertram's hand tightened on the chair-back in front of him. For a moment he could not speak. Then, a bit huskily, he asked:

"Would you dare—risk it?"

"Risk it! Why, Bertram Henshaw, I've meant that picture for the Exhibition from the very first—only I never dreamed you could get it so perfectly lovely. *Now* what do you say about Baby being nicer than any old 'Face of a Girl' that you ever did?" she triumphed.

And Bertram, who, even to himself, had not dared whisper the word exhibition, gave a tremulous laugh that was almost a sob, so overwhelming was his sudden realization of what faith and confidence had meant to Billy, his wife.

If there was still a lingering doubt in Bertram's mind, it must have been dispelled in less than an hour after the Bohemian Ten Club Exhibition flung open its doors on its opening night. Once again Bertram found his picture the cynosure of all admiring eyes, and himself the center of an enthusiastic group of friends and fellow-artists who vied with each other in hearty words of congratulation. And when, later, the feared critics, whose names and opinions counted for so much in his world, had their say in the daily press and weekly reviews, Bertram knew how surely indeed he had won. And when he read that "Henshaw's work shows now a peculiar strength, a sort of reserve power, as it were, which, beautiful as was his former work, it never showed before," he smiled grimly, and said to Billy:

"I suppose, now, that was the fighting I did with my good left hand, eh, dear?"

But there was yet one more drop that was to make Bertram's cup of joy brim to overflowing. It came just one month after the Exhibition in the shape of a terse dozen words from the doctor. Bertram fairly flew home that day. He had no consciousness of any means of locomotion. He thought he was going to tell his wife at once his great good news; but when he saw her, speech suddenly fled, and all that he could do was to draw her closely to him with his left arm and hide his face.

"Why, Bertram, dearest, what—what is it?" stammered the thoroughly frightened Billy. "Has anything-happened?"

"No, no—yes—yes, everything has happened. I mean, it's going to happen," choked the man. "Billy, that old chap says that I'm going to have my arm again. Think of it—my good right arm that I've lost so long!"

"*Oh, Bertram!*" breathed Billy. And she, too, fell to sobbing.

Later, when speech was more coherent, she faltered:

"Well, anyway, it doesn't make any difference *how* many beautiful pictures you p-paint, after this, Bertram, I *can't* be prouder of any than I am of the one your l—left hand did."

"Oh, but I have you to thank for all that, dear."

"No, you haven't," disputed Billy, blinking teary eyes; "but—" she paused, then went on spiritedly, "but, anyhow, I—I don't believe any one—not even Kate—can say *now* that—that I've been a hindrance to you in your c-career!"

"Hindrance!" scoffed Bertram, in a tone that left no room for doubt, and with a kiss that left even less, if possible.

Billy, for still another minute, was silent; then, with a wistfulness that was half playful, half serious, she sighed:

"Bertram, I believe being married is something like clocks, you know, 'specially at the first."

"Clocks, dear?"

"Yes. I was out to Aunt Hannah's to-day. She was fussing with her clock—the one that strikes half an hour ahead—and I saw all those quantities of wheels, little and big, that have to go just so, with all the little cogs fitting into all the other little cogs just exactly right. Well, that's like marriage. See? There's such a lot of little cogs in everyday life that have to be fitted so they'll run smoothly—that have to be adjusted, 'specially at the first."

"Oh, Billy, what an idea!"

"But it's so, really, Bertram. Anyhow, I know my cogs were always getting out of place at the first," laughed Billy. "And I was like Aunt Hannah's clock, too, always going off half an hour ahead of time. And maybe I shall be so again, sometimes. But, Bertram,"—her voice shook a little—"if you'll just look at my face you'll see that I tell the right time there, just as Aunt Hannah's clock does. I'm sure, always, I'll tell the right time there, even if I do go off half an hour ahead!"

"As if I didn't know that," answered Bertram, very low and tenderly. "Besides, I reckon I have some cogs of my own that need adjusting!"